Partners for Peace

edited by George J. Lankevich

The United Nations under U Thant, 1961–1971

Bernard J. Firestone

Partners for Peace, No. 3

The Scarecrow Press, Inc.
Lanham, Maryland, and London
2001

SCARECROW PRESS, INC.

Published in the United States of America
by Scarecrow Press, Inc.
4720 Boston Way, Lanham, Maryland 20706
www.scarecrowpress.com

4 Pleydell Gardens, Folkestone
Kent CT20 2DN, England

British Library Cataloguing-in-Publication Information Available

Library of Congress Cataloging-in-Publication Data

Firestone, Bernard J.
  The United Nations under U Thant, 1961–1971 / Bernard J. Firestone.
    p. c.m.—(Partners for peace ; v. 3)
  Includes bibliographical references and index.
  ISBN 0-8108-3700-5 (cloth : alk. paper)
    1. Thant, U, 1909–1974. 2. United Nations—Biography.
  3. Statesmen—Burma—Biography. 4. United Nations—History. I. Title.
  II. Series.
D839.7.T5 F57 2001
341.23′09′046—dc21   2001020524

Contents

Areas of Interest during U Thant's Term

Introduction

From Hammarskjöld to Thant

The plane crash that killed Dag Hammarskjöld on September 18, 1961, ended an era in the history of the United Nations (UN). For most of its young life, the UN had been shaped, led, and largely populated by the developed nations of Europe and the Americas. These nations had imposed their cold war conflict on the organization's agenda, thereby crowding out issues of greater consequence to much of the rest of the world. But with Hammarskjöld gone, the United Nations stood on the threshold of a dramatic transformation. On September 27, the organization admitted its one hundredth member, Sierra Leone, a third world country much like the vast majority of the UN's newest members. Harboring bitter memories of their colonial experience and beset by profound economic and political distress, the newly independent states of Africa and Asia were determined to wrest control of the UN's agenda from its founders and to refocus global attention and resources on issues such as poverty, dependency, imperialism, and post-colonialism. But who would lead the organization through its momentous transition, and what authority would he enjoy? The first two secretaries-general, Trygve Lie and Hammarskjöld, had been Europeans, and Hammarskjöld, working closely with the United States, had managed to transform the office of secretary-general into a position of enormous status and influence. Yet by 1961, with a burgeoning group of neutralist and anticolonial third world nations making up the largest single voting bloc, the UN was proving itself far more intractable to the positions held both by Hammarskjöld and the United States. Indeed, the office and the person of secretary-general were coming under increasingly harsh attack when death removed Hammarskjöld from the arena.

THE SETTING

The seeds of the UN's transformation had actually been planted in the months and years immediately following World War II. With the United States playing the leading role, the UN's founders had incorporated into the charter a "Declaration Regarding Self-Governing Territories" (chapter XI), guaranteeing just treatment for colonial peoples and requiring that metropolitan states both promote self-government and take "due account of the people's political aspirations." To that end, the UN stipulated a procedure for monitoring each colonial power's adherence to the declaration, through a system of annual reporting to the General Assembly. An elaborate trusteeship system was instituted as well, extending the promise of independence to former League of Nations mandates and the territories of defeated states. Chapter XI did not, however, specify the nature of self-government, and it did not adequately define the term *non-self-governing*. Shielded by the declaration's ambiguities, many colonial powers simply refused to cooperate with the UN and deliberately failed to report on the status of their colonial territories to the General Assembly. The trusteeship system, moreover, could not be applied to the colonial territories of the war's victorious powers without each country's compliance. That left most of the world's colonized peoples protected by word, but still ignored in reality.

Whatever the institutional and legal infirmities of the UN's decolonization system, the political events of fifteen years nonetheless pressed relentlessly toward the breakup of the world's great empires. The Allied victory over fascism had done nothing to abate the prewar drive for independence in the third world; in fact, it had probably accelerated the determination of colonized peoples to share in the freedom that the Allies had won. The war, moreover, had sapped the military and economic strength of Europe's imperial powers, leaving them little able to resist growing nationalist agitation in their colonial territories. In 1947, a reluctant Great Britain relinquished its control over India, long considered the "jewel" of its vast empire. Soon thereafter, other Asian nations joined the growing list of independent states. Over the next decade colonial wars broke out in places such as Algeria, Indochina, Indonesia, and Kenya. Meanwhile, the UN's General Assembly, reflecting the influx of newly created states into its midst, assumed an increasingly hostile stance toward continued colonial rule anywhere in the world.

By the beginning of 1960, there were eighty states represented in the General Assembly, thirty more than the original fifty that had initially formed the organization. Of the eighty, only four were in sub-Saharan Africa, where Western colonialism had proven most intransigent to change. But in 1960, an explosion of independence spread throughout the African continent, and by the end of that year, eighteen new states had joined the United Nations, all but one of African origin. The accretion of these states to the United Nations had an immediate impact on the content of the organization's agenda. On December 14, 1960, a resolution entitled "Declaration on the Granting of Independence to Colonial Countries and Peoples" passed the General Assembly by a vote of 90–0, with nine abstentions. The declaration went vastly further than the United Nations had gone before and clearly stretched the meaning of the charter's chapter XI. It was a recast United Nations, with twice the number of members who had been party to the organization's formation, which overwhelmingly asserted that colonialism was no longer an acceptable form of state behavior.

The enthusiasm surrounding the successful independence movements in Africa could not, however, mask the enormous difficulties facing that continent's infant states. And nowhere did these difficulties emerge with greater force than in the Congo, where independence quickly dissolved into political chaos and where chaos invited cold war combatants to find new arenas for their dangerous competition. The former Belgian Congo, a large, resource-rich territory in the center of Africa, achieved its independence on July 1, 1960. Virtually without preparation in self-government and innocent of economic management, the newly independent Congolese were expected to defer to their former Belgian masters, who still retained control of the economy and the upper echelons of the military. But on July 5, 1960, Congolese troops mutinied against their Belgian officers, thus unleashing widespread domestic violence and inviting the reintroduction of Belgian troops into the country. Taking advantage of the chaotic situation, the pro-Belgian leader of the mineral-rich Katanga province, Moise Tshombe, announced his region's secession from the Congo.

On July 14, 1960, responding to urgent appeals from the Congolese government, the Security Council, with the United States and Soviet Union in accord, ordered the Belgians to leave the Congo and mandated the secretary-general to provide military assistance to restore order to the troubled country. Hammarskjöld was not without experience in this area, having already formed a peacekeeping force in 1957 to police the Egyptian–Israeli frontier. On July 15, 1960, a multinational force, ultimately numbering some eighteen thousand troops, was dispatched to the Congo.

Events in the Congo, however, soon conspired to undermine both the fragile superpower consensus that had supported the operation and the position of Hammarskjöld, who had invested much of his energy and personal prestige in organizing the UN presence in the troubled African nation. The Congolese government represented a pastiche of clashing personalities, ideologies, and tribal loyalties, with the pro-Western President Joseph Kasavubu frequently in conflict with his mercurial prime minister, Patrice Lumumba, widely viewed in the West as a Soviet client. Lumumba, increasingly unhappy with the UN role in the Congo and the continuing secession in Katanga, bitterly attacked Hammarskjöld during an August 1960 visit to New York and then requested military aid from the Soviet Union. President Kasavubu, alarmed at Lumumba's tilt toward the Kremlin and concerned about his own position, fired the prime minister. The prime minister in turn fired the president. Meanwhile, Army Chief of Staff Colonel Joseph Mobuto dissolved the National Assembly and dismissed both Kasavubu and Lumumba. In an ostensible effort to avert full-scale civil war, Hammarskjöld's deputy in Léopoldville, Andrew Cordier, an American who later headed Columbia University, closed the Congo's airports and radio stations. This action effectively crippled Lumumba by denying him military assistance from the Soviets and access to communications where he might plead his case in the developing civil war. His freedom of action broken, Lumumba was soon after arrested by the central government and, in February 1961, murdered. In August 1961, the National Assembly convened again and named Cyrille Adoula the new prime minister.

It was against this background that Hammarskjöld, in September 1961, had flown to Northern Rhodesia to meet with Tshombe. The selection of Adoula had pacified the political situation in the Congo, leaving the Katangese secession as the primary source of political tension in the country. Under a Security Council resolution passed in February 1961 and strongly supported by Afro-Asian nations, ONUC (United Nations Operations in the Congo) had several weeks earlier expelled more than three hundred mercenaries from Katanga. With approximately one hundred Belgian and other European mercenaries remaining in place, the UN, on September 13, mounted a second, more ambitious military assault against the mercenaries. But the UN operation proved a disaster, both for the organization and for Hammarskjöld personally. UN forces met unexpectedly strong resistance, and poor planning allowed Tshombe to flee. Mocking UN officials' initial claim that the secession was over, the Katangese army, led by white mercenaries, launched a successful counterattack against UN headquarters in Elisabethville and trapped an Irish UN contingent at its garrison in Jadotville. To its critics, the use of force by UN forces to end the secession had exceeded ONUC's mandate. The British, in particular, were furious with Hammarskjöld and urged him to meet with Tshombe. The secretary-general, who had arrived in Léopoldville on the day of the UN attack, was deeply embarrassed; he had, after all, earlier asserted that it was not the UN's role to force a solution upon Katanga. Several days later, with his personal role in the operation under sharp criticism, Hammarskjöld was dead.

The UN's search for a secretary-general to succeed Hammarskjöld was launched in the troubled atmosphere of emotional shock over his death and uncertainty over future prospects for the organization. With its Congo operation a political and financial drain, and with its dominant figure already tarnished even before his death, the world body could ill afford a long and contentious delay in the choice of a new leader. But casting a large shadow over the selection process was the cold war, which had been at the center of UN difficulties since 1945 and which continued to resonate ferociously. More complicating still was the entry into the organization of new states whose agenda differed substantially from that of the superpowers and who preferred a secretary-general reflecting their growing prominence in the organization.

Relations between the United States and the Soviet Union were not good in 1961. Despite the promise of a thaw created by the election of a new president in the United States, a series of crises, including the ill-fated American invasion of Cuba at the Bay of Pigs and the Laotian civil war, soured prospects for peace. In June, U.S. President John F. Kennedy met with Soviet Premier Nikita Khrushchev in Vienna in a summit that, rather than improving relations, led to new misunderstandings. Kennedy returned to Washington convinced that the Soviets intended to escalate tensions in Berlin, where the vast exodus of refugees from East to West was embarrassing the Kremlin.

His speculation proved accurate, because on July 8 the Soviets responded to the developing Berlin crisis with the announcement of a 25 percent buildup in their military forces. Then on July 25, with Khrushchev threatening to enter into a separate peace treaty with East Germany, President Kennedy unveiled plans for a major increase in U.S. conventional might. Finally, in a dramatic step to stanch the flow of refugees to West Berlin, the Soviets, during the night of August 12–13, sealed the border dividing the city and erected the Berlin Wall.

Further aggravating superpower tensions was the Soviet decision to resume nuclear testing, which both countries had refrained from doing since 1958, when an unofficial moratorium had begun. On September 1, 4, 5, and 6, the Soviets detonated a series of atmospheric nuclear explosions. Sharply critical of the Kremlin's decision, President Kennedy and British Prime Minister Harold Macmillan urged Premier Khrushchev to join them in signing a treaty that would ban all atmospheric tests. Meanwhile, Kennedy ordered the resumption of U.S. underground testing. On October 23, Russian scientists exploded a thirty-megaton bomb in the atmosphere, and on October 30, in a move that sent political shock waves across the globe, the Soviets detonated an unprecedented fifty-megaton nuclear bomb in the skies over their territory. Khrushchev boasted that Soviet scientists would soon explode bombs with the equivalent yield of one hundred megatons, and Kennedy, responding to domestic pressure to counter the Soviet provocation, ordered American nuclear experts to prepare for an American resumption of atmospheric tests. On October 6, Kennedy and Soviet Foreign Minister Andrei Gromyko met in Washington to discuss the deterioration in superpower relations. At the conclusion of the meeting, when called upon to assess the results of the high-level summit, the president summed up the state of U.S.–Soviet relations with a terse "Zero!"

At the United Nations, superpower tensions were reflected in the bitter conflict over Hammarskjöld's initiatives in the Congo and the future character of the office of secretary-general. UN involvement in the Congo had begun with the great powers in relative accord over the functions and goals of the operation. While the Soviets wanted Hammarskjöld to employ ONUC more aggressively against the Katangese secession, they did not raise serious objections to the secretary-general's more restrained view of UN military operations. They had agreed to the formation of the UN force and applauded in

July 1960 when Hammarskjöld entered Elisabethville in an effort to assert UN authority over Katanga. But President Kasavubu's dramatic dismissal of Lumumba and Andrew Cordier's abrupt closure of the Congo's airports were perceived in Moscow as having dealt twin blows to the Soviet Union's interests. The Kremlin had become convinced that the UN was acting to support the interests of the West in the Congo.

The Soviet response to the changed situation and the UN's role in producing it was quick and implacable. On September 23, 1960, during an unprecedented gathering of world leaders to commemorate the fifteenth anniversary of the United Nations, Khrushchev delivered a blistering personal attack on Hammarskjöld before the General Assembly. He urged that the secretary-generalship be abolished and replaced by a triumvirate, with each of the world's blocs represented with one triumvir. Several days later, Khrushchev renewed his attack against Hammarskjöld and this time called on the secretary-general to resign. In the Soviet leader's words, "If he [Hammarskjöld] cannot muster the courage to resign in . . . a chivalrous way, we shall draw the inevitable conclusions from the situation."[1] Hammarskjöld eloquently defended himself against Khrushchev's attack, and the General Assembly overwhelmingly endorsed his position, but the tension remained. Then in February 1961, Lumumba was killed, probably by officials of the Katanga government. The Russians took advantage of the occasion and the broad outcry against Lumumba's murder to implicate Hammarskjöld in his death. From that point until the secretary-general's own death in September 1961, the Russians refused to recognize Hammarskjöld as secretary-general and refrained from having anything to do with him. Reflecting the depth of the Soviets' bitterness, even after his death, the Russians did not fully endorse the UN's tribute to Hammarskjöld's memory.

The Kremlin's attack on the secretary-general and its formulation of an alternative scheme for the organization of the Secretariat, often known as the "troika" proposal, reflected Soviet anger at the frustration of their objectives in the Congo. But the harshness of the assault suggested that the Russians had grown personally alienated from the secretary-general, a man about whom they had long entertained serious doubts. As the Russians reiterated many times during their sustained attack on Hammarskjöld, "There are no neutral men."[2] Underneath their previous, apparent satisfaction with Hammarskjöld's performance—reflected in their joining a unanimous 1958 recommendation that he be reappointed—lay uneasiness over the kind of person the secretary-general was and the quality of the staff he had assembled. For Hammarskjöld, despite his professed neutrality, was culturally and intellectually a man of the West, a liberal in orientation and deed. In a 1959 visit with Khrushchev he had described, to the premier's annoyance, his role in the Swedish Academy and had defended its award of a Nobel Prize to Boris Pasternak, a writer reviled by Soviet authorities. Hammarskjöld's closest advisers were Westerners as well, and four of them, Ralph Bunche, Henri Labouisse, Heinz Wieschoff, and Andrew Cordier, were Americans. Most critically, the "Congo Club," the inner circle of advisers who orchestrated the Congo operation, was manned exclusively by Westerners. With their own penchant for treating Soviet nationals of the Secretariat as agents of Soviet foreign policy, the Russians were hardly inclined to believe that Hammarskjöld and the Americans surrounding him could deal fairly with their interests.

Thus, the Soviets, by 1960, had grown disenchanted with the very idea of a strong secretary-general. In earlier crises—the 1956 formation of UNEF (United Nations Emergency Force) and during the opening days of the Congo intervention—Hammarskjöld had acted boldly, but always with the support of the superpowers. But the big power consensus collapsed in the Congo shortly after the operation began, and Khrushchev was not about to support a secretary-general who was operating under an outdated mandate. The message the Russians were sending with their troika scheme was that the UN should not and could not operate in the absence of their support. But the troika proposal, by giving each bloc a veto, would, in the opinion of many scholars, have paralyzed the UN. To the emerging third world majority, with so large a stake in the success of the organization, this was not a welcomed prospect.

THE APPOINTMENT OF U THANT

Against this backdrop of uncertainty over the nature of the office, the UN began its search for a successor to Hammarskjöld. East-West battle lines were drawn fairly quickly, with Soviet Foreign Minister Gromyko announcing on September 19 that the Kremlin opposed the appointment of an acting secretary-general, preferring instead full consideration of its troika proposal. President Kennedy forcefully stated American opposition to the Soviet plan in a September 25 speech before the General Assembly: "Even the three houses of the troika did not have three drivers, all going in different directions. . . . They had only one, and so must the United Nations executive."[3] On September 26 delegates of the Big Four nations—the United States, the Soviet Union, Great Britain, and France—met in New York, where Soviet Ambassador Valerian Zorin proposed the formation of an interim executive made up of four UN undersecretaries—with one selected by the other three on a rotational basis—who would be required to reach decisions unanimously. The Soviet plan was rejected.

Despite their hard line and apparent stubbornness, the Soviets were in fact looking for a face-saving exit from their troika position. Khrushchev's proposal had never appealed to third world nations, who viewed a strong UN as being in their collective interest. Moreover, developing nations did not view a single potential triumvir as capable of accurately representing what was a polyglot and diverse group of nations. The Burmese ambassador to the UN, U Thant, represented quite accurately the third world position on the troika when in October 1960 he attacked the Soviet scheme as a recipe for weakening the world organization.

Thant, along with the ambassadors of several other states, was determined to bypass the superpower logjam by promoting a single candidate. The Burmese ambassador favored the appointment of Mongi Slim, ambassador from Tunisia, who had just been selected president of the General Assembly. Slim, widely respected in the world organization, had been a confidant of Hammarskjöld and had consistently supported him during the latter's battle with the Russians. The United States at first supported the candidacy of Irish Ambassador Frederick Boland, who had just been selected as president of the Security Council, but when it became clear that third world nations expected the secretary-generalship to go to one of their own, Washington shifted to Slim, who represented a pro-Western government. Slim, who acknowledged to Thant and several other ambassadors that he would accept a draft to become secretary-general but not acting secretary-general, was not, however, a viable candidate. The Israeli government openly opposed the appointment of an ambassador from an Arab country, and more importantly, the French, involved in a serious conflict with Tunisia over the status of Bizerte, made it clear that Slim was unacceptable to them.

With the Russians advancing a modified version of their troika proposal and the United States adamantly opposed to anything but a single secretary-general, the Kennedy Administration, in an initiative of dubious constitutional legitimacy, actively considered bypassing Moscow by having the General Assembly choose an acting UN chief without a Security Council recommendation. Washington quickly retreated from its maneuver when it became clear that the Afro-Asian bloc, favoring a strong UN, would not support any circumvention of the Security Council. Developing nations insisted on fealty to the charter, especially since the Hammarskjöld regime had shown the difficulties a secretary-general could experience without Russian support. Third world opinion, therefore, frustrated the respective diplomatic efforts of both the United States and Soviet Union. A compromise was reached on October 2, when the Soviet Union relented on its troika scheme and the United States, reconciled to the participation of the Security Council in the selection of the new secretary-general, accepted in principle the Russian position that the UN chief should have advisers representing some configuration of global political interests.

By that date, increasing attention was being focused on Thant as a possible successor to Hammarskjöld. A respected member of the UN community, the Burmese ambassador had served as chairman of the UN Development Fund, presided over the Congo Conciliation Commission, and participated in the organization's Working Committee on Algerian Freedom. The situation seemed ideal for a secretary-general from the Afro-Asian bloc of nations, and Burma, in contrast to some other third world states, was not involved in any festering conflict that could alienate any of the great powers. Even Israel and Egypt, two countries not given to routine agreement on matters of great political import, were quick to accord Thant their backing for the post of acting secretary-general. By October 15, U.S. Ambassador Adlai Stevenson was able to report on American television that Thant had secured the support of both Washington and Moscow.

The superpowers' agreement on Thant did not, however, produce an immediate Security Council vote on his selection. Instead, both nations spent the next several weeks negotiating over the composition and powers of the undersecretariat that would assist any new appointee. At first, the Soviets proposed that the secretary-general be assisted by three deputies—all approved by the Security Council and General Assembly—whom the secretary-general would have to consult and seek agreement with in the fashioning of UN policy. This plan, known as the "sub-troika" scheme, was adamantly rejected by the United States, and the Soviets soon agreed that the new secretary-general should not be bound to consult his subordinates or to secure their agreement. While this concession represented a major break in the United States–Soviet impasse, it did not end it altogether. Instead, the superpowers fought over the number of undersecretaries to be appointed, with each side seeking maximum advantage at the expense of the other. At one point the United States proposed the installation of five undersecretaries, representing different geographic blocs—one each from the United States, Soviet Union, Western Europe, Africa, and Latin America. The Soviets, seeing no political distinction between Western Europe and the United States, argued for the replacement of Western Europe with Eastern Europe. In the face of another American rejection, the Russians proposed the appointment of seven deputies, representing the United States, the Soviet Union, Western Europe, Eastern Europe, Africa, Latin America, and Asia, but the United States rebuffed that suggestion. Finally, on October 30, the exhausted superpowers agreed that Thant should be permitted to select his own undersecretaries. On November 3, Thant was nominated first by the Security Council and then selected by the General Assembly as acting secretary-general. He was to serve until April 1963, the date when Hammarskjöld's term would have expired. In his acceptance speech, Thant took note of the differences that had frustrated the search for a new secretary-general and named Ralph Bunche of the United States and Georgi Arkadev of the Soviet Union to act as his principal advisers. The acting chief of the secretary-general's executive office, C. V. Narasimhan from India, was retained.

THANT'S VIEW OF THE WORLD AND HIS OFFICE

The increasing prominence of third world delegations at headquarters made it probable from the outset of the selection process that the position of acting secretary-general would most likely go to a diplomat from one of the developing nations. Burma, with its colonial past, economic underdevelopment, and severe ethnic schisms, was typical of many of the new states that had recently entered the world body. Through much of the previous century, Burma had been under the thumb of British colonial rule, which had firmly established itself in 1885 after several unsuccessful, earlier attempts to subdue the Burmese. It was in this colonial environment that Thant received his education and formed many of his ideas about the world, ideas that would find forceful expression during his years as secretary-general.

Thant's rise to the secretary-generalship followed a fairly rapid advance through Burmese diplomatic ranks, a rise facilitated by Thant's childhood friendship with U Nu, the country's first prime minister. Burma's growing role in the politics of nonalignment permitted Thant numerous opportunities to engage in international diplomacy in the decade prior to his appointment, and those experiences had made him a very different kind of man from his friend and patron, Nu. In contrast to the mercurial, superstitious, and high-strung Nu, Thant was placid and composed, almost to the point of diffidence. His UN associates called Thant the "Bronze Buddha," since the secretary-general's mood was almost impossible to fathom through the wall of his outward composure. UN official Conor Cruise O'Brien recounted that in November 1961, he received a telephone call from Ralph Bunche in which the undersecretary reported a conversation he had just had with the acting secretary-general. So far as Bunche could tell, Thant was "upset" about a matter relating to O'Brien's performance in the Congo. But, according to O'Brien, Dr. Bunche found the extent of Thant's anger far more difficult to measure than Hammarskjöld's; Thant's personality and mood were not readily accessible.

Thant was not oblivious to his air of serenity. In his memoirs the secretary-general cited his calm reaction to the news that his son, Tin Maung, had died in a Rangoon bus accident, as evidence of his "emotional equilibrium." To Thant, the source of this extraordinary self-control was religion, for, as was the case with most of his countrymen, Thant was a devout believer in the Theravada form of Buddhism, whose philosophy stresses the importance of "equanimity" or "detachment." It was this equanimity, for example, that allowed Thant to accept with composure the death of his only son, for, in the secretary-general's words, "are not birth and death the two phases of the same life process?"[4] To achieve this higher level of cognition and spiritual understanding, Thant practiced daily meditation and credited that discipline with allowing him to achieve the inner peace that characterized his life.

Buddhism taught him as well to be tolerant of all peoples. Compassion and love are fundamental to Buddhist teachings, yet Buddhism is essentially a religion of the individual, where the highest good is achieved by the person's ability to reach a state of spiritual and intellectual equilibrium. This inner directedness encourages a "live and let live" personal philosophy, which, in comparison to many of the world's other major religions, makes Buddhism uniquely tolerant of diversity. Thant's public pronouncements as secretary-general would reflect these beliefs. In 1963, for example, when questioned about the self-immolation of Buddhist monks in a South Vietnam ruled by the Roman Catholic minority, the secretary-general offered the following comment: "As you know, I am a very staunch advocate of religious tolerance. . . . I have a very high esteem and respect for the very noble ethical aspects of many other religions."[5] Thant even found confirmation of Buddhist philosophy in the UN charter, which "calls on us to practice tolerance and live together in peace with one another as good neighbors."[6]

Thant's tolerance, however, did not prevent him from taking sides. Several days before his formal selection as acting secretary-general, he appeared on an American television program hosted by Adlai Stevenson. Sensitive to the Russians' charge that Hammarskjöld had forfeited his claim to objectivity, Thant sought to distinguish between the words *impartiality* and *neutrality*. Even an impartial figure, reasoned Thant, cannot refrain from making judgments about the guilt or innocence of parties to a conflict. Indeed, for all his renowned detachment, Thant was often blunt in his appraisal of world leaders and state policy. He openly criticized French policy in Algeria, and as the 1960s progressed, he frequently attacked American policy in Southeast Asia. On a trip to the Soviet Union in 1962, he shocked his hosts by declaring on Radio Moscow that "the Russian people do not fully understand the true character of the Congo problem."[7] He could be equally blunt, even brutal, about the personal characteristics of his adversaries. About Tshombe, he offered the following startlingly candid observation: "Mr. Tshombe is capable of making any statement. I have a feeling, after consultations with many who know Mr. Tshombe, that he is a very unstable man."[8] In his Moscow address, Thant admitted his penchant for frankness, saying, "I am not a believer in honeyed words."[9]

Thant's bluntness became especially pronounced when he attacked historic injustices perpetrated against third world nations. In a commencement speech at Massachusetts' Williams College in 1962 he said, "the primary motive of the colonial power in developing the natural resources of a colony was its own commercial profit. Consequently, the greater part of the wealth obtained from the colony went into the pockets of the colonial investors."[10] Having experienced colonialism firsthand, Thant was equally eloquent in his description of the social effects of the colonial relationship: "[Colonizers] . . . often kept themselves aloof from native society. Wherever it existed, this aloofness and cultural exclusiveness created resentment, particularly in the minds of the educated subject peoples."[11]

Thant saw the third world nations as a potential "third force" in international affairs. To be sure, the secretary-general recognized the importance of the East-West conflict and, as a pragmatist, understood the limitations of his organization, whose chief peacekeeping agency, the Security Council, depended for its success on the concurrence of two superpowers who profoundly disagreed about issues brought before the world body. As he said in Oslo in 1962, "as far as the political function is concerned the UN apparatus is weak and, if I may say so, inadequate."[12] But the secretary-general, despite his misgivings about the nuclear arms race and continuing tensions between the superpowers, believed, with singular prescience, that the cold war would turn out to be a transitory phenomenon in global affairs. Thant expected that North-South conflict would inevitably assume the center stage of world politics and correctly identified the United Nations as the prime arena of that future conflict. And in that area of world affairs, Thant had no intention of being dispassionate. He intended to employ his position as secretary-general to call for a new world order in which colonialism and its vestiges would be eradicated and economic resources more equitably apportioned. He urged the strengthening of the General Assembly, where third world states now predominated, and strenuously fought all proposals that would have introduced weighted voting into the assembly.

In defining the powers of his office, Thant essentially embraced the Hammarskjöld model, which saw in the charter's article 99 authority for the secretary-general to deal independently with threats to world peace. Article 99 permits the secretary-general to "bring to the attention of the Security Council any matter which in his opinion may threaten the maintenance of international peace and security," but it had been invoked formally by Hammarskjöld only once, in July 1960, during the Congo crisis. Its greater importance lay in the fact that it provided a legal basis for a number of Hammarskjöld's diplomatic initiatives and permitted him to act in the Congo even after the Security Council and General Assembly had become deadlocked by the East-West conflict. While Thant viewed the secretary-general primarily as an agent of the Security Council and General Assembly, he, like Hammarskjöld, did not see the inaction of these organs as bars to action by the secretary-general.

THANT'S EARLY LIFE

U Thant (in Burmese the word *U* is equivalent to the English mister; the secretary-general's name was simply "Thant") was born in Burma in the small town of Pantanaw on January 22, 1909. His father, U Po Hnit, was a landowner of comfortable means and the only man in the town able to read and write English. From his father, Thant and his three younger brothers acquired an early interest in learning, and by the age of twelve the future secretary-general was reading in English the works of Shakespeare and Sir Arthur Conan Doyle. Educated at the National High School in Pantanaw, Thant planned to enter Rangoon University to gain a degree in journalism. When Thant was fourteen, however, his father died, allowing an avaricious relative to swindle Thant's mother out of the family's rightful inheritance to Po Hnit's modest fortune. A long and unsuccessful court fight further depleted the widow's resources. Responsible now for supporting the family, Thant decided to enter the university for only two years and to become a teacher instead of a journalist.

At the university Thant continued his studies in English and took courses in world history and philosophy as well. He was prominently involved in extracurricular activities and was elected an official of both the philosophy and debating societies. Thant was beginning to develop strong opinions about contemporary political issues, and he wrote a series of letters to local newspapers that heaped criticisms on British authorities and Burmese nationalists alike. While Thant was not oriented toward political activism, in college he established a close relationship with U Nu, a young man from a neighboring town who was considerably involved in campus and nationalist politics.

From the university Thant returned to Pantanaw, where he became a teacher in the local high school. He continued his interest in English literature and maintained contact with the English writer J. S. Furnivall, who operated a bookshop frequented by students at the university. Thant continued his writing as well and won several competitions in which he translated English works into his native language. In 1931, Thant achieved the highest score in the national Teachership Examination and was soon appointed headmaster of the Pantanaw school. When the position of school superintendent became available, Thant invited Nu to fill the position. When Nu returned to Rangoon to study law, Thant assumed the job of superintendent in his place.

For the next several years Thant preoccupied himself with teaching and writing. In 1934, he married and began raising a family. But Thant remained relatively insulated from the political upheaval engulfing many of his university colleagues. In 1940, nationalist agitation against the British occupation of Burma escalated, and London, rather than surrender to Burmese demands, imprisoned nationalists such as Nu and other political activists. In December 1941, when Japanese forces invaded Burma, many Burmese welcomed the invasion as a means to rid the country of the hated British. With the British defeated, political prisoners such as Nu were released from prison and invited to participate in an "independent" government under the auspices of the Japanese military occupation. But it soon became clear that Tokyo had no intention of extending real independence to Burma. With the Japanese occupation becoming increasingly brutal, the nationalists now turned against Japan. Nu participated in the formation of the Anti-Fascist People's Freedom League (AFPFL), which united most of the nation's leading political activists in resistance to Japanese rule. Thant, who spent almost the entire war in Pantanaw, did not participate in any formal movement to oust the Japanese, but he engaged in modest expressions of protest against the occupation. He listened to illegal short-wave broadcasts, stored rice for the resistance, and refused, on the grounds that he could not find a teacher, to have Japanese taught in his school.

Notwithstanding his strong political opinions, expressed in numerous freelance articles published in Burmese newspapers over the years, Thant was not a political man. He never, for example, joined a political party. But Thant was an individual of considerable intellectual distinction, and the postwar accession of his friend Nu to the prime ministership of the newly independent Burmese state meant that he would be drawn into governmental service. In 1947, Thant and his family moved to Rangoon, where he hoped to publish a new magazine, but Nu prevailed upon his old friend to become press officer of the AFPFL. There followed a series of high level appointments under Nu, ranging from director of broadcasting and secretary in the ministry of information to secretary for projects in the prime minister's office and executive secretary of the country's economic and social board. The prime minister viewed Thant as the consummate bureaucrat, capable of managing any project, and as time went on Thant became Nu's most trusted lieutenant.

Burma's growing role in the politics of nonalignment coupled with Thant's favored position with Nu soon afforded the future secretary-general opportunities to engage with increasing frequency in international diplomacy. In 1951, Thant was selected to undertake goodwill missions to Thailand and Indonesia, and, in 1952, he visited New York as a member of Burma's delegation to the UN. Thant's travels took him around the globe and exposed him to a variety of powerful world leaders. He attended major third world conferences, including the first two Colombo Prime Ministers' Conferences and the Asian-African Conference in Bandung, Indonesia, which he helped to plan. In 1957, Thant was named Burma's representative to the United Nations, an ambassadorial rank that he held until November 1961, when he assumed the post of acting secretary-general.

Thant's life history, occurring against the background of Burma's struggle for independence, shaped his orientation to many of the problems he faced as leader of the world organization. It influenced his attitudes toward issues such as colonialism, the North-South conflict, and the effort of newly independent states to maintain their territorial integrity in the face of internal, ethnic, and religious tensions. He vigorously attacked continued colonialism in Southern Africa, regularly called for some transfer of wealth from developed to developing countries, and in the cases of the Katangese and Biafran secessions, stood strongly in favor of the threatened central governments. That Thant should take these positions was fully predictable, given both the changing nature of the UN's majority and the formative experiences in Thant's life.

CONCLUSION

Thant's selection as acting secretary-general demonstrated two fundamental facts about the United Nations as it prepared to enter the third decade of its existence. First, it signaled the arrival of the third world as a significant force in the politics of the organization. The appointment of a leader from the ranks of the less-developed nations symbolized the growing presence of these nations in the organization and predicted an expanded UN agenda to consider issues such as economic underdevelopment and colonialism. Over the next decade new UN instrumentalities would be established to confront the needs of its newest members. At the center of these changes would be Thant, both as secretary-general and as a man of the third world, prodding the developed countries to share the planet's wealth, urging the remaining colonial powers to relinquish their imperial possessions, and grappling with a budget swollen by demands the organization could barely meet but that it could not safely ignore.

Looming over these changing circumstances, however, would be the shadow of the cold war, as large and as dark in the 1960s as it had been during the earlier years of the organization's existence. Superpower wrangling over Thant's appointment signaled the cold war's continuing ability to fixate and even paralyze the organization. Over the next decade Thant would learn that despite the evolution of a UN majority impatient with the cold war, hardly an issue confronted by the organization—from the fiscal crisis to the brushfire wars of the third world—could escape the superpowers' near obsession with their ongoing conflict. The history of the United Nations during Thant's years as secretary-general would therefore be a story of transition—as third world concerns consumed more and more of the UN's attention—balanced by continuity, as the organization maintained its preoccupation with the cold war, which tenaciously clung to the center of the UN's agenda.

The new secretary-general faced these two issues, working in an environment almost devoid of consensus and operating with tools that were frequently without power. He could cite UN resolutions opposing colonialism but could organize no military force to dislodge a colonial power. He could arrange conferences calling for the redistribution of global wealth but could not force one penny out of the richest countries. He could bemoan the absence of peace in Vietnam, but not broker a solution that would end the killing. He could call for the dispatching of peacekeeping forces, but, owing to the fiscal crisis, not easily assemble the resources necessary to keep the peace. The changing United Nations afforded new opportunities for its secretary-general to assist in restructuring the organization's agenda. The constraints on the office, however, grew virtually in proportion to the growth in its membership. As the years of Thant's secretary-generalship progressed, he became increasingly frustrated by the limitation of his role and seriously considered not standing for a second term. In the end, though, he served for a little more than ten years. While he did little to strengthen its powers, he did much to restore the superpowers' faith in the impartiality of the office.

NOTES

1. Brian Urquhart, *Hammarskjöld* (New York: Alfred A. Knopf, 1972), 462.

2. Urquhart, *Hammarskjöld*, 462.

3. Richard P. Stebbins, *The United States and World Affairs 1961* (New York: Harper and Brothers, 1962), 357–358.

4. U Thant, *View from the UN* (Garden City, N.Y.: Doubleday, 1975), 23.

5. Andrew W. Cordier and Max Harrelson, eds., *Public Papers of the Secretaries-General of the United Nations, Vol. VI, U Thant* (New York: Columbia University Press, 1976), 367.

6. Andrew Cordier and Max Harrelson, eds., *Public Papers of the Secretaries-General of the United Nations, Vol. VII, U Thant* (New York: Columbia University Press, 1976), 601.

7. Thant, *View from the UN*, 470.

8. Cordier and Harrelson, *Public Papers, Vol. VI*, 37.

9. Thant, *View from the UN*, 470.

10. Cordier and Harrelson, *Public Papers, Vol. VI*, 134.

11. Cordier and Harrelson, *Public Papers, Vol. VI*, 135.

12. Cordier and Harrelson, *Public Papers, Vol. VI*, 179.

1

Early Crises:
The Congo and Cuba

Behind the Soviet effort to weaken the position of secretary-general lay its understandable unhappiness with the UN's performance across fifteen years. At the insistence of the Soviet Union, the charter had assigned to each of the five permanent members of the Security Council a veto over the actions of that eleven-member body, but with France, the United Kingdom, and China firmly allied with the United States, the Russians regularly found themselves isolated in the council's deliberations. The situation in the General Assembly was little better, where the Kremlin and its Eastern European allies could rarely command more than a dozen votes. Consigned to the status of a permanent minority, the Soviets made frequent use of the veto, thus contributing to the perception in the West that the Kremlin was little interested in seeing the United Nations succeed as a peace-keeping instrument.

The weak Soviet position stood in sharp contrast to that of the United States, which enjoyed firm control of both the Security Council and General Assembly and was demonstrably more willing to use the organization to further its national security interests. At the start of the Korean War, for example, Washington took advantage of the Soviets' temporary absence to secure Security Council approval for a largely American police action in Korea. Later, in anticipation of the Soviets' eventual return, America persuaded the General Assembly to pass the "Uniting for Peace" resolution, which authorized the assembly to act in the event of the council's paralysis. Several years later, using this newly legislated constitutional authority, the assembly circumvented the Security Council to condemn the British-

1

French-Israeli invasion of Egypt during the Suez War and to establish a peacekeeping force, its first ever, for the area.

The American role in promoting the "Uniting for Peace" resolution resulted from Washington's frustration at Soviet interference in the work of the Security Council and, conversely, its confidence in its own ability to manipulate the General Assembly. Well into the 1950s and early 1960s the United States almost single-handedly implemented UN resolutions in Korea that it had been largely instrumental in fashioning, supplied valuable financial and logistical assistance to sustain UN peacekeeping operations, and offered to the United Nations its political support in the face of Soviet attacks on international institutions. It was not unnatural for the secretary-general to work closely with the United States—as Hammarskjöld and Lie did—for it was the United States that consistently championed a strong role for the world organization.

The battle over the Congo and the larger question of Hammarskjöld's successor brought Washington's and Moscow's opposing views of an effective United Nations to the fore. The Soviet Union saw in the independence of the secretary-general an obstacle to its goal of spreading communism into the new states of Africa and Asia and looked unfavorably on the UN effort to facilitate the process of peaceful decolonization. The Americans, on the other hand, saw the United Nations as an instrument for promoting stability in newly independent third world nations threatened by Communist takeover. They were, therefore, more inclined to work through the organization and to support the secretary-general's authority to act independently of a Security Council stymied by the Soviet veto. Washington's support for Hammarskjöld was easily transferred to U Thant, as the new secretary-general grappled with novel methods of peacekeeping in a variety of world trouble spots. American support grew stronger in response to the secretary-general's salutary role in resolving the Cuban missile crisis. Only later, as the United States came to appreciate its loss of control over the General Assembly and as Thant's outspoken support of third world concerns began to intrude on America's vital interests, did the relationship between Thant and the United States begin to sour. As Thant assumed power, however, the crisis in the Congo produced close cooperation between the new secretary-general and Washington, cooperation that would allow Thant the power to resolve the lingering civil war.

RESTORING THE CONGO

Military events in the Congo thrust Thant into an immediate mael-strom of activity and crisis. On October 13, 1961, the UN and Tshombe signed a cease-fire agreement compelling ONUC to relin-quish positions seized during its ill-fated September assault on Katangan forces. With its nose bloodied, the world body was in no position to dictate terms to the rebels, and Tshombe convinced him-self that the cease-fire signaled the UN's acceptance of his secession. Troops loyal to the central government continued to move against Katanga, but they proved no match for Tshombe's gendarme, which had become emboldened by the events of September. The Katangese president, recalling his incarceration in Léopoldville several months earlier, even refused to participate in talks with Congolese Prime Minister Cyrille Adoula in the Congolese capital.

On November 11, one week after Thant's selection as acting secretary-general, two UN aircraft were seized and their Italian crews massacred in Kivu Province by Congolese troops. The Kindu atrocity rekindled the UN's interest in pacifying the country, and on November 24, the Security Council, by a vote of 9–0, with Great Britain and France abstaining, authorized the acting secretary-gen-eral to "take vigorous action, including the use of requisite measures of force, if necessary, for the immediate apprehension . . . of all for-eign military and paramilitary personnel and political advisors not under United Nations command."[1] Obviously directed against the Katangese secession, which was largely funded by the Belgian cop-per giant Union Minière, the resolution was designed to give ONUC the requisite authority to suppress the rebellion against the central government. Tshombe naturally chose to interpret the Security Council's latest Congo resolution as a declaration of war against Katanga. On November 25, he called on his countrymen to ensure that "not one UN mercenary must feel himself safe in any place what-ever,"[2] and delivered a blistering public denunciation of the UN. In the supercharged atmosphere that followed President Tshombe's speech, the privileged status of all UN personnel in and around Elis-abethville quickly deteriorated. On November 28, Brian Urquhart and George Ivan Smith, UN officials attending a private dinner party for pro-Tshombe U.S. Senator Thomas Dodd (D-Connecticut), were viciously assaulted by gendarme. Urquhart was incarcerated for sev-eral hours and released only upon Tshombe's personal intervention with his troops. Meanwhile, an Indian major searching for the UN officials was apprehended and killed. During the next several days, UN personnel were seized and roadblocks were installed around Elisabethville in a Katangan effort to impede ONUC's freedom of movement around the city.

Thant, personally sympathetic to the efforts of struggling new nations to secure their independence against internal schisms and colonial interference, was now determined both to enhance ONUC's position and to crush the Katangese rebellion. Even in his capacity as Burma's nonaligned UN ambassador, Thant, had argued for a vigorous application of UN power to restore order to the Congo and had supported Hammarskjöld against the attacks of the Soviet Union. As a member of the UN's Congo Conciliation Commission, he had become familiar with the personalities and issues involved and had developed strong views about the illegality of the Katangese secession. On November 17, 1961, as secretary-general, he presided for the first time over the Advisory Committee on the Congo, composed of ambassadors from countries with military contingents in ONUC, and told the ambassadors of his plans to rid Katanga of all mercenaries. The Security Council resolution of November 24 was much more unambiguous than previous decrees, in that it authorized the acting secretary-general to employ force against the mercenaries. Thant was clearly pleased by the expansion in ONUC's mandate and, in his first speech before the Security Council, pledged to "employ toward that end, and to the best advantage, as much as possible of the total resources available to the United Nations Operation in the Congo."[3]

With Katangese and ONUC forces firing at one another, the Soviet Union pressing him to enforce the Security Council resolution, and the United States agreeable to a real show of force, Thant ordered UN troops into action. Beginning in early December, several thousand ONUC troops moved against key rebel positions in Elisabethville. Well armed and equipped with bombers, the UN forces lifted the roadblocks, captured the main Katangese military base at Camp Massert, and forced the flight of most Katangese officials, including Tshombe. Thant insisted later that the UN operation was intended only to defend ONUC personnel and cited a captured Katangese document threatening destruction of Elisabethville as proof of Tshombe's intentions. But the military operation itself appeared more offensive than defensive in nature, and succeeded in dealing a crushing, albeit temporary, blow to the province's secession.

Notwithstanding his military success, Thant's strong actions in the Congo provoked accusations, primarily from Tshombe's powerful Western allies, that the acting secretary-general was exceeding his mandate. Belgium, the former colonial power, opposed the UN operation, prompting Thant and Belgian Foreign Minister Paul-Henri Spaak to exchange a series of angry letters, the latter accusing UN forces of committing atrocities against Katanga's civilian population. France, a major buyer of Katangese copper and in principle unsympathetic to a strong UN role, was equally harsh in its opposition to the UN offensive. Great Britain was more supportive, despite its large private investments in Union Minière, but Harold Macmillan's Conservative government displayed more ambivalence about the scope of ONUC's operation. On December 8, London agreed to supply ONUC with one thousand-pound bombs, but several days later, while the UN offensive was still in full swing, the foreign secretary, Sir Alec Douglas-Home, called for an immediate cease-fire.

It is unlikely that Thant, for all his belligerence toward the government in Katanga, would have acted without support from the United States, which had provided ONUC with transport planes that proved decisive in the UN war effort. The United States was the UN's largest single contributor, and the acting secretary-general could ill afford to alienate Washington at a time when this uniquely violent peacekeeping operation was running out of money. For its part, the United States wanted to strengthen the centrist government of Cyrille Adoula in Léopoldville and to forestall a pro-Soviet move against the prime minister. With the British calling for a cease-fire, other European allies opposed to the operation, and Capitol Hill conservatives in an uproar, the Kennedy Administration sent its Congo ambassador, Edmund Gullion, to Katanga to expedite a satisfactory end to the fighting. Thant agreed to suspend UN operations on condition that Tshombe fly to the Kitona air base, near Léopoldville and begin discussions with Adoula on the integration of Katangese soldiers into the Congolese army. Tshombe, who had pleaded with the United States to bring the fighting to an end, concurred and was escorted to Kitona by Ambassador Gullion.

On December 20, Adoula and Tshombe, with Ambassador Gullion and Ralph Bunche playing prominent roles, negotiated for more than twenty difficult hours before reaching an agreement. On December 21, Tshombe signed the Kitona Declaration, which signaled his capitulation to the UN. The Katangese president agreed to accept the authority of the central government, President Kasavubu, and the *Loi Fundamentale*. He also pledged to place his Katangese gendarme under the authority of the Léopoldville government and to abide by all appropriate UN resolutions. Despite the UN's stated belief that Tshombe's signature implied Katangese ratification of the agreement, the president informed Ralph Bunche that he was obligated to gain the assent of his cabinet upon returning to Elisabethville.

Thant's willingness to suspend the military operation to allow for negotiations confirmed Soviet suspicions that he, much like his predecessor, was essentially implementing Washington's foreign policy. On December 22, Soviet UN Ambassador Valerian Zorin charged that Bunche had manipulated the Kitona talks in order to save Tshombe. Then in January 1962, Moscow requested that the Security Council consider its complaint that ONUC had deliberately refrained—in contravention of previous Security Council resolutions—from expelling all mercenaries from Katanga. Fearing that a debate would become the occasion for a Russian assault upon Thant's performance in the Congo, a council majority, led by the United States, refused to take up the Soviet complaint. Thant further enhanced Washington's position in the Congo by permitting UN troops to fight alongside soldiers of the central government against the forces of Lumumba loyalist Antoine Gizenga, who had led a secession against the pro-Western Adoula government from Stanleyville. On January 20, 1962, UN forces delivered the captured Gizenga to Adoula in Léopoldville.

The Kennedy Administration deeply appreciated the United Nations' role in subverting Soviet interests in the Congo. Shortly after the successful conclusion of the Kitona talks, American Secretary of State Dean Rusk declared that had the United Nations not become engaged in the Congo, the United States would have had to intervene itself. Linking instability with Soviet opportunism, the secretary of state credited the United Nations with robbing the Soviets of the chance to gain an important beachhead in Africa.

But Tshombe's departure from Kitona to the more secure surroundings of his capital allowed him to retreat quickly from commitments he now claimed had been made under duress. His secessionist cabinet declared itself unable to ratify the document without the support of the National Assembly, and, with Tshombe charging that the American ambassador had forced his assent to the document, drafted a resolution declaring the president's signature null and void. Meanwhile, a letter was sent to President Kennedy, protesting Ambassador Gullion's participation in the talks. UN forces remained in Katanga to promote law and order, and Thant resisted Soviet urging that he resume military operations against the rebels. Nonetheless, the acting secretary-general was growing increasingly frustrated with the obvious foot-dragging in Elisabethville.

Finally, on February 15, 1962, the Katangese Assembly ratified the Kitona Declaration as a basis for discussions between Tshombe and the central government. Over the next several months Katangese and Congolese representatives met in fruitless talks at Léopoldville, while Katangese troops engaged UN and central government forces in sporadic fighting. On June 26, after negotiations finally broke down, Tshombe refused to celebrate the anniversary of Congolese independence in Léopoldville and returned to his own capital, where, on July 11, the Katangese celebrated their own independence. Only days later, a mob of Katangese women and children assaulted UN troops in Elisabethville, reputedly with the concurrence of Tshombe.

Thant, who was traveling in Western Europe and the Soviet Union to explain UN operations in the Congo, was incensed by Tshombe's latest act of defiance. Referring to Tshombe and his colleagues as a "bunch of clowns,"[4] the acting secretary-general returned to New York determined to place new pressure upon the secessionists. In August, after consultation with the United States, Thant offered a Plan of National Reconciliation, which would have created a federal system in the Congo, integrated the armed forces, and arranged for a fifty-fifty split of revenues from the sale of Katanga's resources. After some delay, Tshombe accepted the plan but then characteristically allowed discussions on its implementation to drag on. An angry Thant threatened in September 1962 to impose economic sanctions against the rebellious province. The United States, increasingly concerned about the stability of the Adoula government, supported the proposal and urged its allies to join in sanctions against Tshombe. But Washington met with resistance from the British and French. In October, frustrated by Tshombe's recalcitrance, Thant once again set in motion plans for a military solution to the secession.

In December 1962, Ambassador Stevenson, convinced that Tshombe would never cooperate with the United Nations, advised Thant that the United States would make available a fighter squadron for deployment in the Congo and recommended that ONUC take decisive military action against the secessionists. Thant was pleased by the U. S. offer but countered that he could not accept it in the absence of a Security Council resolution, which the Soviets would surely not endorse. Instead, he asked Washington to provide him with the details of its planned military aid so that he could draft a letter for Adoula requesting U.S. assistance. Kennedy approved Thant's proposal, but before it could be implemented, in late December 1962, Katangese troops once again began firing on ONUC soldiers and setting up roadblocks throughout Elisabethville. Instructed by Thant to remove the roadblocks, UN troops moved quickly against Tshombe's gendarme and in a matter of a few days secured all of the capital. On January 1 and 2, 1963, Tshombe desperately requested that Thant suspend military operations against his forces and permit new negotiations to take place, but Thant refused. The State Department, however, wanted Tshombe to enter talks with Adoula on integrating Katangese forces into the Congolese army and felt that an all-out attack would discourage him from doing so. Washington, therefore, advised Thant to limit the scope of the UN military operation. Although Thant cabled these instructions to his forces in Africa, the message did not get through and UN forces moved relentlessly ahead. On January 3, 1963, ONUC occupied the key mining center of Jadotville. The acting secretary-general, fearful that mercenaries would blow up sensitive mining installations in Kolwezi, the last bastion of the Katangese government, ordered ONUC to stop fighting and instead demanded that Tshombe permit UN troops to occupy the city. On January 21, Tshombe, unable to offer any resistance to ONUC, relented, and UN forces, in a successful climax to "Operation Grand Slam," took Kolwezi. The Katangese secession was finally over.

Despite the years of violence and terror, UN operations in the Congo did succeed in establishing some semblance of political order in the troubled state. But the cost to the UN was high, as more than two hundred people operating in behalf of the organization lost their lives and close to $400 million was expended. While Thant displayed strength in employment of UN troops, the Congo experience actually reduced the organization's capacity for independent activity. Because two of the great powers, France and the Soviet Union, emerged from the Congo operation hostile to further UN peacekeeping, the organization soon found itself near bankruptcy, as both countries refused to contribute funds to future UN operations.

In retrospect, the Congo was hardly different from other newly independent third world states, crippled by tribalism and with a leadership ill-prepared for the responsibilities of government or management of the economy. What thrust the Congo into the forefront of world attention was the intensity of the violence that accompanied the country's political unraveling and the cold war rivalry that brought a global dimension to what was essentially a tribal conflict. Indeed, without the UN peacekeeping operation, it is likely that the superpowers would have intervened themselves. Had the Congo conflict escalated into a direct Soviet-American military confrontation, the consequences for the world might have been far more significant.

From the standpoint of the United Nations, the Congo confrontation demonstrated a fundamental rift over which approach the organization should adopt to hasten decolonization. Following the death of Premier Joseph Stalin in 1953, Soviet foreign policy underwent a perceptible shift, manifesting a greater willingness on the part of the Kremlin to seek the friendship of the new nations of Africa and Asia. This change showed itself in an aggressive Soviet effort to win allies among the world's new states and included as its instruments arms sales, foreign aid, diplomatic support, and in the United Nations, increasingly vocal opposition to the remaining vestiges of colonialism. In January 1961, Premier Khrushchev, rejecting the hard-line view that nuclear war could be fought and won, argued in an East Berlin speech that the Soviets would prevail in the cold war by winning the hearts and minds of third world peoples.

The United States also supported in principle the struggle for independence in the third world, but its interests and objectives were far more complex. Whereas the Soviets had nothing to lose by stridently attacking colonialism and the remaining colonial powers, the United States had to balance its instinctive support for independence with its need to sustain the friendship of European alliance partners who were frequently reluctant to relinquish their colonial control. Whereas the Soviets invariably demanded immediate independence for third world peoples and pushed the United Nations to adopt an aggressive stance against colonialism, Washington favored a more evolutionary approach that typically supported independence in principle but opposed the imposition of sanctions upon colonial powers. This approach frequently placed Washington at odds with the new General Assembly majority, which, for example, regularly voted, along with the Soviet Union, to impose sanctions on Portugal for its colonial policies in Africa.

The Congo proved a perfect battleground for these opposing views. The Soviets had initially joined in the formation of ONUC in order to hasten Belgium's ouster from the Congo and to appear as the champion of the third world's struggle against colonialism. The UN's frustration of Lumumba's ambitions after his disagreement with President Kasavubu, however, quickly turned Moscow against ONUC and the secretary-general. In September 1960, the Soviet Union proposed a Security Council resolution requiring ONUC to relinquish control of the Congo's airports and radio stations, seized earlier under the instructions of UN representative Andrew Cordier. The failure of that resolution and the Soviets' veto of a Tunisian-sponsored resolution affirming the council's confidence in Hammarskjöld effectively stymied the council and forced the issue into the General Assembly. From then until Lumumba's death in February 1961, Hammarskjöld, unable to secure Russian cooperation in the council, proceeded under the authority of the General Assembly, a maneuver that the Soviets claimed to be a violation of the charter. Following Lumumba's assassination and after Hammarskjöld's death, the Russians voted with the rest of the Security Council to authorize more decisive measures against the Katangese secession, and Thant was therefore able to claim council support for subsequent military actions in the Congo. For the most part, though, the Soviets ceased to be a factor in the UN's Congo policy. They had little leverage over the factions in the Congo, and, since Lumumba's death, little hope of influencing the outcome of the power struggle in the troubled African country. With the United Nations and its secretary-general committed to ending the Katangese secession and with the third world majority firmly in support of Thant's policies, the most the Kremlin could do was to periodically criticize the acting secretary-general for not pushing Tshombe harder.

In the United States the Kennedy Administration agreed with Khrushchev's assessment that the cold war arena had shifted to the third world and took very seriously internal struggles in places like the Congo. The Americans viewed ONUC as a means to strengthen the pro-Western government that had evolved in Léopoldville and as an instrument to end the secession in Katanga, which, as long as it lasted, provided Moscow with continued opportunities to declaim against Western colonialism. Ultimately, the American vision prevailed as secession was ended, pro-Soviet political figures were thwarted, and a superpower military confrontation was averted. In the Congo, Thant's objectives paralleled those of the United States, allowing the secretary-general to coordinate his activities with the UN's most powerful member. Thant's strong relationship with Washington, which was characteristic of his early experience at the UN, paid dividends for both parties, as the organization implemented policies consistent with American interests and Thant displayed attributes of leadership that would gain him an early reputation for decisiveness.

The UN role in the Congo did not end with the termination of the Katangese secession, for its troops remained there until mid-1964 while large-scale UN and U.S. economic aid to the central government continued. In one of history's great ironies, when Tshombe became prime minister of the Congo in 1964 his accession triggered a rebellion by secessionists in the Stanleyville area. Once again, European powers intervened on Tshombe's behalf, but this time in his capacity as leader of a "united" Congo. U.S.-provided aircraft transported Belgian paratroopers, now fighting against antigovernment rebels, into battle. In November and December 1964, the UN Security Council again considered the problem of a Congolese secession, but the organization, hopelessly divided and virtually bankrupt, merely urged all members to refrain from intervening in Congolese affairs. In 1965, when General Joseph Mobuto seized power in the Congo, Tshombe was stripped of his parliamentary seat and forced into exile. In 1967, his private airplane was hijacked and commandeered to Algeria where he was imprisoned until his death in 1969.

THE CUBAN MISSILE CRISIS

While the Congo necessarily occupied a large portion of the acting secretary-general's time, it was not the most dangerous international crisis to demand his attention. In October 1962, events in the Caribbean placed the superpowers on the precipice of nuclear war and thrust Thant into his most sensitive and important role as secretary-general. It also demonstrated the usefulness of the office of secretary-general as a potential broker between the superpowers.

The immediate catalyst for the Cuban missile crisis was the American intelligence discovery that the Soviets were in the process of placing offensive nuclear missiles in Cuba, ninety miles from American shores. The U.S. obsession with Cuba had actually begun several years earlier with avowed socialist Fidel Castro's rise to power in Havana. Castro's growing friendship with the Soviet Union, coupled with American cuts in sugar imports and Cuban nationalizations of

American-owned companies, culminated in January 1961 in a severance of diplomatic relations between the two countries. When Kennedy assumed office, he inherited a plan for the invasion of the island by Cuban exiles, and in April 1961, he authorized execution of the plan. The ill-fated fiasco at the Bay of Pigs resulted, and, over the next several years, the United States sponsored efforts to oust the Castro regime through internal subversion and assassination.

Cuban efforts to raise the matter of U.S.-Cuban relations before the Security Council were consistently stymied by U.S. insistence that the issue lay more properly with the Organization of American States (OAS). In January 1962, the OAS issued its "Final Act" at Punta del Este, Uruguay, and effectively excluded the Cuban regime from the inter-American system. Cuba demanded that the Security Council obtain from the International Court of Justice an advisory opinion regarding the legality of the OAS action, but the Security Council, bowing to U.S. adamancy, refused to consider the question. Cuba thereupon charged that the OAS resolution was a prelude to a full-scale American invasion of the island.

Throughout the summer of 1962, rumors circulated that Moscow was placing offensive missiles in Cuba, but President Kennedy, unable to substantiate the reports, downplayed the seriousness of the threat. Finally, on October 14, 1962, a high-flying U-2 reconnaissance aircraft photographed clear evidence that Soviet installations were being equipped with offensive nuclear missiles. This revelation triggered an extraordinary and highly secretive decision-making process in Washington, climaxing in President Kennedy's announcement, on the evening of October 22, that the United States would impose a naval quarantine around the island.

As late as September 17, Thant had dismissed the possibility that the United States and Soviet Union would actually risk war over Cuba. Kennedy's announcement did not, however, catch Thant by surprise. On Saturday, October 20, Thant's military adviser, General Indar Jit Rikhye, had informed him that the Kennedy Administration possessed irrefutable proof of the existence of Soviet missiles in Cuba. Nonetheless, the harshness of the president's speech and Kennedy's decision to air the problem publicly rather than through secret diplomatic channels convinced Thant of the seriousness of the evolving confrontation. As he said in his first public statement on the crisis, "If today the United Nations should prove itself ineffective, it may have proved itself so for all time."[5]

On October 23, the Security Council first met to consider the crisis. Ambassador Stevenson, who during the previous week had participated in high-level Washington discussions to plan a response to the Soviet action, introduced an American draft resolution calling on the Soviets to remove their missiles from Cuba and authorizing the acting secretary-general to dispatch observers to supervise the withdrawal. Soviet Ambassador Valerian Zorin, who by chance was acting as president of the Security Council, bitterly rebutted the American delegate's charge that there were offensive missiles on the island and instead called on the Security Council to condemn the American naval quarantine. Meanwhile, in a move designed to confer legality on the blockade, the Kennedy Administration arranged for the OAS, which invoked the 1947 Inter-American Treaty of Reciprocal Assistance, to pass a resolution affirming the U.S. stand.

On the evening of October 23, delegates from more than forty countries urged Thant to take immediate action to ease the crisis. On October 24, even as the blockade went into effect, the acting secretary-general, ignoring appeals from the Kennedy Administration that he delay his initiative by twenty-four hours, sent identical letters to Chairman Khrushchev and President Kennedy. Thant appealed to the Russians not to send arms to Cuba for a period of two to three weeks and urged the Americans to suspend the blockade for a similar period of time. In deference to a request by Stevenson, the acting secretary-general, when informing the Security Council on the dispatch of his letters, called on the Soviets to cease construction on the missile sites. His position angered Zorin, who complained to Thant privately that the latter's remarks seemed to prejudge the situation.

Khrushchev, by now perhaps looking for some face-saving measure that would allow him to remove the missiles, responded favorably to the acting secretary-general's request, and a number of Soviet vessels appeared to turn back rather than test the blockade. Kennedy, who was interested not only in halting further shipments of arms but also in gaining the dismantlement of existing weapons, welcomed Thant's intervention but refrained from lifting the quarantine. On October 25, the acting secretary-general once again wrote to the two heads of state. Acting on a recommendation from Stevenson, he asked Khrushchev to postpone testing of the blockade and Kennedy to ensure that his navy would not engage in any hair-trigger action. Both leaders responded favorably to the acting secretary-general's appeal.

Despite the apparent willingness on the part of both sides not to take precipitate action, the continuing pace of missile construction on the island threatened a stronger American response, perhaps even an air strike against the installations. On October 26, bypassing Thant for the first time, Khrushchev sent a long, emotional letter directly to the president, offering to remove the missiles in exchange for an American pledge not to invade the island. Before the administration could respond, another, harsher letter arrived on October 27, suggesting a trade of missiles in Cuba in return for the dismantlement of U.S. Jupiter missiles in Turkey. It was the second letter, according to most accounts, that led a despairing administration to begin preparations for an imminent attack against the Caribbean island. Years later, however, Secretary of State Dean Rusk revealed that Kennedy would not have let the largely obsolete Jupiters stand in the way of the removal of missile sites in Cuba. Unknown to Thant, Rusk, at Kennedy's instruction, telephoned Ambassador Andrew Cordier and dictated a statement—to be read by Thant on further signal from the United States—proposing a trade of Turkish for Cuban missiles. Thant's services, however, were to prove unnecessary, as the Kennedy crisis team chose to respond to Khrushchev's pacific October 26 letter and ignore the bellicose letter of October 27. On October 28, Khrushchev agreed to remove the missiles in return for a U.S. pledge that Cuba would not be attacked.

The dramatic swirl of diplomatic activity involving Washington, Moscow, and the UN occurred without Castro's full knowledge or participation. On October 27, Thant accepted the Cuban government's invitation to visit Havana to discuss the imbroglio. On October 29, with Khrushchev and Kennedy in apparent agreement on a formula for resolving the crisis, Thant embarked for Cuba with the hope of gaining Castro's acceptance of UN or Red Cross supervision of the withdrawal of Soviet missiles. The acting secretary-general discovered, however, that Castro was in no mood to be accommodating. Stung by Khrushchev's unilateral retreat and angered by the flexing of American power against his nation, he issued a "Five Point" plan for resolution of the crisis, which included the withdrawal of all American troops from their base at Guantánamo Bay. Despite pressures from the Soviet Union and clear evidence that the Russians had begun to dismantle the missiles, Castro refused to permit any international inspection. After two lengthy bargaining sessions, Thant returned home empty-handed. The superpower agreement that ended the crisis was monitored by unilateral U.S. surveillance of Cuban shipping, and an important role for international peacekeeping was lost.

Both superpowers recognized that Thant had played a useful role in resolving the Cuban missile crisis, and they rewarded his efforts by offering him a full term as secretary-general. Before the Cuban confrontation the Soviets had still been insisting the post should be reorganized along the lines of their troika scheme. To be sure, the acting secretary-general had not resolved the fundamental difference of opinion between the two sides over Cuba, but he did manage to act as a facilitator, kept lines of communication open, and helped to defuse tensions when they were highest. Thant's role was made indispensable by the inability of the two governments to communicate directly, a problem that was corrected only during the last days of the crisis through the discovery of back channels for communication. Had Thant not demonstrated such scrupulous evenhandedness, despite his personal inclination to view the president's quarantine act as politically dangerous and legally questionable, he could not have played so useful a function.

If there was a disturbing lesson to be drawn from the Cuban missile crisis, it was not in reference to the role of the acting secretary-general. The events of October 1962 raised instead serious questions about the ability of the UN to restrain superpowers when they acted in apparent contravention of the principles of the organization. The Kennedy Administration based its right to blockade the island on the decision of the OAS. As the charter states, "Nothing in the present Charter precludes the existence of regional arrangements or agencies for dealing with such matters relating to the maintenance of international peace and security as are appropriate for regional action." But the charter continues, "no enforcement action shall be taken under regional arrangements . . . without the authorization of the Security Council."[6] It is understandable that the United States, determined to remove the missiles, would not approach the veto-plagued Security Council to authorize an act that Russia must oppose. Nonetheless, it is also clear that the charter, for better or worse, mandates remedies short of the use of force in dealing with international disputes. The missile crisis demonstrated that the superpowers would act unilaterally in defense of their perceived national interest, no matter the wording and intent of the charter. Thant recognized this reality when he commented in a news conference several months after the Cuban crisis, "the United Nations cannot overawe the nuclear powers. I think that is an accepted fact."[7] Nonetheless, Thant seemed pleased with the modest role he was able to play in easing the big power confrontation, and on November 30, 1962, he gracefully accepted a full term as secretary-general. His acceptance speech provided a succinct epitaph for his efforts in the Cuban missiles crisis. "If I now accept an extended term, it is because I do believe that I may be able to play a role, however humble, in the easing of tensions and in bridging the gulf between the major powers."[8]

CONCLUSION

Both the Congo and Cuban missile crises demonstrated that the United Nations was an arena where traditional cold war patterns of superpower interaction and the striving for national self-assertion in the third world would meet. To be sure, significant differences distinguished the two crises. The Congo was a newly independent nation riven by internal war, while Cuba, independent for some sixty years, was united under a strong government. The Soviet-American conflict in the Congo was played out through surrogates, but the Cuban crisis brought the superpowers into a direct military confrontation that threatened nuclear war. The Congo crisis dragged on for several years, while the missile crisis began and ended within two weeks.

Yet there were similarities. The Congo and Cuban crises followed a developing pattern in Soviet-American competition for the friendship of third world states. In both cases, an intensely nationalistic and avowedly Marxist leader faced the hostility of the United States and mobilized the attendant support of the Soviet Union. Both superpowers resorted to extraordinary means to buttress their respective allies and cripple their respective opponents. Third world nations looked toward the United Nations to intervene—in the case of the Congo, to restore the territorial integrity of the state and legitimacy of the central government, and in the case of Cuba, to prevent the escalation of the Soviet-American confrontation into a nuclear conflagration. In both cases, the United Nations helped to avert a superpower shooting war—in the Congo, by making it impossible for either of the nuclear giants to introduce its own troops into the country, and, to a lesser degree, in the Cuban crisis, by providing Kennedy and Khrushchev with mechanisms by which each could retreat from a hard-line position without losing face.

Thant acquitted himself capably in meeting these early tests of his ability to lead the UN in the spirit of Hammarskjöld. He continued his predecessor's policy in the Congo, but managed not to alienate the Soviet Union in the process. He showed himself to be an impartial intermediary during the Cuban crisis and provided the superpowers with a useful channel for communication. Despite Thant's belief that the cold war was of passing consequence next to the quest for self-determination among third world nations, both crises demonstrated the extent to which all the issues at the United Nations became inevitably tangled in the web of Soviet-American rivalry. Thant now appeared to understand this reality and acted accordingly. His early performance won Thant respect from both the superpowers and the third world, and his election to a complete term as secretary-general confirmed their approbation. By January 1963, the politics of the United Nations were considerably less roiled than they had been when Thant assumed office. The interminable Congo crisis was nearing its resolution with the position of secretary-general more secure. Moreover, the superpowers had managed to survive the missile crisis, a confrontation climaxing several years of escalating tension that had followed the erection of the Berlin Wall and the resumption of atmospheric nuclear testing in 1961. The world, nonetheless, remained a dangerous place as new problems centered in the third world assumed increasing prominence. The challenge Thant faced was to manage these problems while steering the United Nations through years of fiscal crisis and doubt about the organization's ultimate ability to survive.

Appendix 1A

The Nuclear Test Ban Treaty, 1963

On August 5, 1963, the foreign ministers of the United States, Soviet Union, and United Kingdom met in Moscow to sign a treaty banning the testing of nuclear weapons in three environments—the air, the sea, and outer space. Agreement on the Partial Nuclear Test Ban Treaty successfully completed five years of difficult East-West negotiations, which witnessed considerable third world agitation favoring a prohibition against testing. While the treaty was ultimately concluded through intensive three power negotiations in Moscow, the United Nations, through the device of an Eighteen Nation Disarmament Committee (ENDC) convening in Geneva, played a key role in prodding the nuclear powers toward agreement, despite the apparent intractability of the issues dividing them.

The United Nations had been a forum for disarmament negotiations since 1946, when the United States used the newly created United Nations Atomic Energy Commission to air its ill-fated nuclear disarmament proposal, the Baruch Plan. Six years later, in 1952, the General Assembly merged the Atomic Energy Commission with the Commission for Conventional Armaments to form the UN Disarmament Commission. In 1954, a subcommittee of the Disarmament Commission was created to allow negotiations among the United States, Soviet Union, Great Britain, Canada, and France. For years, the Western powers and Soviet Union exchanged ambitious disarmament schemes, involving both conventional and nuclear forces, but the wide political gulf between East and West led all negotiations down an endless tunnel.

Adding to the complexity of the talks was the issue of radioactive fallout. In March 1954, the United States exploded a hydrogen weapon in the atmosphere over the Bikini Atoll in the Marshall Islands. Fallout from the American nuclear test extended over a wide area, caused the highly publicized contamination of a Japanese fishing vessel, and generated widespread public concern about the hazards of nuclear radiation. In April 1954, Indian Prime Minister Jawaharlal Nehru, a leader of the nonaligned movement, called for the immediate cessation of all nuclear testing, a demand that exerted tremendous pressure on both nuclear giants, each eager to court the good opinion of the third world.

In 1957, two events occurred that shifted the focus of arms control negotiations from disarmament to a test ban. On June 14, the Soviets offered to accept a limited number of control posts on their territory as part of a treaty prohibiting nuclear testing. The Soviet concession went some way toward meeting Western insistence that any test ban would require international inspection. In response, the United States and Great Britain agreed to decouple the test ban issue from the larger question of disarmament and to focus international attention on the specific issue of nuclear testing. The new position represented an about-face for the Anglo-American allies, who had steadfastly resisted any constraint on their nuclear capabilities so long as the Soviet Union enjoyed a huge advantage in conventional forces. The second major development occurred in the fall, when eleven separate disarmament resolutions were offered to what became known as the "Disarmament General Assembly." A U.S. resolution, which passed the General Assembly by a vote of 56–9, with 15 abstentions, called for a test ban as part of a phased agreement toward eventual disarmament and asked that a conference of scientific experts explore technical means of inspection. The Russians, who wished to separate the test ban issue from the larger disarmament question, were upset at yet another loss in the American-dominated assembly and left both the Disarmament Commission and subcommittee, calling instead for a reconstituted committee comprising all UN members.

The Soviet pullout left the United Nations without an institutional role in disarmament negotiations at a time when East and West were beginning to narrow their differences over the feasibility of negotiating the test ban issue. In the summer of 1958, an East-West Conference of Experts reported that the technical means to police a test ban including underground explosions could indeed be devised. Coinciding with the onset of an unofficial test moratorium, the conference of experts gave impetus to three power Geneva negotiations on the cessation of nuclear testing. Those negotiations began in October 1958 in a UN facility with a UN observer present, but were nonetheless officially outside the auspices of the United Nations.

At the Geneva negotiations, the inspection issue posed the greatest obstacle to agreement, along with the frequent crises in political relations between the United States and the Soviet Union. For example, Premier Nikita Khrushchev's visit to the United States in September 1959 spawned a series of Soviet concessions that raised hopes that the inspections issue would be overcome; but those hopes were dashed by the Soviet shooting-down of an American spy plane in May 1960 and the subsequent cancellation of a scheduled East-West summit. In another example of the sharp twists and turns of nuclear diplomacy, Moscow's unhappiness with Secretary-General Hammarskjöld and the UN's Congo policy led the Soviets to insist on a troika scheme for the proposed international test ban commission. The Soviet decision to resume nuclear testing in September 1961 and the American response in kind further aggravated the course of negotiations.

The first year of the Kennedy Administration did not appreciably improve East-West relations but did lead to a renewed American effort to ignite the Geneva negotiations. As a result, in December 1961 the General Assembly passed a joint American-Soviet statement on principles of disarmament, including provision for the convening of an Eighteen Nation Committee on Disarmament to discuss implementation of the measures outlined in the joint resolution. The eighteen were to include not only five Western and five Eastern bloc nations, but also eight nonaligned governments—Brazil, Burma, Ethiopia, India, Mexico, Nigeria, Sweden, and the United Arab Republic. The inclusion of the nonaligned governments signaled the importance of the issue of nuclear testing to the third world and its hope of acting as a mediating third force between East and West. Nonaligned conferences, such as the Afro-Asian Solidarity Conference of 1958 and the Belgrade Conference of 1961, had made clear that termination of nuclear testing was among the highest priorities of the third world.

The Eighteen Nation Disarmament Committee convened in Geneva on March 14, 1962. While U Thant attended only one session, senior Secretariat officials were always present to lend their assistance. Of the eighteen nations invited to the conference, France, which was determined to continue nuclear testing, did not attend.

The Peoples' Republic of China, two years away from its first nuclear test, was absent as well. The opening of the conference demonstrated the continuing impasse over basic issues, with both sides staking out by now familiar positions. But the inclusion of eight nonaligned nations distinguished the ENDC from the previous three power Geneva talks, and the eight, on April 16, 1962, unveiled a new plan to break the great power stalemate. The suggested plan was deliberately vague, calling for control posts and an international commission but leaving open the question of whether inspections should be voluntary or obligatory. This ambiguity allowed East and West to interpret the memorandum in their own separate ways, and the nonaligned initiative became the basis for continued but futile discussions. In August the Russians rejected two new American draft treaty proposals and soon thereafter the Cuban missile crisis erupted, totally overshadowing the test ban negotiations.

The peaceful conclusion of the missile crisis raised hopes for a breakthrough at Geneva. In November 1962, the General Assembly overwhelmingly endorsed the eight-nation memorandum, and in December, Premier Khrushchev and President Kennedy exchanged conciliatory letters, with the Soviet leader renewing his long-abandoned offer to allow three on-site inspections. Meanwhile, new scientific means to detect underground nuclear tests permitted the United States to reduce the number of annual inspections it would demand. In this hopeful atmosphere, representatives of the United States and Soviet Union met in New York in early January 1963 to discuss the test ban issue. All optimistic forecasts notwithstanding, the negotiations again collapsed in mutual misunderstanding and recrimination, and the resumption of the ENDC, on February 12, found East and West still hopelessly divided over the number of inspections that would be required. At this point, delegates from the eight nations prepared another compromise formula, this time proposing a fixed number of inspections over a five or seven year period, thus allowing nations to bank inspections from one year to the next. According to Indian delegate Arthur Lall, the United States and the Soviet Union prevailed on the nonaligned governments to terminate that initiative, since both states were beginning to retreat from the idea of a comprehensive ban. Each believed that the nonaligned proposal would create unwelcome pressure to actually conclude a comprehensive treaty. In the end, ambassadors from the United States, the Soviet Union, and Great Britain abandoned the

ENDC forum and negotiated a modest ban on atmospheric, under-sea, and outer space testing.

The test ban negotiations demonstrated the strengths and weaknesses of the third world and the UN in compelling the superpowers to restrain the arms race. One major factor pushing the United States toward test ban talks was the pressure exerted by nonaligned states in favor of an end to nuclear testing. As the record demonstrates, the United States entered test ban talks only reluctantly, instead viewing the possession of nuclear weapons as a powerful antidote to the conventional military power of the Soviet Union. Both the United States and the Soviet Union regarded disarmament negotiations—including the test ban—as occasions for propaganda warfare, and both countries struggled mightily to avoid allowing the other to seize the high road of peace.

The other lesson of the test ban is that the superpowers could not be forced to do what was not in their respective interests. For all the moral weight of the nonaligned nations' arguments in behalf of the test ban, it was not they who owned and tested nuclear weapons. When it appeared that another intervention by the eight nonaligned states would push the superpowers toward an underground ban they no longer wanted, the ENDC ceased to be an effective negotiating ground. Instead, the United States, the Soviet Union, and Great Britain reverted to trilateral diplomacy and quickly hammered out an acceptable agreement. In a largely bipolar world, the realities of military power meant that disarmament would ultimately be decided on by those who had the weapons.

NOTES

1. Andrew W. Cordier and Max Harrelson, eds., *Public Papers of the Secretaries-General of the United Nations, Vol. VI, U Thant* (New York: Columbia University Press, 1976), 49.

2. U Thant, *View from the UN* (Garden City, N.Y.: Doubleday, 1975), 136.

3. Cordier and Harrelson, *Public Papers, Vol. VI,* 51.

4. Rames Nassif, *U Thant in New York: 1961–1971* (New York: St. Martin's, 1988), 98.

5. Cordier and Harrelson, *Public Papers, Vol. VI,* 237.

6. Cited in Peter R. Baehr and Leon Gordenker, *The United Nations in the 1990s* (New York: St. Martin's, 1994), 170–171.

7. Cordier and Harrelson, *Public Papers, Vol. VI,* 366.

8. Cordier and Harrelson, *Public Papers, Vol. VI,* 253.

2

Peacekeeping in the Third World

Newfound independence for third world nations inevitably brought with it disorder and strife, as unstable governments struggled to secure their boundaries in the face of grinding and intractable poverty, debilitating ethnic and religious diversity, and continuing confrontation with former colonial powers. As tensions erupted into violence, pressure increased for the United Nations to lend its unique skills to the peacekeeping task. Thant himself favored a vigorous UN response to third world strife; he saw the secretary-general as a trusted figure capable of building bridges between nations in conflict. Two factors, however, limited Thant's capacity to respond aggressively to his turbulent environment. First, the refusal of France and the Soviet Union to pay for peacekeeping obligations incurred by the United Nations in the Congo and the Sinai had thrown the organization into deep financial turmoil. In the early 1960s the UN had barely enough funds to meet its operating budget, let alone to shoulder new and even more expensive burdens abroad. Second, the Soviets, wedded to the principle that authority for peacekeeping resided only in the Security Council and reluctant to engage the United Nations in further peacekeeping missions, opposed ceding that authority to any other instrument, including the secretary-general.

In meeting increasing demands on the organization for peacekeeping assistance, Thant confronted two powerful challenges: first, to find the resources to fund new operations and, second, to circumvent Soviet resistance to expanding the organization's peacekeeping function. This combination of contradictory trends—the increasing need for peacekeeping, on the one hand, and the growing constraints on the UN's ability to provide for it, on the other—occupied much of Thant's time and creative energy during his early years in office. This chapter chronicles five cases of UN involvement in third world strife, in West Irian (West New Guinea), Yemen, Malaysia, Cyprus, and Kashmir. While the circumstances surrounding each operation differed in scope and form, they all tested the secretary-general's ability to employ the organization's peacekeeping machinery in an uncertain political and financial environment.

WEST IRIAN (WEST NEW GUINEA)

The dispute over West Irian involved the governments of the Netherlands and Indonesia in a conflict over West New Guinea (referred to by Indonesia as West Irian), the easternmost portion of the Dutch East Indies and a territory whose status had been left unresolved since 1949, when Indonesia had come into existence as an independent state. For centuries the Dutch had ruled over the East Indies, and they refused to relinquish jurisdiction over West New Guinea until a negotiated settlement could provide the indigenous Papuans some measure of self-determination. Indonesia, arguing that West Irian formed an integral part of the East Indies and proud of its independent status, insisted on immediate cession of the territory and rejected the Netherlands' offer to submit the issue to the International Court of Justice. Beginning in 1954, Djakarta repeatedly referred the dispute to the General Assembly, but resolutions supporting its position failed to garner the necessary two-thirds majority.

By the late 1950s, Holland, recognizing the growth of third world power in the General Assembly and the UN's increasingly vocal opposition to colonialism, offered to relinquish sovereignty over New Guinea in return for a UN-sponsored plebiscite and temporary UN administration over the territory. Indonesia, however, demanded immediate transfer of West Irian to its own authority, with no guarantee that a plebiscite would follow. In December 1961, Indonesian President Sukarno, among the most flamboyant but increasingly influential third world leaders on the international scene, ordered his countrymen to embark upon the "liberation" of West Irian. In an apparent effort to defuse tensions, Dutch Prime Minister Jan Eduard de Quay announced in January 1962 that the Netherlands would begin negotiations on West New Guinea in the absence of an Indonesian commitment to the principle of self-rule for the Papuans. But Sukarno rejected the Dutch concession, instead calling on the Dutch to withdraw from the territory as a precondition for negotiations. With both sides building up their military presence in the area and Indonesia threatening to invade the territory, tensions between the two countries escalated into brief but dangerous military skirmishes, including a naval battle between Indonesian torpedo boats and Dutch vessels.

Acting Secretary-General Thant, alarmed at the increasingly violent nature of the conflict, pleaded with both governments to avoid a major military confrontation and arranged for the return from Dutch custody of Indonesian soldiers taken as prisoners of war. On January 17, 1962, Thant offered to hold talks with both governments, and on January 22 he met separately in preliminary discussions with representatives of each side. He was further encouraged when in February, President Kennedy's brother, Attorney General Robert F. Kennedy, visited Indonesia to discuss with Sukarno the possibility of an American role in brokering the West Irian dispute. Washington was concerned that a war between Holland, a NATO member and ally of the United States, and Indonesia, a leading member of the nonaligned bloc, could push Sukarno closer to the Soviet Union and generate anti-American sentiment among third world nations. Presidential biographer Arthur Schlesinger Jr. wrote that Kennedy, who had little regard for Sukarno, was nonetheless reluctant to make West New Guinea into a cold war battleground. He understood that as had been the case in other conflicts pitting third world nations against European colonial powers, Moscow had nothing to lose by stridently supporting Indonesia against a country allied to the United States. For years the Soviets had encouraged Sukarno's belligerently anti-Western form of nonalignment and were supplying him with arms to fight the Dutch. The United States, on the other hand, stood to lose significant political capital in the third world if a war erupted between Holland and Indonesia, a war that would inevitably compel Washington to support its NATO ally. When Robert Kennedy returned to the United States in March, he, in an obvious gesture toward Djakarta, announced on American television that the Indonesians had "a strong argument" against Holland. Meanwhile, Assistant Secretary of State Averell Harriman lobbied the Dutch to come to the negotiating table. It was at the suggestion of the Kennedy Administration that Thant appointed veteran American diplomat Ellsworth Bunker to act as mediator between the two governments.

Formal negotiations began outside Washington on March 20, 1962, but were suspended on March 26 when Sukarno, contending that the Dutch had no intention of recognizing the Indonesian claim to the territory, recalled his delegation to Djakarta.

With discussions in limbo, fighting broke out between Indonesian paratroopers and Dutch forces on May 15. Dutch Premier Jan Eduard de Quay asked Thant to convene the Security Council to order a stop to the Indonesian paratroop invasion and to send observers to New Guinea; Thant, arguing that such a gesture would entail his taking the Dutch side in the conflict, refused. Bunker and Thant met in New York, agreed on a new diplomatic initiative, and on May 26, the Netherlands and Indonesia agreed to hold discussions on a new U.S. peace plan.

Meeting at Camp David, Dutch and Indonesian negotiators accepted Bunker's plan to temporarily cede Dutch control to the United Nations, pending a transfer of authority to Djakarta and the implementation of a plebiscite for the territory's Papuan population. On August 15, 1962, the two governments signed an accord that resolved their dispute, with Premier de Quay telling his parliament that he was compelled to sign because the United States would not assist the Dutch in a war against Indonesia. A truce went into effect in New Guinea on August 17, and diplomatic relations between Djakarta and The Hague, broken in 1960, were restored. On August 21, Thant's military adviser, Lieutenant General Indar Jit Rikhye, arrived in the disputed territory with twenty officers taken from UN peacekeeping forces in the Middle East and the Congo. On September 21, 1962, the General Assembly voted 89–0–14 in favor of a UN role in easing the transition to Indonesian control over West Irian and gave the secretary-general wide latitude in administering the territory. On October 1, during ceremonies in West Irian, the secretary-general's deputy, José Rolz-Bennett, announced the termination of Dutch rule.

The UN operation in West Irian was extraordinary in two ways. Under provisions of the Indonesian-Dutch accord and subsequent General Assembly resolution, a UN-administered entity, known as the United Nations Temporary Executive Authority in West New Guinea (UNTEA), was established, representing the first such case of direct UN administration of a territory. Backed by a UN security force made up primarily of Pakistani soldiers, the UN administrator, Dr. Djalal Abdoh of Iran, effectively defused the military confrontation between Dutch and Indonesian forces and managed to exercise broad administrative authority over the territory. The second distinctive feature of UNTEA was its funding by the parties to the conflict, a formula that was to be successfully repeated in other trouble spots and that protected the financially troubled UN.

On May 1, 1963, after resisting insistent demands by Sukarno that he step up the timetable for ceding control over West Irian to Indonesia, Thant authorized the formal transfer of UN jurisdiction over the territory to the Indonesian government. The secretary-general then organized a special fund to encourage investment in the primitive area and appointed UN officials to assist in conducting a plebiscite, as provided for in the Dutch-Indonesian accord of August 1962. Indonesia was never entirely happy with the plebiscite provision, and it was not until 1969 that a vote was administered. The election revealed that the inhabitants of West Irian favored maintaining their link with Indonesia.

Thant's role in the West Irian dispute was actually fairly modest. The principal negotiator was American diplomat Ellsworth Bunker, and the chief administrator of the UN operation was the field supervisor, Dr. Abdoh. Moreover, Kennedy's decision not to back the Netherlands against Sukarno forced The Hague into negotiating what it considered to be a capitulatory agreement. Had those in the State Department who favored backing the Dutch prevailed with President Kennedy, it is likely that Holland would have fought a war rather than surrender to Sukarno. Nonetheless, Thant's contributions were useful. He intervened with personal notes to the disputants when the crisis first began to boil over and involved himself again when negotiations threatened to collapse. At all times he made the machinery of the world organization available to the parties to the conflict. Thant considered the West Irian dispute a success on several fronts. UN involvement prevented a nasty military confrontation from escalating, and the organization acted successfully without assuming additional financial encumbrances. Again the UN had demonstrated that it was capable of innovative peacekeeping activities. Finally, UN involvement in West Irian paved the way for decolonization of a specific colonial territory, an objective important to the UN of the 1960s and to Thant personally.

CIVIL WAR IN YEMEN

The resolution of the West Irian crisis coincided with the eruption of a new third world flashpoint, this time in the Middle East. Yemen, a small and arid patch of land occupying the southwestern portion of the Arabian peninsula, was bordered to the north by Saudi Arabia and to the south by the People's Democratic Republic of South Yemen, which until 1967 had been the British colony of Aden. On September 19, 1962, upon the death of Imam Ahmed, the longtime leader of the largely tribal society, Crown Prince Imam Mohammed al-Badr, ascended to the Yemeni throne. Several days later Radio Sana announced that the new imam had been killed in a palace coup and that a republic had been proclaimed by Colonel Abdullah al-Sallal, former commander of the imam's bodyguard. But the new imam had, in fact, not been killed. He had fled Sana to the safety of the country's northern mountains and then proceeded to organize his followers for war against the republican rebels.

The ensuing civil war led to a drawing of battle lines in the already fractious Arab Middle East. Egypt, which had played a hand in inspiring al-Sallal's coup, tendered immediate recognition to the republican government, as did the more radical Arab states of Syria and Iraq. Saudi Arabia and Jordan, however, both governed by conservative monarchs, continued to recognize the threatened imam. Underlying the intra-Arab cleavage over Yemen was a more fundamental dispute, brewing since July 1952, when Egyptian military officers led by Colonel Gamal Abdel Nasser toppled the scandal-ridden regime of King Farouk I. With revolutionary ideology sweeping the Arab world, the Egyptian president played a hand in an aborted overthrow of Jordan's King Hussein and intervened to destabilize a pro-Western government in Lebanon. In 1958, the Iraqi monarchy fell to a military coup and Egypt joined with Syria to form the United Arab Republic. Arab monarchies seemed everywhere under attack, and the outbreak of civil war in Yemen, a state contiguous with Saudi Arabia, now threatened to spill antiroyalist activity into the very heart of the Saudi regime.

Sensing an opportunity to spread his revolution even farther, Nasser, in October 1962, dispatched troops to Yemen to assist the republicans while the Saudis countered with aid to the royalists. It did not take long for the regional conflict to assume global proportions. The Soviet Union, having established a strong relationship with Nasser, who, like Sukarno, espoused a belligerently anti-Western form of "nonalignment," recognized the new regime. Great Britain, still a player in Middle Eastern affairs and concerned about the effect of Nasserism on its colony of Aden, openly favored the royalists. The Kennedy Administration, increasingly active in the arena of intra-Arab politics and interested in improving U.S. relations with Egypt, had recognized the al-Sallal government in December, but since had become anxious that Nasser might threaten the stability of Saudi Arabia, Washington's closest Arab friend in the Middle East and a principal supplier of Western oil. Concerned that continued fighting between Egypt and Saudi Arabia could jeopardize the Saudi monarchy, Kennedy dispatched Ellsworth Bunker, fresh from his success in negotiating a resolution of the Dutch-Indonesian feud in West Irian, to secure an end to the fighting. He also offered Saudi Prince Faisal—a son of the founder of the Saudi kingdom Ibn Saud and brother of the reigning monarch, Saud—a squadron of U.S. Air Force fighters to "deter" Egyptian incursions into Saudi territory.

As the Yemeni civil war grew, Thant was quickly drawn into diplomatic efforts to resolve the conflict. With no authorization from the Security Council but with the consent of the countries involved, UN Undersecretary Ralph Bunche, Thant's closest adviser and overall supervisor of all UN peacekeeping activities, was dispatched to the Middle East in February 1963. He visited both Cairo and Sana—the al-Sallal government having been recognized by the General Assembly—to discuss the civil war and accompanying interventions. At the same time, Ambassador Bunker conducted negotiations with Saudi Arabia's Prince Faisal. After further consultations with Nasser, Bunker was able to secure the three governments' assent to a disengagement agreement. With Washington's concurrence, on April 29, 1963, U Thant announced that a disengagement agreement had been successfully negotiated and that a UN observer mission would be sent to Yemen to monitor implementation of the accord. Under terms of the agreement, Egypt would withdraw its forces from Yemen while Saudi Arabia ended its assistance to royalist forces; a demilitarized zone would straddle the Yemeni-Saudi frontier. Thant appointed Major General Carl Carlson von Horn, chief of staff of the UN Truce Supervisory Organization in Jerusalem, to head what was to be a relatively small team of observers for a task that the secretary-general commented would not extend beyond "three to four months, at the most."[1]

As defined by Thant, the United Nations Observation Mission in Yemen (UNYOM) was to be restricted exclusively to observation and reporting, unlike UNEF or ONUC, whose mandates permitted them to engage in military activities. In a further departure from previous peacekeeping practices, UNYOM was to be financed by the parties to the dispute rather than by the organization as a whole. In May 1963, Thant, who initiated the mission without Security Council authorization but in consultation with Washington, dispatched von Horn to the area to survey the terrain and assess force requirements. Angered by Thant's initiative, the Soviets demanded that the full council meet to consider the Yemen mission. In subsequent council debate, Soviet Ambassador Nikolai Federenko attacked the UN peacekeeping mission as only a disguise for the imperialistic ambitions of Western nations. The Soviet Union did abstain, however, when the Security Council voted on June 11 to send a two hundred-man observer mission to Yemen for a two-month period. The mission formally began its work on July 4, 1963.

From its inception UNYOM was plagued with difficulties. Major General von Horn complained bitterly to headquarters that he did not have sufficient resources to carry out the Security Council's mandate because Saudi Arabia and the United Arab Republic each had contributed only $200,000 to the operation; the general was instructed to make do with the resources available to him. On August 20 von Horn submitted his resignation, and despite his almost immediate second thoughts, was replaced by Thant with Yugoslavian Colonel Branko Pavlovic. There is little doubt that UNYOM did operate under extremely difficult conditions, for the climate was inhospitable, the region remote, and fresh rations in short supply. The mission found itself increasingly hard-pressed and often came under fire as the parties to the conflict stepped up their provocations. Thant had dismissed von Horn's charges as irresponsible, but he himself acknowledged on October 28 that "given the nature of the situation and the terrain, it is not possible for UNYOM with its present personnel, or for that matter, with a much expanded establishment, to observe fully . . . what specifically is being done in the way of disengagement."[2]

Of greater difficulty was the unwillingness of the parties to the conflict to live by the terms of the agreement. While there was evidence that the original Egyptian troops were being withdrawn, there was also proof that fresh recruits were being sent into the country. The Saudis, frustrated by Egypt's apparent violations, continued to supply the royalists. Over the next year, the Saudis regularly threatened not to renew the two-month mandate for the mission, only to pull back in the face of pressure to maintain the UN presence. In the late summer of 1964, after several renewals but with the civil war still raging, both Egypt and Saudi Arabia refused to continue paying for the mission. On September 2, 1964, U Thant announced termination of UNYOM activities.

In announcing the end of UNYOM, Thant put the best light on its difficult mission. "[T]he potential threat to international peace and security represented by the Yemen question has greatly diminished during the existence of the mission and, I believe, to a considerable extent because of its activities."[3] There is no denying Thant's contention that the Yemen issue was far less explosive in 1964 than it had been a year before. But the lessening of tensions could be more accurately attributed to changes in American policy. In March 1963, President Kennedy, concerned that the civil war might spill into Saudi territory, had planned to send U.S. Air Force personnel into the region to protect Saudi territory from Egyptian encroachments. But the president soon had second thoughts about the proposed military mission. The deployment of UNYOM, an agreement brokered primarily by Washington, allowed the United States to pull back from military intervention in favor of a negotiated, albeit flawed disengagement agreement. By 1964 Lyndon Johnson's White House was no longer inclined to make Yemen into a superpower testing ground. With the Saudi monarchy out of serious danger, the situation in Yemen ceased being a significant superpower issue, although it remained a regional problem until the late 1960s.

For his part, Thant was clearly frustrated by the limited scope of UN activities in Yemen. Reflecting that frustration, Ralph Bunche complained that the "tin cup" approach to peacekeeping was a sure recipe for futility, a truism demonstrated in the case of Yemen. But Thant was clearly powerless to expand UNYOM operations. Despite Thant's independent role in initiating plans for the observer mission, the Soviet Union made it quite clear that the heyday of a freewheeling secretary-general had ended with the death of Hammarskjöld. By November 1963, four months after the inception of UNYOM's operations, Thant informally consulted Security Council members on the mission's extension. Thant appeared to understand, despite his contention that the office had grown beyond the boundaries of the charter, that the secretary-general could only act in accordance with the mandates of the Security Council and General Assembly.

MALAYSIA

The UNYOM experience demonstrated to observers both the strengths and weaknesses of the office of secretary-general, and Thant's intervention in the Malaysian crisis accentuated the lessons. The Federation of Malaya, a former colonial dependency of Great Britain, only came into existence in August 1957, and in 1961 the Southeast Asian country, situated at the foot of the Malay peninsula adjacent to the Indonesian archipelago, proposed formation of a Federation of Malaysia to encompass Malaya, British-administered Singapore, North Borneo (Sabah), and Sarawak. The British government of Harold Macmillan agreed to the Malayan proposal, and plans were set in motion for the creation of Malaysia by August 31, 1963. But despite the seeming agreement of all parties, the proposal quickly ran into difficulties.

Malaya's neighbors almost immediately expressed strong reservations about the formation of the new political entity. The Philippines, flaunting a century-old territorial claim to North Borneo, opposed the creation of an expanded Malaya, while Indonesia, led by the redoubtable Sukarno, labeled the proposed federation a cover for British neocolonial ambitions. In June 1963, with the August 31 deadline approaching, representatives of Malaya, Indonesia, and the Philippines, meeting in Manila, affirmed the Malayan proposal contingent upon the support of the people residing in the disputed territories. They invited the secretary-general, who had previously sent his *chef de cabinet*, C. V. Narasimhan, to consult with the three governments, to determine whether such support existed.

In early July, however, the accord threatened to unravel when Malayan Prime Minister Abdul Rahman unilaterally entered into an agreement with Britain to proceed with the creation of Malaysia. Their agreement appeared to prejudge the outcome of the proposed plebiscite in the British-controlled territories, and it was in a crisis atmosphere that Rahman, Sukarno, and Philippine President Disodado Macapagal met in late July and resolved to request formally that Thant play a role in ascertaining the wishes of the residents of North Borneo and Sarawak. Upon consultation with the three governments, the secretary-general decided he could discover evidence of the people's mandate in recent election results from the territories. The governments concerned attached intricate conditions to Thant's study of the election returns but agreed that the secretary-general's conclusions would be binding. On August 12, Thant dispatched an eight-man mission, headed by Secretariat official Laurence V. Michelmore, to North Borneo and Sarawak, and after a brief visit, the team reported to Thant that the residents supported federation. On September 14, the secretary-general announced his findings, and two days later the Federation of Malaysia came into existence.

The willingness of the three states to accept the secretary-general as an "arbitrator," and Thant's inclination to accept such a role without authorization from any UN body, might have represented a major development. Previously, the secretary-general's diplomatic efforts had been confined primarily to mediation, but the willingness of three Asian governments to accept Thant's decision as binding signaled the possible evolution of his office into one with greater authority. But the great expectations generated by the Manila agreement were soon disappointed. Despite Thant's decision and in the face of his acceptance, Macapagal continued to insist on the justice of his nation's claim to North Borneo, while Sukarno even ordered acts of violence against the new federation. In 1965, when Malaysia was elected to serve on the Security Council, Indonesia withdrew in anger from the UN, not to rejoin until 1967, well after Sukarno's ouster by a military coup. Malaysia survived the hostility of its neighbors, but Thant's intervention did not end questions over its territorial and political integrity.

In the case of Malaysia, Thant followed something of the same pattern that had been established with the formation of UNYOM. In both instances, the parties to the conflict financed the operation and the secretary-general appeared to play, at least initially, a role independent of the Security Council. For authority to judge the validity of Malaysian elections, Thant relied on the 1960 "Declaration on the Granting of Independence to Colonial Countries and Peoples," which had stipulated that integration of colonized people into the jurisdiction of an existing state "should be the result of the freely expressed wishes of the territory's peoples . . . expressed through informed and democratic processes. The United Nations could, when it deems it necessary, supervise these processes." Operating under that authority, the Michelmore mission evaluated the legitimacy of recently held elections in Sabah and Sarawak on behalf of the secretary-general. Had the United Nations been called upon to organize its own elections, however, Thant would have been required to obtain a grant of authority from the Security Council or General Assembly. Thant admitted, on June 28, 1963, that if he were asked to conduct a plebiscite "a clear mandate from a competent organ of the United Nations will be necessary."[4] Moreover, the secretary-general made his involvement in the crisis contingent upon British acceptance of his role. Thant showed that when called upon, and in the absence of significant opposition from the world organization's most

important powers, he could act independently and achieve worth-
while results. But the Malaysian case made abundantly clear that his
ultimate success depended on the willingness of member states, even
relatively small ones, to accept his rulings in good faith.

CYPRUS

Thant's intervention in West Irian, Yemen, and Malaysia involved
the United Nations in novel kinds of peacekeeping activities. The
world organization's intervention in Cyprus in 1964, which was to
become the UN's longest-running peacekeeping operation, more
faithfully followed precedents set in earlier peacekeeping operations
in the Middle East and Africa. But the intractable Cyprus crisis
demonstrated as well the limits of UN authority when it runs counter
to the interests of sovereign nations.

Cyprus is an island state situated in the eastern portion of the
Mediterranean Sea. Located some forty miles south of Turkey and
five hundred miles from the Greek mainland, its six hundred thousand people in 1964 were approximately 80 percent Greek and 20
percent Turkish. The Greeks traced their presence on the island to
1400 B.C., while the Turks, who had first arrived as soldiers during
the Ottoman conquest of Cyprus, dated their roots from the sixteenth
century. The Turks' rule over Cyprus lasted until 1878, when a weakened Ottoman Empire was compelled to cede administration of the
island to Great Britain. After World War I, Turkey relinquished all its
claims to sovereignty over Cyprus and, in 1923, the island was formally incorporated into the British Empire. Two years later Cyprus
was accorded the status of a Crown Colony.

Over the next several decades, British rule over the island was for-
ever complicated by the bitter strife between the two ethnic Cypriot
communities. The Greek population of Cyprus overwhelmingly supported enosis, or union of the island with Greece. The minority Turks
just as resolutely opposed unification with Greece and preferred
either continued British rule or partition of the island into Greek and
Turkish political entities. The Greek and Turkish governments, as
might be expected, invariably aggravated the intercommunal strife
by supporting the contesting claims of their respective nationals.

Throughout forty years of colonial rule, British authorities were
forced to oppose efforts by Greek nationalists on the island to achieve

enosis. Convinced of the strategic value of the island and unwilling to offend the government of Turkey, London resisted the notion of Cypriot independence, which would have certainly led to enosis and intercommunal warfare. But stimulated by the anticolonialism fervor of the 1950s, Greek Cypriots stepped up their long fight against the colonial authority. Bolstered by an informal plebiscite of the Greek community, revealing almost unanimous popular approval for enosis, Cypriot Archbishop Makarios III launched a bloody revolt against British rule. Violence was escalated when the National Organization of Cypriot Struggle, headed by former Greek Army Colonel Georgios Grivas, mounted a terrorist campaign against British soldiers. The Greek government, now officially committed to enosis, attempted to bring the matter before the United Nations, but Great Britain insisted that the Cyprus problem was an internal question and blocked all discussion. Attempts to resolve the crisis by North Atlantic Treaty Organization officials, alarmed about the prospect of war between two of its members, proved equally fruitless.

In January and February 1959, the government of British Prime Minister Harold Macmillan hosted bilateral talks between Greek Prime Minister Konstantinos Karamanlis and Turkish Prime Minister Adnan Menderes. After consultation with leaders of the Greek and Turkish communities on Cyprus, the two leaders reached an accord at Zurich. Shortly thereafter, representatives of the three governments, along with Makarios III and Dr. Fazil Kuchuk, leader of Cyprus's Turks, met in London to endorse the Zurich Agreement. The accord granted Cyprus its independence but also prohibited enosis. An elaborate scheme for power sharing between the two communities required that the president be a Greek and the vice president, a Turk. Archbishop Makarios III was elected president of the new republic, which achieved its independence on August 16, 1960.

Despite the formal agreement, the new constitution soon unraveled because the power-sharing scheme granted the president and vice president veto authority over one another's acts. The Greek majority saw the constitution as a device for protecting the Turks. Almost at once, Greek and Turkish radicals, who had rejected the Zurich Agreement, began to stockpile weapons in anticipation of intercommunal warfare. In December 1963, when Makarios suggested a plan to scrap the presidential and vice presidential vetoes, open warfare erupted between the two communities.

The 1959 Treaty of Guarantee that accompanied the Cyprus constitution gave Great Britain, Greece, and Turkey power to secure the accord by military means if necessary. All three countries had military garrisons on the island, but given the discord between Greeks and Turks, they could not serve as a joint peacekeeping force, especially with Ankara threatening an invasion to protect its compatriots. The British therefore proposed the creation of a NATO force to police Cyprus, but Makarios refused. Violence continued and finally, on February 15, the governments of the United Kingdom and Cyprus separately requested the Security Council to consider the question.

Debate on the Cyprus crisis followed predictable lines, as the Soviet Union attempted to create fissures in the Western alliance by condemning Turkey, Great Britain, and the Treaty of Guarantee. The United States, for its part, defended London's right to be involved on the island, but was critical of the violence. On March 4, the Security Council passed a resolution authorizing the secretary-general to appoint a mediator and organize a peacekeeping mission of three months' duration. The governments of Czechoslovakia, France, and the Soviet Union objected to paragraph four of the resolution— empowering Thant to determine the composition and size of the force—on the grounds that it represented an abdication of Security Council responsibility for peacekeeping. Both the Soviet Union and France had long-standing reservations about peacekeeping operations by the UN, and, joined by Czechoslovakia, they abstained on the critical paragraph. With the UN in the midst of a serious financial crisis, in large part traceable to Paris and Moscow's refusal to pay for UNEF and ONUC, financing of UNFICYP (United Nations Force in Cyprus), as the peacekeeping force was to be known, was to come from governments contributing military contingents. Voluntary contributions from others would be solicited, but there would be no mandatory assessments.

Conditions on the island rapidly deteriorated during 1964, and Thant, who was content with a large behind-the-scenes role in fashioning UNFICYP's mandate, was compelled to move quickly in creating a force. Continuing clashes between Greeks and Turks on Cyprus led the Turkish government to warn Makarios that it might intervene militarily to protect the Turkish minority. With Greece threatening to repel a Turkish invasion, the Security Council convened again to reaffirm the terms of the March 4 resolution. The crisis was eased on March 27 when UNFICYP began operations under the command of Indian Lt. General P. S. Gyani, who had been on the scene since January as Thant's personal representative. Thant appointed Sakari S. Tuomioja of Finland to serve as UN mediator after Ankara rebuffed his first choice, Secretariat official José Rolz-Bennett, and in May, the secretary-general dispatched Galo Plaza Lasso, former president of Ecuador, as his personal observer on Cyprus.

In June, at the end of the force's first three-month mandate, UNFICYP numbered 6,238 military personnel recruited from Austria, Canada, Denmark, Finland, Iceland, and Sweden. The United Kingdom, Greece, Turkey, Cyprus, and the United States, along with a number of other countries, contributed money to finance the operation, which by late June had consumed approximately $5.5 million. But nothing had been resolved, and in requesting Security Council authorization for extension of UNFICYP's three-month mandate, Thant complained that the method of financing the force "is most unsatisfactory."[5] Later in 1964, requesting yet another extension of UNFICYP's mandate, the secretary-general warned that the Security Council's failure to deal effectively with the force's funding problem could compel him to terminate the peacekeeping operation before the end of its three-month mandate.

In fashioning UNFICYP's mission, Thant was careful not to give the UN force any role in pressing a political solution on the island's troubled population. The peacekeeping force's principal function, according to the secretary-general, was to prevent a recurrence of fighting, and UNFICYP was therefore authorized to fire only in self-defense; it would patrol and observe rather than control. In his typically frank style, Thant noted, "It would be incongruous, even a little insane, for that Force to set about killing Cypriots, whether Greek or Turkish, to prevent them from killing each other."[6] Thant hoped that UNFICYP could eventually move beyond preventing outbreaks of new fighting toward creating conditions "under which an ordinary man may move freely and carry on his day's work without fear or hindrance."[7] In late April, he unveiled his own peace plan calling for freedom of movement, disarming of civilians, and participation of the Turkish minority in the affairs of government.

The hostility between the two communities was so great, however, that UN forces were little more than a buffer between opposing armies. Thant's June 1964 report to the Security Council credited UNFICYP with having prevented all-out fighting, but acknowledged that tension on the island remained very high; he accused both communities of arming themselves for future battles. Meanwhile, the United States attempted to prevent the deteriorating situation from erupting into a war between two NATO allies. President Lyndon Johnson sternly warned the Turkish government not to invade Cyprus and then, in conjunction with Thant, dispatched former U.S. Secretary of State Dean Acheson to Geneva to meet with Greek and Turkish officials. In August, Makarios, determined to subdue the Turkish community once and for all, ordered his forces to attack a number of Turkish towns and villages and restricted UNFICYP from moving into Turkish enclaves to restore order. Ankara responded with massive bombing of Greek positions on the island. Once again, the Security Council was convened and a truce was achieved, but a political solution remained elusive.

Over the next several years the situation on Cyprus remained roughly the same. UNFICYP was periodically renewed, for six-, rather than three-, month mandates, and Thant as regularly complained that the financing formula was inadequate. All mediation proved ineffective, and in 1965, the Turkish government successfully forced the removal of Galo Plaza Lasso as mediator, because he had filed a report with Thant critical of the Treaty of Guarantee. Efforts by Thant to renew negotiations through Plaza Lasso's successor, Dr. Carlos Bernardes, proved equally fruitless.

In November 1967, the situation on Cyprus took a turn for the worse after a local battle between Cypriot National Guardsmen and Turkish Cypriots escalated into large-scale fighting. Soldiers attached to UNFICYP were beaten by members of both organizations, and UN property was damaged. As in previous crises, tension on the island threatened to erupt into a war between Greece and Turkey, and Thant moved quickly to establish lines of communication with the disputants. He appealed to the governments of Cyprus, Greece, and Turkey to demonstrate restraint and sent Rolz-Bennett to the region to act as a mediator. President Johnson dispatched veteran American diplomat Cyrus Vance to the area as well. In late November, the president of the Security Council read a statement expressing satisfaction with the secretary-general's efforts in easing the crisis.

While Thant and Vance succeeded in reaching a temporary resolution of the conflict, the secretary-general felt that the time had come for fashioning a long-range solution to the Cyprus problem. Thant attempted to convince the parties to the dispute and the Security

Council that all non-Cypriot forces, including large contingents of Greek and Turkish military personnel, should be removed from the island under the supervision of UNFICYP. Yet on December 22, 1967, when the Security Council voted to extend the UN force's mandate, it refrained from advocating a military disengagement schedule or broadening UNFICYP's mandate to facilitate withdrawal of non-Cypriot forces from the island. Thant was clearly disappointed by the council's timidity. As he said on December 22, 1967, "Bearing in mind the sharply divergent views of some of the parties in regard to the issues that may be raised during their forthcoming discussions with me . . . I would have welcomed clear guidance. . . . The weight of the Council's views would have been invaluable to me . . . and in its absence I deem it my duty to forewarn the Council of the difficulties that lie ahead."[8]

The Cyprus issue was still unresolved upon the completion of Thant's tenure as secretary-general in 1971, and remains so today. While relations between Greeks and Turks appeared to improve during the late 1960s, the underlying tensions remained strong. In 1974, a coup against the military junta in Greece once again fanned enosis feelings on the island and this time fostered a Turkish reaction. In July 1974, Turkey invaded Cyprus and established a de facto partition—the Turks call it *taksim*—between the two communities. Several years later, the Turks established a puppet Cypriot government, recognized as sovereign only by the government of Turkey. As of this writing, UNFICYP remains deployed between Turks and Greeks on the divided island of Cyprus.

Thant did play a significant role in preventing the Cyprus civil war from erupting into a full-scale conflict between Greece and Turkey. Whenever tensions threatened to boil over, he acted to find a diplomatic common ground between the antagonists, usually by dispatching a mediator to the region. Thant frequently wrote directly to the parties involved and coordinated his organization's efforts with the efforts of the U.S. government, which consistently played a constructive role in seeking a diplomatic solution. Thant also played a decisive role in organizing and directing the UN peacekeeping mission on Cyprus and was instrumental in keeping it financially viable despite the unsatisfactory nature of UNFICYP's funding mandate.

Where Thant and the international community failed were in their efforts to reach beyond temporary palliatives to a long-range resolution of the conflict. UNFICYP does act as a buffer, but, despite the secretary-general's best intentions, the UN has not been able to restore normal life to the island's troubled inhabitants. Nor could Thant, who in contrast to Hammarskjöld tended to work almost exclusively through mediators, force the parties to the conflict to overcome the profound sectarian and ethnic suspicions that had brought them to civil war. For its part, the Security Council showed itself willing to have the UN act as a barrier against further fighting and even to authorize the secretary-general to appoint mediators. But riven by divisions over the nature and financing of peacekeeping operations, the council was not prepared to expand the size or mandate of UNFI-CYP to compel Turkish and Greek troops to leave the island.

KASHMIR

In West Irian, Yemen, Malaya, and Cyprus, Thant worked through subordinates or in conjunction with American diplomats to achieve limited results for UN peacekeeping. In the early fall of 1965, however, violent events on the Asian subcontinent thrust Thant into perhaps his most active role as secretary-general. The issue was Kashmir, a territory contested by India and Pakistan since the creation of both countries in 1947. Populated primarily by Muslims, who identified with their coreligionists in Pakistan, the bulk of Kashmir's territory was nevertheless occupied by India, which rested its title on a succession agreement with the territory's last Hindu maharajah. The Kashmir question had come before the United Nations on many occasions since 1948, but owing to Indian recalcitrance and its prestige as a leader of the third world bloc, a plebiscite involving the region's inhabitants had never materialized. Major fighting had been averted through the presence of a UN observer mission, formally named the United Nations Military Observer Group in India and Pakistan (UNMOGIP), but the situation along the border between the two large countries remained tense for almost two decades.

The fragile cease-fire in Kashmir collapsed in August 1965 when Pakistani soldiers dressed as civilians infiltrated Indian controlled territory, which in turn precipitated an Indian military response. Before long, both sides were engaged in heavy fighting, involving artillery exchanges, infantry probes, and air attacks upon one another's territory. India then expanded the war by attacking the Punjab, far from the original war theater, and so threatening the Pakistani city of Lahore. Thant attempted to prevent the fighting from escalating by interceding directly with the combatants, but the Pakistanis would not allow him to issue a public call for a cease-fire. Furthermore, both governments attached such impossible conditions to the dispatch of Ralph Bunche to the region that a planned mission by the UN official never materialized. The always-cautious Thant was ever careful to secure support before undertaking any important initiative. When Thant recalled Lt. General Robert H. Nimmo of Australia, head of UNMOGIP, to New York to receive a firsthand report on the fighting, he was appalled by scale of the violence in the region.

In response to Nimmo's bleak report, Thant sent identical messages to President Mohammad Ayub Khan of Pakistan and Prime Minister Sri Lal Bahadur Shastri of India, warning both nations of their obligations under the charter. On September 4, U.S. Ambassador Arthur Goldberg, who along with other council members had previously consulted with the secretary-general, convened an urgent meeting of the Security Council, which unanimously called on India and Pakistan to observe an immediate cease-fire. When reports reached New York that the council resolution was being ignored, the council passed a new resolution urging Thant to visit the area.

Thant's visit, first to Rawalpindi, then to New Delhi, in mid-September 1965 produced no tangible results. After long negotiations, Thant issued three separate messages to Ayub Khan and Shastri in a futile effort to secure both governments' agreement to a cease-fire. Pakistan, however, insisted that no cease-fire could be accepted in the absence of a UN effort to trace the political roots of the Kashmir problem. India maintained that a cease-fire should not limit Indian soldiers from firing on irregulars crossing the Pakistani border into Kashmir. The secretary-general returned to New York on September 16 without an agreement to end the fighting, but, in appreciation of his effort, he was met at the airport by an unprecedented gathering of all Security Council delegates.

Conceding the failure of his mission, Thant, in an extraordinary request, urged the Security Council to order India and Pakistan to stop fighting or face UN sanctions. The council, whose members were unwilling to alienate the two warring parties, stopped short of adopting so drastic a measure and instead called for an immediate cease-fire and a return of troops to positions held before the outbreak of fighting. But international pressure was now making itself felt, and the two governments acceded to the council's demand. Secretary-General Thant then used funds earmarked for emergency peacekeeping operations to augment UNMOGIP's presence in Kashmir and organized another observer force, the India-Pakistan Observation Mission (UNIPOM), to supervise the cease-fire on the western border between the two nations. By October, however, UN observers were dealing with numerous complaints of cease-fire violations, and in November, the Security Council met yet again to demand that India and Pakistan meet with a representative of the secretary-general to discuss plans for mutual troop withdrawals. Meanwhile, in order to counter the influence of China, which was encouraging Pakistan in its war against India, the Soviet Union, which for years had been working diligently to expand its influence on the Indian subcontinent, offered to act as a mediator. In December Ayub Khan and Shastri announced that they would meet in the Soviet city of Tashkent to discuss their differences. On January 10, 1966, the two leaders signed the Tashkent Declaration, which signaled their acceptance of a cease-fire and return to the status quo ante bellum. Shortly afterward UNIPOM was disbanded and UNMOGIP reduced to a corporal's guard. While the ultimate credit for ending the India-Pakistan war went to the Soviet Union, the crisis saw Thant playing perhaps the most vigorous role of his career as secretary-general. Departing from routine procedure, Thant himself traveled to the region to deal directly with the disputants. He urged decisive action upon the Security Council and played an important behind-the-scenes role in the fashioning of council resolutions. Thant swiftly organized UNIPOM, strengthened UNMOGIP, and publicly rebuked both sides when they failed to live up to their charter obligations. In addition, when the secretary-general, through his personal representative Brigadier-General Tulio Marambio of Chile, helped to implement the troop withdrawal, both sides agreed to in the Tashkent Declaration.

As was the case in previous crises, Thant closely coordinated his activities with the United States. Washington was deeply troubled by the war and concerned that the Chinese Communists might be drawn into the conflict. Ambassador Goldberg, with whom Thant enjoyed a solid and mutually respectful relationship, happened to be president of the Security Council in September 1965, and the two worked closely to plot Security Council action. President Johnson, in fact, offered Thant use of *Air Force One* for the secretary-general's visit to Asia, but Thant declined, fearing he might be perceived as acting for Washington. Nonetheless, he did accept Johnson's offer of an

American aircraft attached to the Embassy in Tehran as a means to travel from Pakistan to India. Thant's recommendation that the Security Council consider ordering Pakistan and India to halt their war enjoyed the strong backing of the United States as well. But the Soviets were less supportive of Thant's role. Moscow backed the Security Council's cease-fire call but, in keeping with its general policy, attacked the secretary-general for organizing and directing UNIPOM without proper Security Council authorization. France backed the Kremlin's stand, but other members of the Security Council, led by the United States, supported Thant, and the secretary-general prevailed.

CONCLUSION: THANT'S NEW TERM

Despite the relative success of Thant's intervention in Kashmir, the secretary-general was becoming increasingly frustrated with his role. His term was due to expire in November 1966, and there was near unanimous agreement among the UN members that he should continue in his post. But Thant, for both personal and political reasons, was reluctant to stand for a second term. Throughout the summer he hinted that he would not seek another term, and on September 1 he announced that he would definitely relinquish his post after November. He cited as reasons for his refusal to continue as secretary-general the unresolved financial crisis, the inadequacy of UN peacekeeping operations, and the continuing tragedy of war in Vietnam. Several weeks later, however, Thant began to relent. In a press conference, he offered to extend his term by two months to aid the organization, even though he found it "increasingly difficult to function as Secretary-General in the manner in which I wish to function."[9] Observers believed that Soviet efforts to limit the scope of the secretary-general's authority, coupled with Washington's reluctance to permit him a role in ending the Vietnam War, inhibited Thant's enthusiasm for the job. Having sent this message to the great powers, Thant then allowed himself to be persuaded to accept a second term. On December 2, the Security Council recommended unanimously that U Thant be reappointed for a second full term as secretary-general. The president of the council read a statement praising Thant for having brought before it "basic issues confronting the Organization and disturbing developments in many parts of the world."[10] Thant, for his part, noted with "particular appreciation" the council's statement of respect. On December 2, 1966, the General Assembly unanimously affirmed the Security Council's recommendation that U Thant serve as secretary-general until December 31, 1971.

NOTES

1. Andrew W. Cordier and Max Harrelson, eds., *Public Papers of the Secretaries-General of the United Nations, Vol. VI, U Thant* (New York: Columbia University Press, 1976), 330.

2. Cordier and Harrelson, *Public Papers, Vol. VI*, 475.

3. Cordier and Harrelson, *Public Papers, Vol. VI*, 638.

4. Cordier and Harrelson, *Public Papers, Vol. VI*, 370.

5. Cordier and Harrelson, *Public Papers, Vol. VI*, 579.

6. Cordier and Harrelson, *Public Papers, Vol. VI*, 565.

7. Cordier and Harrelson, *Public Papers, Vol. VI*, 564.

8. Andrew W. Cordier and Max Harrelson, eds., *Public Papers of the Secretaries-General of the United Nations, Vol. VII, U Thant* (New York: Columbia University Press, 1976), 611–612.

9. Cordier and Harrelson, *Public Papers, Vol. VII*, 295.

10. Cordier and Harrelson, *Public Papers, Vol. VII*, 306.

3

Man of the Third World

The violent third world conflicts that occupied so much of Thant's time and energy during his first several years in office obscured the social and economic tensions plaguing so many of the world's new states. But the increasingly large disparity in incomes between developed and less-developed peoples, and the poorer nations' inability to compel any reallocation of global wealth, soon made the third world realize that the UN might become an instrument of redistributive policy. Increasingly conscious of the advantage conferred by their numerical superiority in the General Assembly and other UN organs, developing states saw the organization as a means to effect changes in a world order that had negatively dominated their destinies for more than a century.

The centrality of the United Nations to third world interests coincided with its emergence as a coherent bloc, with an ascertainable political and economic agenda. In April 1955, when leaders of twenty-nine African and Asian nations assembled at Bandung, Indonesia, to form the nonaligned movement, the conferees affirmed the role of the United Nations as an engine of political and economic liberation. Several years later, in September 1961, nonaligned nations meeting in Belgrade, Yugoslavia, heard their host Marshal Tito characterize the United Nations as the best hope for addressing the grievances of the third world. During the 1960s, as the membership of the United Nations increased to include many of the world's poorest states, developing nations began to flex their muscles within the organization. And as the institution's agenda naturally changed to accommodate the interests of its newest members, the well-being and even survival of the United Nations became central foreign policy concerns of third world states. As Thant wrote in the early 1970s, "Most of the new members, who are nonaligned and uncommitted, are motivated by the one major objective of preserving the United Nations as the guardian of their rights and liberties."[1]

Thant himself enthusiastically supported the growing third world pressure for political and economic change. His patron, U Nu, had been a leading figure in the nonaligned movement, and through Nu he had met a large number of the world's most distinguished third world leaders. Thant had attended the Bandung and Belgrade conferences, and his memoirs described the impact of nonalignment on his political philosophy:

> I shall be less than honest if I say that such experience and contacts had no impact on me. In the fifties, I found myself increasingly identified with the cause of small nations, poor nations, newly independent nations, and nations struggling for independence. Soon my conception of the United Nations was primarily from the vantage point of the Third World.[2]

As ambassador to the UN, Thant had played a leading role in the nonaligned movement and was even credited, albeit erroneously, with coining both *third world* and *developing nations* as terms to describe newly independent states that were aggressively pressing their concerns upon the United Nations. In September 1960, he became chairman of the UN's Afro-Asian group, and one year later, he succeeded Hammarskjöld, with solid third world support. As secretary-general he was a vigorous and articulate champion of third world causes and always wished to strengthen the General Assembly, where developing nations enjoyed a huge majority.

With or without Thant at its helm, the United Nations during the 1960s would have reflected in its agenda and power structure the emergence of the third world as a major force in world politics. In 1960 alone, seventeen new states, all but Cyprus from Africa, were admitted to the world organization. During Thant's decade as secretary-general, another thirty-two nations, all of third world origin, entered the UN. By August 1965 the assembly had 114 members, and to reflect the changing membership, the charter was amended to expand Security Council membership from eleven to fifteen and the Economic and Social Council from eighteen to twenty-seven. As former British diplomat Evan Luard has noted, the enlargement of the Security

Council, with a guarantee that certain seats would be allocated to states from designated geographic areas, was specifically designed to ensure representation on the executive level for the UN's third world. Under the arrangement established in the immediate aftermath of World War II, two nonpermanent seats on the council had gone to governments from Latin America, one to a government from Western Europe, one to an Eastern European government, one to a government from the Afro-Asian bloc of nations, and one to the government of a Commonwealth country. Under the new arrangement mandated by the General Assembly, the Commonwealth seat was dropped and five Afro-Asian states were included, two from Asia, two from Africa, and one from among the world's Arab nations.

Thant believed that the emergence of an active third force in the United Nations, situated between the two great ideological blocs, would make the secretary-general, "particularly in his role of representing the philosophy he shares with almost all of the small and medium states,"[3] a much more powerful figure. But the success of decolonization made it certain that whoever occupied the position of secretary-general, whether of third world origin or not, would only remain effective with the support of the developing nations, who now constituted the largest single bloc in the world organization.

THE STRUGGLE FOR SELF-DETERMINATION

Colonialism was the issue that carried the greatest emotional resonance for third world peoples, and it was in that area that the UN was unusually active during the decade of Thant's tenure. The charter's chapter XI had encouraged colonial powers to treat non-self-governing peoples with dignity and respect and had obligated them to facilitate the transition of dependent territories to self-determination. Nonetheless, prior to 1960, virtually no machinery existed for holding colonial powers accountable to the standards set by the charter. In December 1960, however, the third world majority in the General Assembly achieved, by a vote of 90–0, a Declaration on the Granting of Independence to Colonial Countries and Peoples. That declaration, which the United States did not vote for, essentially confirmed what had been obvious since the end of World War II—that is, that colonialism was no longer a legitimate form of state behavior. Less than a year later, in 1961, unhappy at the failure of several colonial powers to implement its resolution, the General Assembly established (97–0) the awkwardly named Special Committee on the Situation with Regard to the Implementation of the Declaration of the Granting of Independence to Colonial Countries and Peoples. That committee, expanded in 1962 from seventeen to twenty-four members, monitored the decline of colonialism and vigorously attacked the policies of states such as Portugal and South Africa for violation of the new standards.

In many respects the aggressiveness of the anticolonial movement in the UN reflected the disintegration of the very evil against which it was directed. Decolonization swelled the membership of the world organization with newly independent states, and these states were determined to root out the last vestiges of the colonial system. But certain cases, such as Portugal's control over vast colonial territories in Africa, the unresolved status of South-West Africa (renamed Namibia in 1968), and the increasing tensions associated with the policy of apartheid in South Africa, remained intractable. To these issues, the UN's new majority and its secretary-general turned their attention.

Portuguese dominion over Angola, Mozambique, and Portuguese Guinea represented the last vestiges of overt colonial rule in Africa. During the 1950s, African nations regularly obtained General Assembly resolutions urging Portugal to divest itself of its colonial holdings or, at the very least, to relax its repressive policies in those territories. The Portuguese insisted, however, that their African territories were simply "overseas provinces" of the mother country and refused to apprise the United Nations as to the status of the territories' inhabitants. In December 1960, the General Assembly listed the Portuguese territories it considered to be non-self-governing and demanded that the Lisbon government grant immediate independence to their peoples. In May 1961, the Kennedy Administration reversed the policy established under President Dwight D. Eisenhower and joined African countries in urging Lisbon to permit a process of self-determination in its African dominions. The new American policy reflected Ambassador Stevenson's victory over a State Department reluctant to jeopardize U.S. relations with Portugal, America's staunch ally and a strategically important country. Stevenson's vigorous support of the African position on Angola won the United States many friends in that continent, and, despite the warnings of the State Department's Europeanists, Portugal did not deny the United States basing rights in the Azores. Beyond rhetoric, there was little the secretary-general could do. Thant's annual reports ritually reproved the Portuguese government for its failure to abide by UN resolutions, but the Portuguese-African conflict remained unresolved when he left the UN in 1971. Several years later, however, after a military coup in Portugal overthrew the Salazar dictatorship, Lisbon bowed to years of adverse opinion in the United Nations and its increasingly untenable military situation. In time, three more third world states joined the world organization—Angola, Guinea-Bissau, and Mozambique.

Of equal concern to African nations was the status of Namibia, a vast mandate granted by the League of Nations to South Africa after World War I. Pretoria, despite urging to the contrary by the General Assembly, had refused to place the territory under the UN trusteeship system after World War II. In 1950, the International Court of Justice (ICJ) ruled in an advisory opinion that the league mandate was still in effect and that South Africa was answerable to the United Nations for its behavior in the territory, but that ruling was ignored by South Africa. In 1960, Liberia and Ethiopia brought suit against South Africa before the ICJ, claiming that Pretoria had failed to comply with its mandatory obligations, but the court ruled that the plaintiffs had no legal standing to sue South Africa. Having become impatient with futile legal remedies, in October 1966 the assembly voted to terminate the mandate and to place the territory of South-West Africa under UN control. In 1967, the United Nations Council for South-West Africa was created and given responsibility for administering the affairs of the territory until independence; the assembly also recommended the appointment of a commissioner to implement terms of the resolution. Thant hailed the General Assembly's action as one that offered "a fresh point of departure, a new possibility of reconciliation, a chance to stem the growing racial hostility in that part of the world," and implored "all member states . . . to heed the General Assembly appeal."[4] South Africa, however, remained unmoved. In 1969, with South Africa refusing to cooperate with the UN Council, the Security Council (France and Great Britain abstaining) affirmed the termination of the mandate and ordered South Africa to withdraw from Namibia by October 4. The assembly and Security Council showed themselves willing to take strong action against South Africa, and the United States, with Ambassador Goldberg playing a leading role, helped to fashion resolutions acceptable to both African and Western interests. But the United States refused to support the imposition of economic sanctions against the South African government. It abstained in the General Assembly on a resolution sponsored by African states calling on the Security Council to "take all appropriate measures" to ensure the implementation of the resolution transferring authority over Namibian affairs to the UN Council on South-West Africa. With Western powers unwilling to impose sanctions and with South Africa in control of Namibia, little could be done to force Pretoria's hand.

The same problem arose in regard to South Africa's policy of apartheid. In the 1940s and 1950s the General Assembly had heard complaints against South Africa's treatment of its Indian and black populations, respectively. Not until 1960, however, under growing pressure from third world nations and in the shadow of the brutal Sharpeville massacre, in which more than two hundred blacks were killed by South African police, did the Security Council abandon the posture that apartheid was a purely internal matter. On April 1, 1960, with the United Kingdom abstaining, the Security Council passed a resolution declaring apartheid a possible threat to peace. On August 7, in a further show of UN resolve, the Security Council, with Paris and London abstaining, voted to bar the sale of arms to South Africa. Finally, on December 4, 1963, it authorized the secretary-general to appoint a council of experts to study the problem of apartheid and to make recommendations leading to its elimination. Despite these actions, the council's posture on apartheid fell far below, in both substance and tone, the outrage evident in the General Assembly, which voted numerous resolutions against South Africa during the decade of Thant's tenure. In November 1962 the General Assembly set up the Special Committee on Apartheid and in 1965 a UN Trust Fund was created to financially assist families of South Africans incarcerated for their activities against the South African government. The assembly authorized funding for the creation of annual seminars on apartheid and regularly called on a reluctant Security Council to impose harsh economic sanctions upon South Africa and to consider its expulsion from the United Nations.

Thant personally condemned South African apartheid, but with the third world nations playing so active a role, he confined himself largely to following the policy mandate of the UN. On March 27,

1964, in response to resolutions from both the Security Council and General Assembly, he wrote South Africa's UN ambassador, Matthys I. Botha, urging that Pretoria not execute three black men condemned to die for their antiapartheid activities. He organized the annual seminars on apartheid and convened the Panel of Experts but studiously refrained from unilaterally taking concrete steps in the absence of a decision by at least one of the UN's political bodies. When specifically asked whether he supported proposals to expel South Africa from the United Nations, Thant always deferred to the authority of the General Assembly and Security Council.

Thant understood that the UN's ability to eliminate apartheid was contingent upon the willingness of the Western powers, tied to South Africa through a web of economic links, to endorse punitive action against the white regime. While speaking to reporters in 1966, Thant suggested that only the big powers could deal effectively with the situation in South Africa. But he seemed to concur with a report by the Special Committee on Apartheid that cited continued South Africa trade by France, the United Kingdom, and the United States as an impediment to resolution of the apartheid crisis. In 1966 he called for the imposition of strict economic sanctions upon Pretoria, and an unusually long section of his 1969 report noted almost universal condemnation of the "abhorrent" practice of apartheid. Such moral uniformity made it imperative that all nations support "full and effective implementation of measures already decided upon by the competent United Nations organs."[5] Thant called for the "full cooperation of the main trading partners of South Africa including some permanent members of the Security Council,"[6] but nothing was done to fulfill his hope.

Similar frustration awaited Thant regarding the case of Southern Rhodesia, where white extremists led by Ian Smith declared their independence from Great Britain on November 11, 1965, and then proceeded to draft a constitution modeled along the lines of the South African system of apartheid. The UN had first intervened in the Southern Rhodesian situation in June 1962 when the General Assembly had declared the area a non-self-governing territory, but the unilateral declaration of independence and establishment of a renegade white regime spurred the UN to further action. On November 20, 1965, the Security Council called on London to end the rebellion and prohibited other governments from recognizing the new state. It also imposed selective, mandatory economic sanctions on the Smith regime and charged the secretary-general with the task of choosing the items to be embargoed. Later, in 1968, with the white government even more defiant and the British in support of UN action, the council imposed broader sanctions upon Rhodesia.

Thant viewed the situation in Southern Rhodesia as little more than an attempt by South Africa to "extend the influence of its philosophy of racial discrimination and segregation."[7] The secretary-general, whose childhood had been characterized by discrimination based on racial distinction, considered that race discrimination was in the long run the greatest threat to world peace. "In my view, the tensions generated by racial discrimination or disparity in treatment among the whites and the blacks, is much more dangerous—I think, in the long run, much more explosive than the division of the world on ideological grounds. This is, in my view, potentially one of the most serious threats to international peace and security."[8]

But there was little Thant could achieve other than to implement General Assembly and Security Council resolutions and use the bully pulpit of his office to inveigh against the Smith regime and its supporters. He could not even function as a mediator, since it was Great Britain that was primarily involved in negotiating with the Smith regime, and neither government desired UN intervention. Nor was Thant's leadership necessary, for both the General Assembly and Security Council were clearly outraged by the Rhodesian action. When asked how the United Nations could impose sanctions upon a government it did not recognize, the secretary-general coyly summed up the situation. "As you know, I am not a jurist or constitutional lawyer. As the Secretary-General I have to comply with the decision of the principal organs of the United Nations. The Security Council in its wisdom has adopted a resolution—a historic resolution. Whether it is legal or illegal is not my business to argue. I have to comply with the decision of the Security Council."[9]

Whatever his thoughts on the legality or illegality of UN actions, the words Thant spoke against the Smith regime were uttered with conviction and determination. In condemning the Rhodesian government's so-called referendum on a new constitution for Rhodesia in 1969, the usually temperate Thant employed words such as *deplorable, abhorrent,* and *racist.* He was no less outspoken in describing the complicity of South Africa and Portugal in undermining UN sanctions through continued and open trade with Rhodesia.

NORTH-SOUTH CONFLICT

Colonialism and racism were issues that carried tremendous symbolic weight in an institution dominated by newly independent, non-white countries, but their practical significance lessened with the passage of time and the decline of colonialism and white minority rule. What succeeded as the primary concern of third world countries was the ever-widening economic gulf between rich and poor countries, a situation Thant considered to be a major source of world tension.

Developed nations seemed to recognize in principle their moral obligation to facilitate economic maturation in the developing world. Speaking before the assembly in September 1961, President Kennedy called for the proclamation of a development decade, and that December, shortly after Thant's accession as acting secretary-general, the General Assembly endorsed the proposal. Thant was ordered to formulate specific plans and targets for the development decade. Upon consultation with a large number of governments and specialized agencies affiliated with the United Nations, the Secretariat prepared a detailed proposal that the secretary-general presented to the ECOSOC (Economic and Social Council) on July 9, 1962. The centerpiece of Thant's address was a recommendation that developed countries transfer 1 percent per year of their national incomes to developing nations and that economically advanced states assist third world nations in the formulation of sound development plans. Thant, in addition, set 5 percent per year annual economic growth as a goal for all developing states by 1970. The secretary-general's plan was endorsed by ECOSOC and later by the General Assembly, and the Secretariat was given considerable responsibility for developing follow-up procedures and monitoring UN development activities.

The program did indeed enjoy some success. With General Assembly authorization, the secretary-general developed a UN institute to train development cadres in poor countries; the United Nations Institute for Training and Research succeeded in educating thousands of young people in the arts of administration and diplomacy. In addition, previous development programs such as the Expanded Program of Technical Assistance (EPTA) and the Special Fund, once modestly funded, were combined into a larger, better-capitalized program known as the United Nations Development Program (UNDP). A new agency, the United Nations Industrial Development Organization (UNIDO), was approved by the General Assembly in 1965.

Chapter 3

In general, however, the results of the First United Nations Development Decade fell far short of expectations. In 1965, Thant noted in a progress report that the gulf between rich and poor countries had, in fact, grown larger, not smaller. Not only was the target of 5 percent per year growth rate not met, but the growth that did occur was vitiated by huge increases in population. Thant laid most of the blame for the failure of the First Development Decade on the unwillingness of the industrialized countries to transfer even a modest portion of their wealth to the third world. Economic aid in absolute numbers did grow from 1961 to 1971, but the actual proportion of assistance relative to GNP fell from 0.79 percent of GNP in 1960 to 0.66 percent in 1969. But others found cause for unhappiness in the performance of the UN itself. As A. Leroy Bennett notes, "Planning for the First Development Decade was inadequate and poorly executed. Most of the measures were in the form of exhortations in vague terms, lacking any specificity of procedures, priorities, or commitments by which the aims could be achieved."[10] Thant was not known to be a particularly effective administrator, and, despite the strength of his belief that a radical redistribution of income was necessary, the organization was not up to the task.

The emphasis on ideals to the virtual exclusion of effective implementation is clearly demonstrated in the early history of the United Nations Conference on Trade and Development (UNCTAD). ECOSOC had voted on August 3, 1962, to form a preparatory committee to plan a conference to study the impact of world trade on developing nations. On December 8, 1962, the General Assembly affirmed ECOSOC's proposal, but expanded the size of the preparatory committee to include a wider group of third world states. The United States and other Western, industrialized nations were unenthusiastic about another conference to discuss trade when a more established framework, the General Agreement on Tariffs and Trade (GATT) already existed. But the developing states were determined to define the trade agenda in terms of their own concerns, and GATT did not afford them that opportunity. The United States calculated that it would be better to attend the conference and attempt to moderate the final product than to boycott it. In the end, more than 120 governments attended the first UNCTAD in Geneva during the spring of 1964.

The conference resolutions reflected the third world's concern over its declining share of world trade during an era of rising global wealth. Heavily dependent on the sale of primary commodities, whose price fluctuations could wreak havoc with developing economies, third world nations demanded commodity price stabilization and tariff reductions. The conference endorsed the General Assembly call for a transfer of wealth from developed to developing states and established machinery for the consideration of future trade issues. UNCTAD became a permanent, semiautonomous organization with its own secretariat.

Thant's function at Geneva was limited primarily to exhortation. After he spoke eloquently about trade imbalances and their contribution to widening the North-South gulf, he played a distinctly secondary role. The conference's conceptual master was the former executive secretary of the Economic Commission for Latin America, Raul Prebisch, a Latin-American economist whose work on trade questions and their impact on developing nations had gained him a wide following throughout the third world. Prebisch championed the use of third world political power to realign economic relationships, and he envisioned a permanent UNCTAD as the third world's means to move from the "periphery" to the "center" of the world economy. Prebisch's influence at the Geneva deliberations was so decisive that Thant later named him UNCTAD's first secretary-general.

In order to succeed, UNCTAD required the cooperation of developing and developed states alike, but the proceedings at Geneva demonstrated the real and the psychological gulfs between North and South. UN scholar Leroy Bennett has demonstrated that of twenty-seven principles passed by the conference, only five were voted unanimously. In all others, a third world majority labeled the "Group of Seventy-Seven" prevailed over the objections or abstentions of the developed states. While their numerical dominance of the conference ensured third world nations a huge propaganda victory, UNCTAD's ultimate success would depend on the willingness of developed states to comply with objectives they opposed. A second UNCTAD scheduled for New Delhi had to be delayed two years because of continuing differences between developed and developing states. When it finally convened in 1968 the deliberations were so contentious that Thant began a postmortem on the conference with the words, *"What went wrong at New Delhi?"*[11]

CONCLUSION

The UN's continuing struggles over colonialism and income redistribution during the 1960s represented a monumental awakening of political consciousness among third world peoples. While General Assembly resolutions did not effect instant results in the most intractable colonial situations—that is, in Angola and Namibia—or succeed in immediately toppling apartheid in South Africa, they contributed to the evolution of a new international morality that eventually prevailed; Angola became independent in 1974, and Namibia achieved its freedom in 1990. A negotiated settlement produced majority rule in Rhodesia, which became Zimbabwe in 1980, and early in the 1990s South Africa experienced a shift to majority rule as well. The effects of the evolving UN consensus around the inadmissibility of colonialism and racism cannot be underestimated as a contributing factor in the settlement of these seemingly intractable issues.

Of more dubious effect was the UN's effort to achieve a redistribution of global wealth, away from the industrialized countries of the North to the less-developed nations of the South. As in the case of the UN's fight against colonialism, a consensus did develop around the need for some measure of redistribution, as demonstrated by the General Assembly's call for a UN development decade and by the convening of UN-sponsored conferences and the establishment of new UN agencies. But agreement on principles could not overcome the harsh reality that sovereign states will promote their own, selfish interests. Without a consensus on how to implement grand principles of income redistribution, and lacking the authority to compel a transfer of wealth, the UN proved largely ineffectual. Not only did no major redistribution of wealth occur; instead, the gap between rich and poor grew even larger.

Whatever the actual performance of UNCTAD, its creation, along with the establishment of the UN Development Decade, UNDP, and UNIDO, testified to the growing priority of third world concerns in the United Nations. To be sure, the proliferation of new agencies taxed the UN's already strained financial and administrative capabilities, the latter never particularly strong under Thant's indifferent management. But the ability of the third world to redefine the UN's agenda, to capture some of its institutional machinery, and to organize into a formidable political bloc represented a significant departure for the world organization. To many, the UN itself had been fundamentally altered. Thant, as secretary-general, by no means led in this historic movement toward third world prominence, but both in word and deed he identified himself with it completely.

NOTES

1. U Thant, *View from the UN* (Garden City, N.Y.: Doubleday, 1975), 35.

2. Thant, *View from the UN*, 36.

3. Thant, *View from the UN*, 35.

4. Andrew W. Cordier and Max Harrelson, eds., *Public Papers of the Secretaries-General of the United Nations, Vol. VII, U Thant* (New York: Columbia University Press, 1976), 519.

5. Andrew W. Cordier and Max Harrelson, eds., *Public Papers of the Secretaries-General of the United Nations, Vol. VIII, U Thant* (New York: Columbia University Press, 1977), 297.

6. Cordier and Harrelson, *Public Papers, Vol. VIII*, 297.

7. Cordier and Harrelson, *Public Papers, Vol. VIII*, 245.

8. Cordier and Harrelson, *Public Papers, Vol. VII*, 234.

9. Cordier and Harrelson, *Public Papers, Vol. VIII*, 368.

10. A. Leroy Bennett, *International Organizations: Principles and Issues*, 5th ed. (Englewood Cliffs, N.J.: Prentice Hall, 1991), 287.

11. Cordier and Harrelson, *Public Papers, Vol. VIII*, 57.

4

The New Majority and the United States: The Fiscal Crisis and Vietnam

The shift in the character of the United Nations from an organization composed primarily of Western states to one populated by large numbers of third world nations created significant confusion and discomfort in American foreign policy circles. The United States, for so long the dominant state on Turtle Bay, seemed unable to create a policy to respond to the changed circumstances of its power. In November 1960, the assembly debated a resolution that was to become the UN's "Declaration on the Granting of Independence to Colonial Countries and Peoples." That resolution, sponsored by forty-three third world countries, demanded that the colonial powers grant dependent peoples their immediate independence. The United States, officially concerned that the resolution could be used to challenge the status of Puerto Rico, its own dependent territory, supported the United Kingdom's position that article 73 of the United Nations Charter, titled the "Declaration Regarding Non-Self-Governing Territories," effectively encouraged the process of decolonization and that a new declaration was both superfluous and inflammatory. Washington joined the United Kingdom in abstaining on the resolution, which otherwise garnered the unanimous support of the nonaligned bloc of nations.

American isolation from the newly evolving third world majority stemmed, in large part, from traditional cold war concerns about the correlation of East-West forces. In 1959, one year before the General Assembly's adoption of the declaration, political scientist Inis Claude had described the United States as part of the "colonial bloc" of UN members, along with the United Kingdom, Belgium, France, the Netherlands, Australia, and New Zealand. Despite Washington's principled opposition to colonialism, the bloc's "centrifugal pulls [were] somewhat offset . . . by the recognition of the need for avoiding the alienation or weakening of the colonialist members of the anti-Soviet front, and the fear the anticolonial game may emancipate dependent peoples right into the hands of new Communist masters."[1] Fear of the Soviet Union resonated strongly in the policy-making deliberations of the Europe-centered Eisenhower Administration, and Moscow's strong backing for the anticolonial declaration only intensified American concerns that decolonization would create a group of volatile states vulnerable to Communist subversion. Indeed, because a speech to the General Assembly by Premier Khrushchev in September 1960 had given rise to the resolution, Washington could easily justify its decision to abstain.

The inauguration of John F. Kennedy as president of the United States in January 1961 brought a new look at America's relations with the third world, and by extension to the role of the United States in a changing United Nations. Kennedy and his advisers were much more inclined than their predecessors to see the third world as an East-West battleground of virtually equal significance to that of Central Europe. In their rhetoric, they were much more willing to balance the well understood interests of their European allies with the increasingly critical need to win support from the newly independent peoples of Africa and Asia. That meant, among other things, endorsing third world opposition to continued colonial rule. This innovation in American policy became clear in May 1961 when the United States supported a General Assembly decision to set up a commission to monitor implementation of the declaration on the granting of independence to non-self-governing peoples. In further reflection of that shift, Washington forged a close relationship with U Thant during his and Kennedy's early days in their respective offices to encourage peaceful evolution to independence in the third world, even if that meant distancing the United States from the policies of some of its European allies. In the disputes over the Congo and West Irian and in its opposition to Portugal's continued ill treatment of dependent people in Africa, the Kennedy Administration found itself in frequent disagreement with its traditional European friends still wedded to some degree to a colonial mentality. Ambassador Adlai Stevenson led the way as the United States abandoned the Eisenhower Administration's reflexive aversion to the promotion of third world views on decolonization. Instead, the Kennedy Administration attempted to outflank the Soviets by supporting third world self-determination and using the instruments of the United Nations to direct that drive into a pro-Western path.

The American role in helping to resolve the Congo, West Irian, and Yemen disputes demonstrated the success of the Kennedy Administration's realistic new approach toward the UN. As Ambassador Stevenson stated in January 1962, the United Nations remained critical to Washington's foreign policy. But as time went on, the growing preponderance of third world nations in the world organization and their loud chorus of economic and political grievances against the West began to drown out stories of American successes. The American public, more accustomed to a United Nations in which Washington exercised near total control, had difficulty appreciating the new shape of the organization and a more limited American role. The altered situation was reflected in increasingly strong criticisms of the United Nations, particularly from among right-wing elements of the American political system. In June 1961, the Republican Policy Committee, representing Republican officeholders, called for a system of weighted voting in the General Assembly that would redress the emerging power shift in favor of the United States. Ambassador Stevenson quickly rebuffed the Republican proposal, citing the principle of sovereign equality. Nevertheless, in December 1961, after the UN had failed to condemn India for its invasion of Portuguese-held Goa, the ambassador warned of the dire consequences that could flow from the UN's refusal to criticize India, a leading member of the nonaligned bloc. Over the next several years, continuing third world criticisms of America's reluctance to share its great wealth, coupled with the widely held expectation in the third world that the United States should shoulder the lion's share of the burden of financing the United Nations, contributed further to American unhappiness with the world organization.

This chapter examines the two events that effectively sealed the evolution in American perceptions of the United Nations, the fiscal crisis and Thant's efforts to end the Vietnam War. The fiscal crisis demonstrated to Americans the extent to which the United States had lost control over the organization it had dominated for so many years and led Washington to reevaluate its status within the world organization. The Vietnam War, and Washington's opposition to a UN role in brokering its end, indicated that the United Nations had ceased to be seen in Washington as an effective tool of American foreign policy. Both crises occurred as the organization moved toward third world supremacy and as the United States fell in the power structure of the UN. Taken together, they firmly ended the American era in the United Nations.

THE FISCAL CRISIS

Most peacekeeping activities undertaken during Thant's first several years in office were financed by the parties to the conflicts, thus relieving the world organization of potentially crippling financial encumbrances. But the financial burdens created by the ongoing deployment of the United Nations Emergency Force (UNEF) in the Sinai and the enormous military costs of the Congo operation, coupled with the Soviet and French refusals to pay for peacekeeping, thrust the world organization in the early 1960s into a situation of fiscal crisis. The UN's experience in Cyprus, an intervention dependent on voluntary contributions to finance UNFICYP, demonstrated that the United Nations could no longer assume that resources to carry on its work would always be available.

Fiscal crisis had actually been apparent well before Thant assumed the post of acting secretary-general. In order to finance UNEF, a separate fund had been established outside the regular budget of the world organization. Hammarsjköld, however, with support from the United States, had maintained that the existence of a special UNEF account did not diminish from each government's responsibility to finance peacekeeping forces. All such activities, he reasoned, fell under article 17 of the charter, which allocated responsibility for financing UN activities to all member states. The Soviet Union, however, claimed that only France, Great Britain, and Israel, the "aggressor" states at Suez, should pay for UNEF. The General Assembly, with the USSR and its allies dissenting, voted in favor of the principle that all states were obliged to pay for the organization's peacekeeping activities, although it promised rebates to poor states unable to pay their full assessments. The United States fully complied with its quota to support the General Assembly's formula, but the Soviet Union refused to pay its assessment.

The Security Council's decision in 1960 to authorize a new peacekeeping operation, ONUC, further strained scarce UN resources. Despite the Soviet Union's affirmative vote on ONUC, the Kremlin persisted in its argument that aggressor states, in this case, Belgium, should pay for peacekeeping. The Fifth Committee of the General Assembly affirmed several times in 1960 and 1961 that financial responsibility for peacekeeping fell under article 17 of the United Nations Charter, and the General Assembly regularly accepted the recommendations of the committee. But after Patrice Lumumba's death, the Soviet Union had soured on ONUC and now argued that fiscal arrangements relating to peacekeeping should be made in the Security Council, where the Soviets enjoyed a veto power. The General Assembly rejected the Soviet argument but was unable to force Moscow to pay its assessment. The United States became the chief contributor to both operations, but by late 1961, as many states adopted Russia's stance, the peacekeepers were more than $80 million in debt.

It was against this background that Thant became acting secretary-general in November 1961. According to U.S. Ambassador Philip Klutznick, Thant had "little interest in, or understanding, of UN finances,"[2] and happily endorsed a 1961 U.S. delegation proposal that the UN float bonds to pay its expenses—although Thant later claimed credit as "father" of the scheme. On December 20, 1961, the General Assembly passed the bond issue by a vote of 58–13, with 28 abstentions. Among the negative votes were Moscow's and Paris's. The Kennedy Administration, after a bruising political battle with Capitol Hill conservatives, agreed to match bond purchases by other states up to $100 million. Over the next two years, $154.7 million in bonds were sold to alleviate the UN's short-term fiscal problems, but the long-range problem remained ominous.

The General Assembly's decision to authorize a bond issue was coupled with a UN request to the World Court that it render an advisory opinion on the critical article 17 issue. On July 20, 1962, the International Court of Justice ruled that paying expenses for peacekeeping operations was incumbent upon all members of the organization, a decision the General Assembly gratefully voted to accept in December. As a consequence, many minor states in arrears paid their assessments, but the Soviet Union and France remained unmoved. They continued to refuse financial responsibility for peacekeeping operations they regarded as inconsistent with their respective national interests.

Efforts to resolve the funding crisis in 1963 and 1964 proved futile. Working groups of the General Assembly regularly met, worked out compromise formulas, and then had them rejected, as both sides rigidly adhered to their respective positions. The United States, bearing the financial brunt of the organization's debts, insisted that article 17 obligated Moscow to pay for all the organization's expenses, including peacekeeping. The Soviet Union, in the face of General Assembly resolutions and a World Court advisory opinion to the contrary, argued just as resolutely that article 17 did not apply. The secretary-general used his speeches, press conferences, and annual reports to warn that the world organization was in jeopardy of collapsing over the fiscal issue. The General Assembly followed his lead, and in May 1963, a special session discussed what Thant called the "most vital [problem] before the United Nations."[3] The assembly urged all members to make good on the arrears, which by then had reached $114 million. Meanwhile, with the millions raised through the sale of bonds nearly gone, the secretary-general implemented belt-tightening measures on the world body. With the situation in the Congo more stable, funds for ONUC were cut and UNEF was streamlined as well. Staff expenditures were contained, despite the growing activities of the United Nations in the developing world.

By September 30, 1964, ONUC and UNEF were in arrears by $112.3 million. The secretary-general reported that the organization had cash reserves of $24.8 million and a deficit of $113.3 million, owed by twenty-nine member states. The Soviet share of the deficit was enormous. The Kremlin owed $54.8 million to the two peacekeeping accounts, while Paris was in arrears on ONUC in the amount of $17.8 million. Thus, the stage was set for a political showdown in the General Assembly. Under article 19 of the charter, when a member's arrears equaled or exceeded the assessed amount of its contributions due for the preceding two years, it "shall have no vote in the General Assembly."[4] The United States asserted that since the Soviet Union could not demonstrate that its failure to pay was due to conditions beyond Moscow's control, the terms of the charter automatically disqualified the Kremlin from voting.

Washington pressed the article 19 issue, supported by General Assembly resolutions and the International Court of Justice ruling on the financing issue, in the hope that other governments would apply sufficient pressure on Moscow to force a favorable resolution of the crisis. During the congressional fight over the bond issue in 1962, Kennedy had pledged to Capitol Hill conservatives that he would exert all efforts to compel governments in arrears to pay their UN assessments, and it was President Lyndon Baines Johnson, who succeeded the assassinated Kennedy in November 1963, who inherited that policy. In 1964, with the General Assembly's Working Group of Twenty-One stymied by continued Soviet and French refusals to pay their UN debt, Johnson decided to force the issue by threatening to invoke article 19.

Whatever the moral persuasiveness of the American argument in behalf of the charter, and no matter how much the organization needed the money, it was also clear to the secretary-general that a crisis over Soviet and French voting rights in the General Assembly could destroy the organization. In August 1964, Thant visited Moscow, Paris, and Washington in a personal attempt to stave off disaster at the nineteenth General Assembly. Fortunately, because the nonaligned nations were convening their own conference in Cairo and had requested that the General Assembly delay its annual September opening, Thant gladly agreed to reschedule the UN session to December 1. This delay allowed Thant, the United States, and the Soviet Union to cooperate behind the scenes to rescue the organization from imminent political collapse. The secretary-general first proposed the creation of a "peace fund," an account in which member states that refused to pay for specific peacekeeping operations could contribute without appearing to compromise on the principle of peacekeeping. The proposal, however, failed to generate substantial support. Instead, Thant was forced to rely on stopgap measures that would permit the organization to function but without precipitating a potentially ruinous showdown on article 19.

On November 20, Ambassador Federenko and Secretary Rusk agreed to avoid a great power explosion in the General Assembly by allowing the assembly to convene without taking formal votes. The General Assembly met on December 1, and under the agreed formula a number of new third world states were admitted, a credentials committee was appointed, and a new assembly president was elected—all without forcing a confrontation over article 19. The scheme worked because the General Assembly majority was not eager to invoke the charter on so sensitive and politically charged a matter. Washington had recognized the reality of its declining power in the General Assembly and decided to go along with the obvious charade. On February 18, 1965, after Albanian Ambassador Halim Budo insisted that a vote be taken on his motion that the assembly return to its normal procedure, the United States allowed the assembly to vote on Assembly President Alex Quaison-Sackey's ruling that the motion was out of order. Although it claimed that the matter was purely procedural, the United States was perceived by many to have retreated from its insistence that article 19 be invoked against the Soviet Union. The nineteenth session of the General Assembly, the shortest in history, was then adjourned.

Over the next several months, efforts to solve the financing problem and avoid a repetition of the events surrounding the nineteenth General Assembly session proved fruitless. Then, on August 16, 1965, the new American ambassador, Arthur J. Goldberg, declared that the United States would drop its insistence that the assembly invoke article 19. Goldberg asserted the moral rightness of the American position but admitted that the assembly was clearly unwilling to take the necessary measures against delinquent states. The cost for the organization was high, however, for the ambassador now put into the record an American reservation to the principle of collective security: "The United States reserves the same option to make exceptions [to collective financial responsibility] if, in our view, strong and compelling reasons exist for doing so."[5] Indeed, in private communications with the Kremlin, President Johnson, in a futile effort to induce the Soviets to make good on their arrears, had already deferred to the Russian view that future peacekeeping operations would have to originate in the Security Council. There each "big power" retained a veto over UN action, and their interests were secure.

The American decision to avoid confrontation over article 19 saved the organization from political collapse. The twentieth assembly voted to resume normal operations and urged member states, particularly those from the developed world, to increase their voluntary contributions to the organization. Over the next several years, Thant continued to struggle with the problem of funding UNFICYP, but in the 1970s, peacekeeping forces for the Middle East proved easier to fund. In the final analysis, though, the United Nations, despite its ability to survive, was damaged mightily by the fiscal crisis. As political scientist John G. Stoessinger observed in his useful study of the UN, the battle over funding was never a battle over the existence of the organization, but instead a struggle over the UN's role. The Soviets, angered by the Congo operation, were determined to prevent the organization from instituting collective security operations over their objections and viewed the funding issue as a means to assert their position. The United States, traditionally employing the UN to further its foreign policy interests, had long supported mandatory peacekeeping assessments and the principle of collective security and saw the fiscal crisis as a test of the UN's ability to continue in that role. The irony of the article 19 crisis is that the American failure to prevail in the General Assembly led Washington to a conclusion the Soviets had reached a long time before. A General Assembly dominated by third world votes, and even the United Nations itself, was becoming an unreliable foreign policy tool. Thant's view of the UN as a peacekeeping instrument had to suffer in the process. By 1965, American attitudes toward the UN were perceptibly changing. The American retreat on article 19 certified that shift, as did Washington's decision to employ the Organization of American States to legitimize its May invasion of the Dominican Republic and the Johnson Administration's corresponding frustration of UN involvement in the Caribbean country. It was Vietnam, however, which decisively demonstrated the UN's failure to resolve international conflict and Washington's alienation from the world organization.

THE WAR IN VIETNAM

America's role in Vietnam reflected the Kennedy and Johnson administrations' belief that to compete against communism in the third world required a vigorous American stance, including the actual commitment of troops to the field of battle. Under President Eisenhower, the American commitment to South Vietnam had been limited to economic aid and covert military assistance, but under Kennedy the American role had expanded to include military advisers and then troops. Escalation increased dramatically under Lyndon Johnson, who in 1965 significantly increased American troop strength and combat involvement in an effort to win the war. Johnson's escalation of the war produced an American troop presence in South Vietnam of close to 550 thousand soldiers by 1968.

U Thant's opposition to American military involvement in Vietnam stemmed from his strong belief, first articulated in the mid-1950s, that the Vietnam War could only be resolved by political means. The governments of South Vietnam were neither democratic nor stable, and to portray the conflict there as a struggle between freedom and totalitarianism struck the secretary-general as ridiculous. Thant, with his own background in the struggle against British colonialism, viewed Ho Chi Minh of North Vietnam primarily as an Asian nationalist, only secondarily a Communist. His emphatic comment in July 1967 summarized his stance. "I am convinced that the war cannot be brought to an end until the United States and her allies recognize that it is being fought by Vietnamese, not as a war of Communist aggression, but as a war of national independence."[6]

The enormous human cost of the Vietnam War was of particular concern to the secretary-general. In December 1965, he referred to American involvement as "more violent, more cruel, more damaging to human life and property . . . than at any other time during the generation of conflict that country has known."[7] In a calculated slap at the Johnson Administration, Thant expressed astonishment at American policy in terms deliberately reminiscent of his criticism of the Soviet Union's Congo policy: "I am sure that the great American people, if only they knew the true facts and the background to the developments in South Vietnam, will agree with me that further bloodshed is unnecessary."[8] Referring to Senator Barry Goldwater's proposal that the United States use nuclear weapons in Vietnam, Thant reminded his American audience that Asians had been the first victims of atomic bombs and would not easily be reconciled to their renewed use against fellow Asians.

Despite his strong feelings, Thant was uncertain about any role the United Nations could play in mediating the Vietnam conflict. While Ambassador Stevenson hoped to use the Security Council to achieve a negotiated settlement, U.S. Secretary of State Dean Rusk worried that the Soviets would inevitably frustrate American interests in the council. Thant seemed to concur with Rusk and told Stevenson that the Russians would not permit the United Nations to be used as a vehicle for a cease-fire and negotiations. Contributing further to Thant's feeling of helplessness was the absence of key parties to the conflict—North and South Vietnam and the People's Republic of China—from membership in the United Nations. The secretary-general could only urge—unsuccessfully—the reconvening of the 1954 Geneva Peace Conference, which had first divided Vietnam and set terms for the eventual reunification of the country.

Thant's concern with Vietnam began during the summer of 1964. He visited several foreign capitals and, at the urging of Soviet Party Chairman Khrushchev and Burma's new ruler Ne Win, approached Washington with fresh ideas about breaking the negotiating stalemate. At a State Department luncheon on August 6, 1964, Thant had suggested to Secretary Rusk that an American emissary meet with a representative of North Vietnam. Encouraged by what he took to be a positive response from the American secretary of state, the secretary-general asked a high-ranking Soviet official in the Secretariat, Vladimir Suslov, to elicit Hanoi's reaction to the proposal. In September, Thant received a positive reply from Hanoi, through Suslov, which he then relayed to Ambassador Stevenson. The American ambassador notified Thant that a reply from Washington would have to await the results of the presidential election. After Johnson's election, Stevenson informed the secretary-general that a well-connected Canadian member of the International Control Commission had persuaded the administration that North Vietnam was not interested in direct talks. Convinced that Washington was lending too much credence to a questionable report, in December, Thant approached Soviet Foreign Minister Andrei Gromyko and was again told that Hanoi would pursue direct negotiations with the United States. In mid-January 1965, Stevenson, impatient with his own State Department's refusal to reply to the secretary-general, asked Thant where talks could be held; Thant replied that Rangoon would both welcome the talks and ensure their secrecy. What happened in Washington remains diplomatically murky, but on January 30 Stevenson notified Thant that the United States, fearful of undermining the government in Saigon, would not participate in the talks. On February 7, the United States substantially escalated the war by initiating sustained bombings of the north and increasing American ground combat operations.

Thant never forgave Washington for spurning his 1964 efforts at peace, and an interview with Stevenson, published in the *Saturday Evening Post* several months after the ambassador's death in July 1965, revealed a similar bitterness at America's failure to capitalize on the opportunity to negotiate. While meeting with President Johnson on June 25, 1965, an amazed Thant listened as the president launched into an attack on his UN ambassador and criticized the secretary-general for his own comments on Vietnam. The meeting convinced Thant that Johnson had not been apprised of the peace initiative as it was unfolding. Secretary Rusk later sought to blame Stevenson for the collapse of the peace effort by telling Thant that the ambassador had not been authorized to turn down the proposal. In Thant's view, however, his 1964 initiative failed because Washington was in the midst of planning an escalation of the war, which could not have materialized had the administration been forced into negotiations.

Thant's vigorous attention to the war stemmed both from his strong aversion to American policy and from his conception of the secretary-general's role. Like Hammarskjöld, Thant maintained that article 99 of the UN Charter empowered a UN chief to engage in preventive diplomacy, without the sanction of the Security Council. But Washington was clearly unhappy with Thant's attitude toward its war, and relations between the secretary-general and the Johnson Administration quickly deteriorated. While he liked President Johnson personally, Thant was stunned by the apparent simplemindedness of the president's views on Vietnam, characterized by Johnson's alleged assertion to him that a victory for the Communists in Vietnam would jeopardize Hawaii. Stung by the secretary-general's persistent and increasingly bitter attacks on their policies, administration officials resented Thant's meddling in areas they regarded beyond his competence and outside his impartial role. They ridiculed his belief that Ho Chi Minh was anything but a dedicated Communist. They mocked Thant's ignorance of the fact that the United States had supplied his native Burma with millions of dollars to fight a Communist insurgency. By 1967, the tension between Thant and Washington was so severe that Rusk publicly wondered whether Thant's exertions were designed to win a Nobel Prize for the secretary-general.

Despite deep strains over Thant's Vietnam attitude, the administration at least formally maintained its interest in the secretary-general's efforts to bridge the gap between Hanoi and Washington. In March 1965, a State Department source suggested that the United States would support a role for the secretary-general in the peace process. In April, when Thant proposed to visit Hanoi, both North Vietnam and China, angered by the secretary-general's relatively favorable response to President Johnson's April 7 Johns Hopkins Address on Vietnam, rejected his overture. Then shortly after Stevenson's death, in July, the president and Thant exchanged warm letters that left open the door to further UN intervention over Vietnam.

In the spring of 1966, following President Johnson's failed effort to combine a bombing halt with a diplomatic offensive to bring about peace talks, Thant, in Europe, announced a three-point peace plan for Vietnam. In a television broadcast aired in Paris, the secretary-general listed three essential steps toward initiating peace negotiations: a halt in American bombing of North Vietnam, the de-escalation of all military activities in South Vietnam, and a willingness "on the part of some of the parties primarily concerned to speak to those who are fighting, to discuss with those who are fighting."[9] The Thant peace plan met objections from both sides. North Vietnam supported the concept of a bombing halt but refused to reduce its military activities in the south. The United States, while it accepted aspects of the Thant formula in principle, would not cease bombing without Hanoi's commitment to scale down its military activities against the Saigon government. Throughout 1966, Thant both attacked American policy in Vietnam and publicized his peace plan, but neither side moved enough to allow peace negotiations to begin.

In December 1966, Ambassador Goldberg asked Thant to help arrange a cease-fire in Vietnam, and Thant expressed his appreciation for the American statement of support for his efforts. Following the Tet truce of February 1967 and in response to a resumption of American bombing and the mining of North Vietnamese waters, the secretary-general arranged, through the good offices of the French ambassador to the United Nations, to meet with high-ranking North Vietnamese officials during an ostensible vacation to Burma. On March 2, Thant met in Rangoon with a delegation from Hanoi and proposed a three-point formula that included a truce in place, preliminary talks between the United States and North Vietnam, and a reconvening of the Geneva Peace Conference. The secret talks soon became public knowledge, and before he left for New York, Thant acknowledged that he had indeed met with North Vietnamese representatives.

Despite the expectations raised by Thant's initiative, Hanoi regarded the new proposals as a retreat from the secretary-general's often stated contention that the United States should unconditionally halt its bombing. Even as the United States welcomed the call for a mutual cease-fire, North Vietnam bitterly assailed the proposal and the secretary-general himself. South Vietnam, following Washington's lead, generally supported Thant's new formulations but objected to being left out of the negotiating process. Thant himself insisted that the new plan was not designed to supplant the previous program and continued throughout 1967 to call on the United States to cease bombing of the north.

It was not until early 1968, in the aftermath of the Tet offensive of January 30, that Thant's long effort began to show results. Encouraged by conciliatory statements from Hanoi and Washington, Thant visited a number of foreign capitals and met on February 8 with a representative of the North Vietnamese government in New Delhi. On February 14, a North Vietnamese diplomat in Paris informed the secretary-general that Hanoi would begin talks with the United States in return for an unconditional cessation of American bombing; all questions, including North Vietnamese military activity in the south, could be discussed in negotiations. Thant interpreted Hanoi's response as an affirmation of his March 1967 peace efforts, and, upon his return to the United States, he met with both Ambassador Goldberg and President Johnson. Johnson regarded Thant's report as "interesting but hardly conclusive"[10] and continued to argue that a bombing halt would allow North Vietnam to improve its military position in the south. Thant's efforts coincided, however, with a major reassessment within the administration over the future direction of the war. On March 31, after further signals from Hanoi corroborated the secretary-general's report, President Johnson announced that he would not seek reelection to the presidency and ordered a cessation of the bombing north of the twentieth parallel. On the basis of this partial bombing halt, Hanoi agreed to participate in negotiations with the United States.

Throughout the summer, American and North Vietnamese diplomats wrangled inconclusively in Paris over preliminary issues. Thant was certain that only the absence of a complete bombing halt prevented a diplomatic breakthrough, and in September, responding to Hanoi's plea that he involve himself in the peace process, he publicly rebuked the United States for continuing the bombing. In a further slap at the United States, he also asserted that the General Assembly backed his stand. Thant's personal intervention in the Paris talks drew a sharply negative response from Washington, where UN Ambassador George Ball called the secretary-general "naive." Only on October 31, with the American presidential election several days away, did Johnson announce a complete bombing halt and so pave the way for National Liberation Front (NLF, or Viet Cong) and South Vietnamese participation in the Paris negotiations. By January 1969, two of Thant's March 1966 conditions had been met: a complete bombing halt was in effect and all parties to the conflict, including the NLF, were involved in negotiations.

When Thant left his position as secretary-general in December 1971, American intervention in Vietnam was winding down, and the war was attracting less international concern than it had several years earlier. The Nixon Administration's policy of decreasing

America's troop presence in Vietnam while simultaneously widening the war through heavier bombing and incursions into Cambodia and Laos nevertheless gave Thant frequent occasions for further criticisms of American policy. During these years, Thant occasionally voiced optimism about the chances for peace in Indochina, but, for the most part, his voice was raised in criticism of American policy.

It is difficult to assess the record of Thant's involvement in the Vietnam War. The secretary-general had been a strong opponent of the war even before the huge American military escalations of 1965–1966, and the conflict dragged on after the conclusion of his tenure in New York. It does not appear, therefore, that his unequivocal opposition to the war had any immediate effect on either American or North Vietnamese policy. The United States, for the most part, did not welcome Thant's involvement in the peace process, and when a breakthrough did occur, in 1968, it had little to do with the secretary-general. Thant's diplomatic efforts were, in fact, being denigrated by the president, and when negotiations began, Washington excluded Thant from the process.

Nonetheless, it would be incorrect to dismiss the secretary-general's efforts as inconsequential. Over time, dissension in the United States over the war policy and widespread opposition abroad weakened the Johnson and Nixon administrations' determination to fight the war through to a military conclusion. To the extent that world public opinion played a role in ending the war, Thant's persistent criticisms had an effect, especially among third world nations where his influence was greatest.

CONCLUSION

The fiscal crisis signaled a fundamental change in the distribution of power within the United Nations—away from the United States. Ambassador Seymour Maxwell Finger, who served during the mid-1960s in the United States Mission to the United Nations, remembered that "at USUN we were convinced that the Soviets would find a way to pay if the Third World countries stood firm,"[11] but Moscow's escalating threats to leave the organization weakened third world support for the American position. Developing states had long championed the United Nations, and they recognized in the continuing impasse over article 19 a profound threat to the vitality and even existence of the organization. Despite their moral support for the United States, they were not about to, in the words of one African diplomat, "blow up the world Organization on the altar of a principle founded upon Charter provisions of an admittedly ambiguous character."[12]

If the fiscal crisis indicated that the United States had lost control over the world organization, then the war in Vietnam demonstrated the extent to which the United Nations was no longer regarded by Washington as a useful instrument of American foreign policy. A decade earlier, during the fortuitous absence of the Soviet Union from the Security Council, the United States had used a similar situation—the North Korean invasion of South Korea—to obtain validation of its policy from the UN. But the situation was different in Vietnam. The Soviets were firmly ensconced in the Security Council, the vast majority of the General Assembly was hostile to American policy, and the secretary-general was openly critical of the American war effort. In this atmosphere, the United States not only did not seek UN intervention, it openly discouraged it.

Taken together, the fiscal crisis, Vietnam War, and the United Nations' role in dealing with the American invasion of the Dominican Republic in 1965 signaled a transformation in the world organization. America had lost control over the United Nations' agenda and so lost faith in the utility of the organization as an instrument of foreign policy. In 1969, the United States cast its first veto in the Security Council, an act that perhaps more than any other symbolized Washington's changing view of the world organization. In the 1950s, when the Security Council had been stymied by the Soviet veto, the United States had turned to the General Assembly to ensure effective UN action. In the early 1960s, with a revived Security Council careful to protect its prerogatives under the charter and the General Assembly a less predictable forum, the United States had used Thant to resolve disputes in third world nations and coordinated its diplomacy with his. In the mid-1960s, with Thant publicly hostile to America's most important foreign policy commitment, the United States sought to keep even the secretary-general at arms' length. Just as the Soviets had relied on their Security Council veto to protect them from the effects of their minority status, the United States, now also in the minority, took refuge in the Security Council and its veto power.

Appendix 4A

The Dominican Crisis, 1965

In the spring of 1965, unrest in the Dominican Republic triggered a large-scale American military intervention into the tiny, Central American country. Coinciding with significant American military escalation in South Vietnam, the invasion of the Dominican Republic reminded America's critics that "carrying a big stick" had been a persistent feature of Washington's policy toward Central and Latin America. But President Lyndon Baines Johnson was determined to prevent the spread of communism in the Western Hemisphere, and the intervention extended into the summer and fall. During the crisis, the United Nations was virtually deadlocked by Soviet-American acrimony on the Security Council and stymied by a conflict in jurisdiction between itself and the Organization of American States, and so proved largely ineffective in settling the conflict.

The Dominican civil war erupted in April 1965, when troops loyal to former President Juan Bosch, ousted in a 1963 military coup, launched an insurrection against the ruling junta, led by Donald Reid Cabral. The rebels were leftists who demanded restoration of the 1963 constitution, and the ensuing fighting pitted pro-Bosch, forces led by Colonel Francisco Caamano Deno against high-ranking military officers, including General Antonio Imbert Barreras, opposed to Bosch's return. After intense fighting in the Santo Domingo area proved inconclusive, the two factions each established a government and claimed control over the country.

On April 27, ostensibly out of concern for the lives of Americans trapped by the fighting, President Johnson ordered marines to evacuate approximately one thousand American citizens to vessels located in the Caribbean. On April 28, after being told that the leftists were gaining the upper hand in the fighting, Johnson ordered more marines to the island, with instructions that they interpose themselves between the warring factions. Eventually, some twenty thousand American troops were sent to the Dominican Republic to contain what the administration regarded as an effort by Communists loyal to Fidel Castro to establish another beachhead in Central America.

Charging the United States with the "cynical violation of elementary norms of international law,"[13] Soviet Ambassador Nikolai T. Federenko on May 1, 1965, requested an emergency meeting of the Security Council. Federenko initiated debate on May 3 with a blistering attack on American policy in Central America. In reply, Ambassador Adlai Stevenson, plagued by doubts about the wisdom and morality of American policy, characterized the civil war as a joint effort by the Soviet Union and Cuba to establish influence in the Western Hemisphere. He appealed that the council permit the Organization of American States (OAS), an organization much more likely than the Security Council to follow Washington's lead, to deal with the problem. On May 4, a Soviet resolution calling on American troops to withdraw and end their "gross violation of the UN Charter,"[14] was defeated. On May 14, in response to an urgent letter from the Dominican rebel foreign minister, Jottia Cury, to U Thant, the Security Council unanimously approved a Jordanian resolution calling on the secretary-general to send a personal representative to the troubled Caribbean island and urging the warring parties to observe a cease-fire. Thant appointed veteran Venezuelan diplomat Jose Antonio Mayobre, who had been with the UN Secretariat since 1951, as his personal representative.

The Mayobre peace mission arrived in Santo Domingo on May 18 and immediately confused the diplomatic situation on the island. Also in Santo Domingo were a four-man American diplomatic team, headed by Johnson's national security adviser, McGeorge Bundy, and a five-man OAS Peace Commission, dispatched to the Dominican Republic on April 29. The latter group was so frustrated by the UN intervention, that its members called UN involvement "an unfortunate event that powerfully affected the course of events," because it "compromised and interfered with the OAS Commission."[15] The entire commission resigned in protest against U.S. and UN interferences, and the OAS sent its secretary-general, Jose A. Mora, to visit Santo Domingo.

Mayobre too was experiencing frustration in his efforts to negotiate a peaceful settlement. On May 19 the Security Council unanimously endorsed a recommendation by the council president that the UN diplomat engineer a twelve-hour truce to permit the Red Cross to withdraw the dead and wounded from the war theater; the humanitarian truce took effect on May 20. But on May 21 the Soviet Union introduced two new resolutions—one condemning the United States for its invasion of the Dominican Republic, the second calling for the withdrawal of all foreign troops. Both were defeated in the Security Council. On May 22, however, the council approved by a vote of 10–0–1 a French resolution calling for an expansion of the truce into a permanent cease-fire and inviting the secretary-general to report on implementation of the resolution. Ambassador Stevenson explained that the United States abstained because the resolution made no mention of the OAS role. By May 23, an Inter-American Peace Force formed by the OAS and consisting primarily of U.S. Marines with small military contingents from selected Latin American countries, began fanning out through Santo Domingo in three-man teams to supervise the truce.

The USSR continued to use the Security Council as a means to get involved in the dispute. The council reconvened on June 3 to hear a Soviet complaint that junta forces were summarily arresting and executing rebel sympathizers in Santo Domingo. On June 7, the Soviet Union joined France, Jordan, and Uruguay to recommend that Mayobre be given the authority to investigate human rights abuses in the Dominican Republic. The United States, with the support of Great Britain, Bolivia, and Malaysia, countered that the OAS was effectively monitoring human rights abuses on the island. On June 16, in response to new violence, Federenko recommended that Thant himself visit Santo Domingo, a suggestion U.S. Ambassador Charles Yost called "mischievous." The Soviets' unsuccessful effort to expand Thant's role in the Dominican Republic represented an ironic departure for a government that for years had sought to limit the discretionary power of the secretary-general.

The open split between the United States and the Soviet Union in the Security Council made decisive UN action impossible in the Dominican crisis, and the jurisdictional disputes between Mayobre and the OAS further complicated the situation. It was a new three-man OAS mission, headed by American diplomat Ellsworth Bunker, that managed over the summer to secure both factions' acquiescence

to a new peace formula. Under the "Act of Dominican Reconciliation," junta and rebel forces agreed to the establishment of a provisional government and new elections. In June 1966, an election, with
Bosch in the running, produced a victory for former President
Joaquín Balaguer. The UN ended Mayobre's mission in October 1966.

Secretary-general Thant, while acknowledging the usefulness of
regional security organizations and their constitutionality under the
charter, entertained strong reservations about the wisdom of the
OAS's, and by extension, Washington's Dominican role. The secretary-general warned that regional organizations ought not to act
without Security Council consent and, three years later, he drew a
parallel between OAS action in the Dominican Republic and the Warsaw Pact's decision to invade Czechoslovakia. As a third worlder
whose country had managed to maintain its independence despite
the presence of Communist China on its borders, Thant was extremely
sensitive to the vulnerability of small states to the caprices of regional
superpowers. His general aversion to the use of force to resolve international disputes motivated Thant to express opposition to U.S. policy in the Dominican Republic, although not to the point of denounc-
ing Washington to the world organization. For its part, the United
States correctly felt that it had more control over the OAS than it did
over the Security Council, an assumption given credence by Soviet
efforts to use the council as a forum for excoriating Washington. The
administration resented Thant's view of its Dominican policy, and in
a June 1965 meeting, Johnson severely criticized the secretary-general for Mayobre's actions. Thant's harsh criticism of the American
effort in South Vietnam, joined with his publicly articulated reservations about Washington's Dominican intervention, had the effect of
estranging him from the Johnson Administration. It effectively ended
the cooperative relationship with America that had helped Thant
during his earlier years in office.

NOTES

1. Inis L. Claude, Jr., *Swords into Plowshares* (New York: Random House,
1959), 358.

2. Seymour Maxwell Finger, *Your Man at the UN: People, Politics, and
Bureaucracy in the Making of Foreign Policy* (New York: New York University
Press, 1980), 133.

3. Andrew W. Cordier and Max Harrelson, eds., *Public Papers of the Sec-*

retaries-General of the United Nations, Vol. VI, U Thant (New York: Columbia University Press, 1976), 345.

4. Cited in Peter R. Baehr and Leon Gordenker, *The United Nations in the 1990s* (New York: St. Martin's, 1994), 164.

5. Andrew W. Cordier and Max Harrelson, eds., *Public Papers of the Secretaries-General of the United Nations, Vol. VII, U Thant* (New York: Columbia University Press, 1976), 168.

6. Cordier and Harrelson, *Public Papers, Vol. VII,* 508.

7. U Thant, *View from the UN* (Garden City, N.Y.: Doubleday, 1975), 81.

8. Cordier and Harrelson, *Public Papers, Vol. VII,* 39.

9. Cordier and Harrelson, *Public Papers, Vol. VII,* 224.

10. Lyndon Baines Johnson, *The Vantage Point: Perspectives of the Presidency 1963–1969* (New York: Holt, Rinehart and Winston, 1971), 395.

11. Finger, *Your Man at the UN,* 136.

12. Finger, *Your Man at the UN,* 137.

13. *Facts on File Yearbook 1965* (New York: Facts on File, 1966), 155.

14. *Facts on File Yearbook 1965,* 155.

15. *Facts on File Yearbook 1965,* 178.

5

Final Disappointments: The 1967 Arab-Israeli War and the India-Pakistan War of 1971

Thant's December 1966 appointment to a second five-year term demonstrated his success in lifting the uncertainty surrounding the office of the secretary-general. In his first five years as secretary-general, Thant brought the UN's intervention in the Congo to a largely successful conclusion, involved the United Nations in innovative and cost-effective peacekeeping operations, and helped reshape the agenda of the world organization to take into account the concerns of third world countries.

But these successes were offset by disappointments and difficulties. During Thant's first years in office, the United Nations barely escaped financial and political ruin as the conflict over financing escalated into a major and near catastrophic East-West showdown on article 19. The peacekeeping activities of the UN were inevitably affected, as financial constraints limited the organization's ability to consider new peacekeeping operations. His struggle to rearrange the global agenda toward the solution of third world political and economic problems foundered as well, as colonialism persisted in Southern Africa and an intractable poverty continued to grind away at developing economies. And perhaps most troubling, the cold war continued to shadow the work of the United Nations and the secretary-general. The Soviets and later the Americans lost confidence in the organization's capacity to act neutrally when dealing with the respective interests of the great powers, and both acted toward the UN accordingly.

During the later years of Thant's tenure as secretary-general, two events occurred to change both his fortunes and those of the United

Nations. The first was the Arab-Israeli War of June 1967, an event that propelled Thant into a thicket of such emotionally charged controversy that it ultimately led to questions about his own competence and fair-mindedness. The second was the India-Pakistan conflict of December 1971, a war whose vast toll in human suffering ultimately led to the dismemberment of a sovereign state. Both events involved long-standing conflicts—reaching back almost to the creation of the United Nations—in which the organization had early on assumed some truce supervisory role, and in the case of the Arab-Israeli conflict, a peacekeeping function as well. Both events witnessed Thant exerting himself to prevent war, but ultimately failing in the face of a Security Council paralyzed by the East-West standoff. Neither produced a situation of anxiety and strife within the UN equivalent to the turmoil that had surrounded it during Hammarskjöld's last days, but both, taken together, symbolized the deep sense of futility that had come to characterize the organization's peacekeeping efforts.

THE 1967 ARAB-ISRAELI WAR

The Arab-Israeli conflict had commanded the attention of the United Nations since November 1947, when, on the basis of a recommendation from the United Nations Committee on Palestine, the General Assembly had voted to partition Palestine into a Jewish state and an Arab state, with Jerusalem internationalized under a UN trusteeship. The UN action did little to lessen tensions between Palestine's Arab and Jewish communities and instead provoked what amounted to a civil war. The withdrawal of the British mandatory authority from Palestine in May 1948 was followed by the immediate creation of the State of Israel by the Jewish community of Palestine. A subsequent invasion by neighboring Arab countries produced the first in the seemingly endless series of Arab-Israeli wars. In 1949, with both sides militarily exhausted, UN mediator Ralph Bunche managed to secure a lasting respite to the fighting, which was eventually monitored by the newly created United Nations Truce Supervisory Organization (UNTSO). Israel emerged from the war secure and with more territory than had originally been allotted under the UN partition plan. Jordan absorbed the territory designated for a Palestinian state, while Jerusalem was divided into Israeli and Jordanian sectors. Meanwhile, huge numbers of Palestinian refugees fled into neighboring Arab countries. The Arab states who fought Israel, unreconciled to the presence of a Jewish state in their midst, refused to make peace with the fledgling country, and Israel, concerned about the delicate demographic balance between Arabs and Jews within its borders, rebuffed UN demands that the refugees be repatriated into Israeli territory.

The next eighteen years witnessed a recurring pattern of violence between Israel and its Arab neighbors; guerilla raids led to Israeli reprisals followed in turn by Security Council condemnations. The only exception, in terms of the magnitude of the violence employed, was the Suez War of 1956, which led to the creation of the United Nations Emergency Force, a contingent first deployed in 1957 and still faithfully in place on the eve of the crisis that produced the Six Day War of 1967. It was in January 1967, that Secretary-General Thant, responding to Israeli-Syrian conflict over cultivation rights in the demilitarized zone separating the two countries, called upon Israel and Syria to reconvene the Israeli-Syrian Mixed Armistice Commission, which had not met since 1960. But when the commission met, the two sides were unable even to negotiate their differences. By early April, escalating tensions led to Israeli and Syrian aerial dogfights that resulted in the loss of six Syrian aircraft. The events along the Israeli-Syrian frontier placed particular pressure upon Egypt's President Gamal Abdel Nasser, a third world hero and the putative leader of the Arab world. Linked to Syria since November 1966 by a mutual defense treaty, Nasser had previously shown little inclination to join in a military adventure against the Jewish state. Nasser's caution, however, earned him the ridicule of other Arab states, and Jordan's prime minister accused him of hiding behind the shield of UNEF to avoid confrontation with Israel. Together with the prestige-damaging effect of his inconclusive intervention in Yemen and the declining fortunes of his pan-Arab appeal, the violent situation along the Israeli-Syrian border compelled Nasser to act in a more adventurous fashion.

In May 1967, belligerent statements by Israeli Prime Minister Levi Eshkol, coupled with Soviet-circulated rumors that Israeli troops were massing for an attack against Syria, produced a war fever throughout the Arab Middle East. In early May, a concerned Thant sent a letter to General Odd Bull, chief of staff of the UNTSO, encouraging him to pacify the border between Israel and Syria. Several days later, on May 11, the secretary-general specifically condemned Arab terrorist attacks into Israel and warned that the situation in the Middle East was assuming crisis proportions, but his alarm failed to rouse the concern of the Security Council. On May 14, Egyptian General Mahmoud Fawzi visited Damascus to assess the evolving military situation, and on May 15, Egyptian troops publicly moved through Cairo from their deployments in the south. On May 16, despite affirmations by officials of UNTSO that no evidence of an impending Israeli invasion could be found, the Egyptian government declared a state of military emergency. On the same day, Fawzi requested that the United Nations Emergency Force (UNEF) be removed from the Sinai, where it had kept the peace for close to eleven years.

Egypt's demand heightened the sense of crisis enveloping the Middle East. UNEF's commander, Indian General Indar Jit Rikhye, had no authority to evacuate the force on his own but quickly transmitted Cairo's ultimatum to Thant, who had been planning a July visit to the region. Thant, in New York, immediately met with Egypt's UN ambassador, Mohammed Awad El-Kony, whose aide-mémoire to the Egyptian government indicated that any request for the removal of UN forces should be made directly to the secretary-general rather than to Rikhye. Although Cairo was requesting only the transfer of UN soldiers from the border to less-sensitive positions, Thant informed El-Kony that he could not permit UN forces to "stand aside in order to become a silent and helpless witness to an armed confrontation between the parties."[1] If, on the other hand, Cairo desired a complete removal of UN forces, which the secretary-general viewed as consistent with Egypt's sovereign right, Thant indicated that he would reluctantly comply with the request.

UNEF's military position began to disintegrate shortly after Thant's meeting with El-Kony. On May 17–18, Egyptian forces replaced UNEF units in three frontier positions, and on-site efforts to convince the Israelis to accept UNEF forces on their territory then failed. By the time a formal Egyptian request for UNEF's total removal arrived at noon on May 18, the force, in Thant's estimation, had ceased to be functional. Warned by El-Kony not to request a reconsideration of the Egyptian decision, Thant convened UNEF's advisory committee (composed of nations that had supplied troops to the peacekeeping operation). The committee was sharply divided on the wisdom of Thant's decision to comply immediately with Cairo's request, with Western nations such as Canada urging that the matter be brought before the General Assembly. Yet third world nations friendly to Egypt, such as Yugoslavia and India, backed the secretary-general. With no vote taken in the Advisory Committee, Thant notified Egyptian Foreign Minister Mohammed Riad that UNEF would withdraw from the area. Only then, on the evening of May 19, were the General Assembly and Security Council formally apprised of Thant's decision.

Israeli and Egyptian forces now faced one another directly in the Sinai Peninsula, as the secretary-general initiated an intense diplomatic effort to avert war. On May 22, in Paris en route to Cairo, Thant was informed that Nasser had closed the Straits of Tiran to Israeli shipping, thus effectively blockading the Gulf of Aqaba and Israel's southern port of Eilat. The secretary-general was certain that Egypt's action would be viewed in Israel as an act of war and pressed Nasser to accept a three-week moratorium. During that period no Israeli ships or ships bound for Israel could enter the gulf, but the Egyptians would refrain from inspecting vessels navigating through the straits. The Egyptian president signaled his agreement, but the Israelis, convinced that Thant was only forestalling the inevitable, refused to either accept the terms of the moratorium or honor the secretary-general's request that a UN representative visit the region. On his return from Egypt Thant continued to promote his moratorium in the Security Council, where the United States worked behind the scenes to prevent the outbreak of war. The Soviet Union, however, adopted a hard-line position designed to win friends in the Arab world and refused to go along with the secretary-general's plan for a "breathing spell." Russia also spurned French President Charles de Gaulle's proposal for a "Big Four" conference to consider ways of averting war. On June 5, as the deadlocked Security Council was mulling over two different resolutions, the Israeli air force struck swiftly and effectively against Egyptian and Syrian air bases, to win Israel complete mastery of the air. Israeli ground forces then quickly penetrated Arab defenses, and within two days Egyptian forces were driven back across the Suez Canal; Jordanian forces were expelled from all territory west of the Jordan River, including East Jerusalem. The Israeli army then turned to its border with Syria and within days secured the strategic Golan Heights overlooking Israel's fertile agricultural valleys. Although the Security Council passed three resolutions calling for a cease-fire, the war continued until Sunday, June 11, when a fourth UN-sponsored cease-fire call finally went into effect. After only six days, Israel found itself in control of the entire Sinai Peninsula, the Gaza Strip, the West Bank of the Jordan River, and the Golan Heights. What the Arab side had envisioned as a war to eradicate Israel turned instead into a massive political and human catastrophe, with established governments discredited and even more civilians displaced.

Arab governments were not, however, the only casualties of the war. Israeli Foreign Minister Abba Eban, in an obvious allusion to the withdrawal of UNEF, rhetorically asked the General Assembly on June 19, "What is the use of a fire brigade which vanishes from the scene as soon as the first smoke and flames appear?"[2] Coinciding with the General Assembly debate, Ernest Gross, a former official in the United States Mission to the United Nations, publicized a ten-year-old aide-mémoire from Hammarskjöld in which the late secretary-general had indicated his understanding that the Egyptians could not unilaterally request the termination of the UNEF mission—a direct contradiction to Thant's argument that UNEF could remain on Egyptian territory only at the sufferance of the government in Cairo. Other Americans were equally critical. President Johnson noted years later in his autobiography that even the Egyptians were surprised at the alacrity with which the secretary-general responded to their request for UNEF's departure. The war and Thant's role in not preventing it left the secretariat demoralized. Brian Urquhart recalled "those days as one of the most wretched periods in all my time at the UN. We all labored under a crushing sense of failure."[3]

In retrospect, even those who accept the secretary-general's argument that Egypt had the sovereign right to request the removal of UNEF question Thant's hasty acceptance of Cairo's demand. Could he not have stalled by taking the matter before the General Assembly, as some on the Advisory Committee recommended? The secretary-general countered that delay would have jeopardized the lives of UN troops, whose camps were being overrun by Egyptian forces even as Cairo was awaiting Thant's reply to its formal request. Artillery attacks on UN camps before May 18 had led both the Yugoslavian and Indian governments to make clear that they would remove their contingents unilaterally. According to Thant, both the removal of the UN force and its timing were sensible responses to the legitimate demands of the Egyptian government and UNEF's deteriorating military situation.

If Thant hoped to bluff the Egyptians into withdrawing their demand for UNEF's redeployment by insisting that Egypt formally request the removal of the UN force, then he miscalculated badly. Raging war fever in Cairo gave Nasser no choice but to carry through with his May 16 ultimatum. But Thant's tactical misjudgment can hardly be blamed for precipitating a war that both sides had been sliding toward since 1964, when the Arab states threatened war in retaliation for Israel's decision to divert the waters of the Jordan. Superpower tensions only added fuel to the fire, since the Soviets cynically spread rumors of an Israeli invasion and then hindered the secretary-general's efforts to achieve a "cooling off" period. The United States failed to coordinate Western efforts to test Egypt's blockade of the Gulf of Aqaba and thus left Israel to its own devices during a vital time in the crisis. Finally, if history bitterly remembers Thant for his decision to remove UNEF, it ignores the efforts he made to move the Security Council toward some concerted action. Thant's failure only documents the inability of the Security Council to operate effectively when the big powers are divided or when faced with animosities such as those that perennially divide and roil the Middle East.

After Israel's complete victory, the secretary-general argued that the United Nations would have to redirect its energies to deal with the Arab-Israeli conflict. Convinced that the world organization had a role to play in a dispute where the principal antagonists could not deal directly with one another, Thant urged that the United Nations move from its traditional role of arranging and supervising "cease-fire[s], truce[s], and armistice agreement[s]" and begin making "progress . . . towards removing the root causes of the conflict."[4] In June and July 1967, an emergency session of the General Assembly debated the war and its consequences but managed only to pass a resolution condemning Israel's "annexation" of East Jerusalem and its largely Arab population. Artfully bypassed were most of the critical issues dividing Arabs and Israelis. Serious skirmishes between Egypt and Israel soon broke out across the cease-fire line, and in October an Israeli naval vessel was sunk by Egyptian forces. Thant convinced both sides to allow UN observers to monitor the cease-fire, and in December, despite by then standard Soviet objections to his acting without Security Council authorization, he increased the size of the truce supervisory force from forty-three to ninety men. By that time, the Security Council, convened after a complaint against Israel lodged by Egypt, had passed resolution 242 on November 22, regarded by virtually all parties to the conflict, then and since, as a basis for a final peace settlement. Addressing in somewhat ambiguous terms all aspects of the Arab-Israeli conflict and calling for the relinquishment by Israel of territories captured in 1967 in return for peace, the resolution also requested the secretary-general to "designate a special representative . . . to establish and maintain contacts with the states concerned in order to promote agreement."[5] Thant always considered the appointment of a special representative as essential to the expanded role he envisioned for the United Nations, and he quickly named Sweden's ambassador to the Soviet Union, Gunnar Jarring, to act as his agent in the region.

The secretary-general, rather than travel to the Middle East himself, entrusted diplomatic affairs to Jarring, who devoted the better part of the next three years to the Arab-Israeli conflict. But Jarring's efforts were undermined by conflicting perceptions of his role. Israel predicated substantive negotiations on the Arabs' willingness to engage in face-to-face discussions and so attempted to limit Jarring's diplomacy to procedural matters. Jordan and Egypt, while hinting they might someday recognize Israel's right to exist, refused to accept direct contacts, instead attempting to use Jarring as a go-between for substantive negotiations. All Arab states were reluctant to enter into a permanent peace with Israel, yet remained insistent on Israel's withdrawal from all territories captured in 1967; Israel, almost completely distrustful of Arab intentions, was equally determined to hold on to some strategic portions of the territory conquered in the war.

Jarring's endless difficulties finally persuaded Thant to endorse French President Charles de Gaulle's 1969 call for a Big Four conference on the Middle East. But Israel adamantly opposed an "imposed solution," and despite several meetings, the Big Four were unable to create a constructive negotiating formula. Meanwhile, tensions between Israel and Egypt intensified, and by mid-1969 a devastating artillery war across the cease-fire line heralded the "War of Attrition." The fighting added new urgency to diplomatic efforts, and in December, the Big Four endorsed a peace plan arranged by Washington and Moscow. But Jerusalem, stung by Secretary of State William Rogers's December 1969 suggestion that Israel fully relinquish the territories in return for peace, refused even to meet Jarring, who had been deputized by the Big Four to communicate the plan to the warring parties.

The first months of 1970 witnessed greater escalation of the Egyptian-Israeli war, as Israeli jets carried out deep penetration bombings against Egyptian targets. It was at the initiative of the United States that, in July, Egypt, Israel, and Jordan agreed to a ninety-day cease-fire and the beginning of indirect negotiations under the auspices of Ambassador Jarring. Thant was ecstatic at the news of Israel's decision to engage in indirect talks that were based on the principle of territorial withdrawal. His enthusiasm turned to disappointment, however, when Jerusalem, citing the alleged emplacement of Russian strategic ground-to-air missiles on Egyptian territory as a violation of the cease-fire agreement, decided in September 1970 not to participate.

After several months' hiatus, highlighted by the Jordanian Civil War, in which King Hussein expelled the Palestinian fighters living under his rule, and Nasser's death, Jarring resumed his frustrating mission. In February 1971, he asked Israel, Jordan, and the United Arab Republic to respond to a comprehensive peace proposal under which Israel would withdraw to the pre-1967 Israeli-Egyptian boundary in return for a formal peace. Cairo's new leader, Anwar Sadat, agreed to the Jarring initiative, but the Israeli government of Prime Minister Golda Meir rejected it because of Jarring's apparent departure from the role of a strict mediator. The United States staunchly supported Jarring's effort, but the Swedish diplomat, convinced that he had accomplished as much as he could, returned to Moscow as Swedish ambassador on March 25, 1971. The last real opportunity for peace had been lost, and in October 1973, two years after Thant left the United Nations, the fourth major war between Israel and its Arab neighbors broke out.

Since 1967, resolution 242 has remained fundamental to all Middle East peace proposals. Yet the UN role in brokering an Arab-Israeli peace agreement came to an end with the failure of the Jarring mission. Future diplomatic breakthroughs—such as the Sinai and Syrian disengagement agreements and Camp David accords—were instead achieved through the good offices of the United States. The decline in the UN's role can be attributed to two factors. First the Jarring mission depended on the support of the great powers, but the United States and the Soviet Union had very different ideas about what constituted a just peace settlement. The Soviets, in particular, appeared more interested in employing the peace process to score debating points against Israel and winning friends in the third world. Second, while resolutions condemning Israeli policy did not originate with the war, the intensity and frequency of Security Council and General Assembly pronouncements against Israel increased after 1967. As a consequence, Israel came to see the United Nations, dominated by a third world and Soviet bloc majority hostile to its interests, as an advocate rather than an impartial broker. As for the secretary-general, his actions during the prelude to war convinced Israel that he favored the Arabs. In reality, Thant's views were substantially more complex, for he had for a long time admired the Jewish state and found ideological kinship in Israel's socialism and development struggle. But the secretary-general also reflected—as he did in so many other instances—the evolving third world consensus on the inadmissibility of Israeli territorial aggrandizement and sympathy for the condition of Palestinian refugees. As the gap between Israeli policy and UN opinion grew, so too did the distance between Thant and Israel. In his last year as secretary-general, Thant did little to hide his frustration with the refusal of the Israeli government to negotiate under UN auspices.

THE CREATION OF BANGLADESH

The Six Day War of June 1967 clouded Thant's last years as secretary-general. It was, however, the perennial conflict between India and Pakistan that provided Thant with his last major crisis and demonstrated once again the weakness of the United Nations as an agent of world peace. The conflict that erupted in December 1971 had its roots not only in the long-standing enmity between the two nations but also in the developing turmoil in East Pakistan. In that section of the nation, Bengali separatists, encouraged by their stunning triumph in nationwide parliamentary elections, were agitating for greater autonomy from West Pakistan, more than one thousand miles away. The refusal of leading West Pakistani politicians to participate in an assembly dominated by Bengalis and the decision of Pakistani President Mohammed Yahya Khan to defer opening of the newly elected assembly inflamed passion in the eastern part of the country, where a general strike was declared. On March 25, 1971, in response to growing civil insurrection, Yahya Khan banned the separatist Awami League, ordered the arrest of its leader, Sheik Mujibur Rahman, and instructed his army to suppress what had become a full-fledged secessionist movement. The result was a brutal massacre of Bengalis by their own army and the flight of hundreds of thousands of refugees into nearby India.

Thant was sickened by the carnage in Pakistan and cognizant of growing demographic pressure on an India ill-equipped to absorb so large and desperate a population. On April 22, Samar Sen, New Delhi's ambassador to the UN, urged Thant to provide humanitarian aid to the East Pakistani refugees. The secretary-general immediately wrote Yahya Khan with an offer of UN assistance, but on May 3, a reluctant Pakistani president told Thant that his government was capable of carrying out relief efforts by itself. If UN assistance became necessary, Yahya Khan continued, "it will be administered by Pakistan's own relief agencies."[6] On May 22, however, Pakistan's UN mission notified Thant that the government would permit the world organization to provide relief assistance. The secretary-general then dispatched his assistant secretary-general for interagency affairs to Islamabad and Dacca, and placed the UN's high commissioner for refugees in charge of relief efforts in India. By then, the toll in human suffering had grown enormously and the number of refugees had multiplied to approximately ten million.

As the crisis escalated, Thant was ever mindful that the refugee issue might fuel another war between the traditional Asian antagonists. Under article 99 of the UN Charter, the secretary-general enjoyed the right to bring potential breaches of the peace to the attention of the Security Council, but Thant was concerned that without the prearranged compliance of India and Pakistan the matter would die in the council and the secretary-general would suffer irreparable damage to his prestige. In July Thant dispatched an aide-mémoire to both governments and to the president of the Security Council, requesting that the council meet to consider the crisis, but with little enthusiasm apparent among the council's members, no meeting was held. Thant also consulted behind the scenes with former Malaysian Prime Minister Tunku Abdul Rahman, a leading Muslim dignitary, in an effort to employ Tunku as a go-between for India and Pakistan. That effort, much like his July aide-mémoire, proved unproductive.

As Thant waited for an opportunity to bring about a political settlement, the UN's relief efforts intensified. On July 31, the United Nations and Pakistan agreed to an American plan creating a 103-man UN relief team for East Pakistan. Seventy-three monitors were to be deployed in Dacca, Chittagong, Rajshahi, and Khulna to report on conditions in the east, while the remaining UN personnel (recruited from UNICEF, the FAO, WFP, and WHO) would conduct relief efforts. On August 6, Thant announced that relief would be coordinated out of UN offices in Geneva, and on August 9, Secretary of State William Rogers handed Thant a check for $1 million toward the cost of relief efforts.

The political impasse remained, however, intractable. On August 2, New Delhi had rejected a Thant proposal calling on the two governments to allow the high commissioner for refugees to operate on both sides of their common border. Over the next several months, in messages to President Khan and Indian Prime Minister Indira Gandhi, Thant continued to warn both governments about the dangers of imminent war as tensions between the two countries escalated. Then, in late November, Pakistan declared a national emergency. On November 29, Yayha Khan sent Thant a letter asking the secretary-general to dispatch observers to Pakistan's side of the border with India. Declaring himself powerless to decide unilaterally on Islamabad's request, Thant referred the letter to the Security Council. On December 3, full-scale war erupted, and on December 6, with Indian forces advancing on Dacca, the Bengali capital, New Delhi formally recognized the existence of an independent state of Bangladesh.

In response to the fact of war, the Security Council finally met to discuss issues Thant had wished it to consider several months earlier. But the council was hopelessly deadlocked because the Soviet Union, which had aggressively courted New Delhi for years, refused to permit any condemnation of Indian policy. For its part, the United States suspended $87.6 million in development aid to India and openly labeled New Delhi the "main aggressor." The People's Republic of China, newly admitted to the United Nations, used the occasion to denounce Soviet foreign policy and to threaten India, against whom it had fought a major war fewer than ten years earlier. On December 6, a resolution calling for a cease-fire and Indian withdrawal from East Pakistan was defeated in the Security Council by a vote of 11–2–2, with the Soviet Union and Poland voting against and Great Britain and France abstaining. The Chinese delegate, Chiao Huan-hua, scornfully referred to the Soviet government as "the boss behind the Indian aggression" since "The Indian expansionists usually do not have much guts!"[7]

Since the council was unable to act, Thant had the issue referred to the General Assembly. Despite India's traditional role as leader of the nonaligned world, the assembly surprisingly voted, by a margin of 104–11–0, for an immediate cease-fire and troop withdrawal. Yet New Delhi, determined to establish Bengali independence once and for all, ignored the cease-fire call and proceeded to complete its military victory in Dacca. On December 12, when the Security Council reconvened, a representative of the new government of Bangladesh attempted to appear before the panel. But the council president, A. J. Pratt of Sierra Leone, declared that he was not yet satisfied that "a new state called Bangla Desh [*sic*] existed."[8] When another resolution calling for a cease-fire and Indian withdrawal was vetoed by the Kremlin, on December 15, Pakistani Foreign Minister Ali Buttho accused the UN of legalizing Indian aggression and dramatically walked out of the council. Only after the surrender of Pakistani forces on December 16 did India announce its acceptance of the cease-fire. On December 21, one day after Yahya Khan was replaced as president of Pakistan by Ali Buttho, the Security Council successfully voted in favor of a cease-fire and troop withdrawal. Both countries now accepted the UN resolution. Three years later, on September 17, 1974, Bangladesh was admitted into the United Nations.

Thant was immensely troubled by the UN's impotence in the face of so large-scale a human tragedy as the Bengali secession. He was revolted by the brutality of Pakistan's effort to suppress the insurrection and pleaded with President Khan on a number of occasions to exercise restraint in asserting his government's authority over the rebels. But Thant was intensely critical of India's role as well. While he sympathized with New Delhi's unhappiness over the influx of refugees into Indian territory, he objected to India's violation of Pakistan's sovereignty and its use of armed force to truncate Pakistan into two weaker states. As for the United Nations, Thant's memoirs were brutally frank. "Throughout the struggle, the United Nations had made no move to act; my pleas and warnings to the Security Council, both privately and publicly, fell on deaf ears."[9]

CONCLUSION

The conflicts in the Middle East and the Indian subcontinent demonstrated the UN's incapacity to deal with wars between third world states in an organization dominated by the Soviet-American conflict. Their intense jockeying for influence in the third world had made it impossible for the superpowers in either case to find common ground and avert war. The Soviet Union seemed more intent on showing its support for two leading members of the nonaligned bloc,

Egypt and India, than in forcing moderation on rivals. In the case of the Six Day War, the Security Council met numerous times between May 24 and June 14. In the period leading up to the war, the Kremlin refused to support U Thant's call for a moratorium, despite Nasser's acquiescence in the secretary-general's proposal, and no council resolution emerged. During the war itself, Moscow, alarmed at its clients' huge military losses, joined the other members of the council in voting for a succession of cease-fires. In the period immediately following the war, the Soviet Union put forward a resolution specifically condemning Israel for its conduct and calling on that country to relinquish territories taken during the war. This decidedly one-sided resolution failed to garner the necessary majority for passage. The Security Council, stymied by the dynamics of Soviet-American rivalry, could neither avert war nor take steps to prevent a future conflagration.

The Security Council's fecklessness in the case of the India-Pakistan War was even more pronounced, first, because the crisis that produced the war unfolded over a longer period of time, thus giving the council ample time to respond, and second, because Thant had appealed to the council, through his July 20 aide-mémoire, to convene—with no success. The council, reflecting its members' wishes not to offend either India or Pakistan, did not meet until December 4, after the war had begun, and was then paralyzed by a Soviet veto designed to protect the Kremlin's clients in New Delhi.

The Security Council's inability to act led in both cases to referral of the problem to the General Assembly. In the case of the Arab-Israeli conflict, the nonaligned nations voted as a bloc to support the Arab position, while the Soviet Union, continuing its single-minded pursuit of third world influence, actively opposed Israel. Their respective resolutions placed a heavy emphasis on condemnation of Israel and Israel's unconditional withdrawal from the conquered territories. Although the remainder of the UN's membership was more disposed to an evenhanded approach, linking withdrawal to a comprehensive treatment of the entire Arab-Israeli conflict, the emergency General Assembly session ended in deadlock. Similarly, the Security Council referred the India-Pakistan War to the General Assembly under terms of the Uniting for Peace Resolution. Confronted by a war between two of its members, as distinguished from the Arab-Israeli conflict, which pitted its members against an outsider, the nonaligned nations overwhelmingly condemned India and called on its forces to withdraw to their prewar borders. But India was too close to victory to be constrained by the UN, and the cease-fire call went unheeded. In neither case could the General Assembly, with limited authority under the charter, act effectively in place of the Security Council.

The two war crises left Thant totally dispirited. In the Six Day War he believed himself unfairly criticized because of his decision to remove UNEF. Then the India-Pakistan War occurred, despite all his warnings, and seemed to underline the futility of the United Nations. Over the last four years of his tenure in office, Thant involved himself in many ongoing problems and some new ones as well, but neither the organization nor his reputation ever recovered completely from the events surrounding the Six Day War. The tragedy accompanying the creation of Bangladesh served as a sad valedictory to the undoubted low point of Thant's secretary-generalship.

Appendix 5A

The China Question, 1961–1971

The issue of Chinese representation in the United Nations recurred annually during Thant's tenure as secretary-general. Each autumn, from 1961 to 1971 (with the exception of 1964 during the fiscal crisis), the General Assembly discussed and then voted on resolutions favoring some form of Communist Chinese representation in the world body. The issue was not finally resolved until two months before Thant left office.

The question of which China belonged in the United Nations had its genesis in 1949 when Chiang Kai-shek's Koumintang was exiled to Taiwan, where it established a nationalist government. Both Taiwan and the victorious Marxist revolutionary government of Mao Tse-tung in Peking now claimed sovereignty over the Chinese mainland. In January 1950, by a margin of three to six with two abstentions, the Security Council voted down a Soviet resolution calling for the ouster of Chiang's delegation in favor of representatives of the Peking regime. At that time, Washington had not yet decided on a firm policy toward the China question, although its closest ally, Great Britain, had already recognized the Communist regime. Reflecting its indecision, the Truman Administration treated the Russian resolution of 1950 as a procedural question—thus forgoing the use of a veto—and refrained from attacking the Peking government in the debate that preceded the vote. The political context was altered in June 1950, however, when North Korea invaded South Korea and precipitated a war that would eventually involve the United States and Communist China as combatants. The Korean "police action" and subsequent Communist threats against Taiwan solidified Washington's opposition to the admission of Peking to the United Nations. For the next decade the United States used its dominant position in the UN to prevent the issue of Chinese representation from reaching the agenda of the General Assembly.

Only in the late 1961 did Washington permit a discussion and vote in the General Assembly on the representation question. The Kennedy Administration recognized that the Chinese issue could not be kept off the General Assembly's agenda indefinitely. The Non-Aligned Nations, convened at Belgrade in September 1961, had passed a resolution urging the General Assembly to recognize the Peking regime as the only legitimate UN representative, and third world states demanded open discussion of the China question. Sensing that it no longer controlled the votes to prevent discussion of the issue, Washington agreed to a debate in December 1961.

But permitting debate did not mean that the United States was willing to admit a regime it opposed. On December 15, 1961, the Soviets introduced a resolution calling for the expulsion of the nationalists and their replacement by the Communists. The United States contended that Chinese representation was an important question, necessitating a two-thirds vote, and its position carried by a tally of 61–34–7. The Soviet resolution was then defeated by a vote of 48–37–19. A third motion to admit the People's Republic of China without expelling the nationalists was defeated by margin of 45–30–29. Supporting the United States against the Soviet resolution were most of its European allies, except for Great Britain, Denmark, and Norway; all Latin American states other than Cuba; France and several of its former colonies; all members of the Southeast Asia Treaty Organization (SEATO); and Canada. Thus a pattern of delay based on procedural power was established—it would endure for a decade.

Over the next two years, the American position on the China question strengthened, as votes calling for the expulsion of the nationalists were defeated in the General Assembly. Erosion of support for Communist China was largely the result of China's October 1962 invasion of India, even though New Delhi did vote to seat Peking. After the 1963 vote, Chinese Foreign Minister Chen Yi referred to the UN as a "monkey show" manipulated by the United States. In 1964, in deference to the no-vote procedure occasioned by the fiscal crisis, no vote was taken.

When the General Assembly next considered the Chinese representation issue in November 1965, the United States succeeded in securing "important question" status for the substantive vote only by a margin of 56–47–11. The closeness of the procedural vote demonstrated a substantial decline in General Assembly support for America's position on Chinese membership, and the assembly then deadlocked at 47–47–20 on an Albanian resolution to oust the nationalists in favor of the Communists.

Peking had made substantial gains, in part, because its October 1964 detonation of an atomic bomb had underlined the importance of China's membership in an organization whose agenda included the search for a workable disarmament formula. But the turmoil that the mainland experienced during the Cultural Revolution that began in 1966 led to a reversal in China's fortunes in General Assembly voting. As the mainland slipped into chaos, China itself stated it was not interested in joining the UN, and from 1966 to 1968 the United States easily won a series of "important question" votes and managed to keep Peking out of the UN.

During this period, the most consistent advocate of Peking's membership in the United Nations was U Thant, who argued in September 1966 that, "In the long run, the organization cannot be expected to function if one-quarter of the human race is not allowed to participate in its deliberations."[10] Thant viewed Chinese Communist membership as essential to resolving critical issues, such as the war in Vietnam and the arms race. He tended to minimize the harshness of Peking's rhetoric and suggested the idiosyncrasies of Chinese Communist behavior might be because of Peking's exclusion from the world community. As he said, "When a country is regarded as an outcast, as an outlaw, as the villain of the peace, if I may say so, I think that particular country is apt to act in a rather strange way."[11] Nonetheless, in public Thant carefully distinguished between "two U Thants," one a "private individual," the other a UN public servant who "cannot say things which [he wants] to say because of [his] position."[12] The private Thant clearly favored membership for Communist China; the public Thant has "no views of [his] own, except in the context of General Assembly resolutions."[13]

Despite confusing signals from Peking and the continued failure of its supporters to gain the Communist government's entry into the United Nations, the late 1960s witnessed a change in the General Assembly's approach to the admission issue. In 1967, France backed Peking's entry into the United Nations, and in 1969, Belgium, Chile, and Italy switched their votes from "no" to "yes." In that same year, several African countries, including Ghana, Libya, Mauritius, and Niger, which had previously abstained on the question, voted in favor of Peking's entry. There was apparent change in American policy as well, with the advent of the Nixon Administration. The 1969 annual resolution in favor of the expulsion of the nationalists was defeated by a vote of 48–56–21, but the United States did considerably less canvassing in favor of its position. Significantly, in June 1970, a ritual U.S. House of Representatives rider opposed to a UN seat for Peking was removed from a foreign aid bill. Then on October 25, 1970, White House Press Secretary Ronald L. Ziegler announced that the "United States opposes the admission of the Peking regime into the UN at the expense of the expulsion of the Republic of China,"[14] thus hinting at United States acceptance of a "two China" stance. On November 20, when the annual resolution favoring the seating of Peking over Taipei actually gained fifty-one votes against, forty-nine opposed, and twenty-five abstaining, the State Department announced that it favored "universality" of UN membership, including Taiwan.

By 1971, American opposition to Chinese Communist membership in the United Nations had become untenable. So many states were now on record as favoring Peking's entry that Secretary-General Thant predicted the Communists would gain UN admission in 1972. Changes in American foreign policy toward China, occasioned by the increasingly bitter Sino-Soviet split, climaxed in July 1971 with President Richard Nixon's announcement that he would visit Peking in 1972. American policy could no longer logically be based on excluding China from the UN. Nonetheless, the United States persisted in its efforts to retain a seat for Taiwan. On September 16, 1971, President Nixon announced that the United States would support Taipei's replacement by Peking in the Security Council but oppose any effort to expel Taiwan from the General Assembly. The mainland Communists insisted that they would not enter the United Nations so long as Taiwan was still represented.

The final debate opened on October 19, 1971. On October 25, the General Assembly defeated by a vote of 59–55–15 the usual motion, this time introduced by United States Ambassador George Bush, that China's admission be treated as an "important question." After the United States was defeated on the procedural question, the nationalist delegates led by Ambassador Liu Chieh, walked out of the assembly hall, with despair and defiance etched on their faces. The Albanian-sponsored resolution to expel the nationalists and admit the

Communists, its outcome by now a foregone conclusion of the vote, the assembly floor, in a display deeply offensive to President Nixon, erupted into cheers and applause.

While Thant "felt sad at the departure of the Republic of China from the halls of the UN,"[15] he nonetheless valued the inclusion of a government, which at the time he had predicted would be among the world's four big powers, along with the United States, the Soviet Union, and Europe. On October 27, 1971, the secretary-general sent a telegram to Peking urging the Communist government to select a Security Council delegation as soon as possible. On October 31, Thant was informed that the Communist government would be known as "China, People's Republic of" and on November 15, 1971, Chinese Ambassador Chiao Huan-hua, chairman of the Chinese delegation to the United Nations, made his government's first speech in the world organization.

NOTES

1. U Thant, *View from the UN* (Garden City, N.Y.: Doubleday, 1978), 222.

2. Andrew W. Cordier and Max Harrelson, eds., *Public Papers of the Secretaries-General of the United Nations, Vol. VII, U Thant 1965–1967* (New York: Columbia University Press, 1976), 420.

3. Brian Urquhart, *A Life in Peace and War* (New York: Harper and Row, 1987), 215.

4. Cordier and Harrelson, *Public Papers, Vol. VII*, 535.

5. Cordier and Harrelson, *Public Papers, Vol. VII*, 604.

6. *Facts on File Yearbook 1971* (New York: Facts on File, 1972), 343.

7. *Facts on File Yearbook 1971*, 942.

8. *Facts on File Yearbook 1971*, 962.

9. Thant, *View from the UN*, 436.

10. *Facts on File Yearbook 1966* (New York: Facts on File, 1967), 373.

11. Cordier and Harrelson, *Public Papers, Vol. VII*, 231.

12. Cordier and Harrelson, *Public Papers, Vol. VII*, 230.

13. Cordier and Harrelson, *Public Papers, Vol. VII*, 230.

14. *Facts on File Yearbook 1970* (New York: Facts on File, 1971), 818.

15. Andrew W. Cordier and Max Harrelson, eds., *Public Papers of the Secretaries-General of the United Nations, Vol. VIII, U Thant* (New York: Columbia University Press, 1977), 681.

6

Assessment

Thant's frustrations over the latest and most brutal Indo-Pakistani war were matched by disappointments in other areas, as protracted problems remained unsettled. The sectarian strife on Cyprus continued to simmer, the Vietnam War, despite the advent of negotiations, widened, the financial miseries of the organization deepened, and the Arab-Israeli conflict showed few signs of progressing toward a peaceful resolution. Personal problems also mounted. In December 1971, the secretary-general's trusted aide, Ralph Bunche, died after a long and debilitating illness, and Thant, plagued throughout his UN tenure with stomach ulcers, experienced a deterioration in his own physical condition. The secretary-general was nonetheless pressed by member governments of the United Nations to assume a third term as leader of the organization. But Thant, beset by personal problems and exhausted after ten years at a job he considered the world's most difficult, could not be moved. Expressing before the General Assembly his "great relief bordering on liberation, upon [his] impending retirement,"[1] Thant relinquished the post to Kurt Waldheim in late December 1971. He died in 1974.

As secretary-general, Thant projected the image of an honest but unimaginative civil servant, reluctant to test the limits of his office and its prerogatives. In contrast to the UN's first secretary-general, Trygve Lie, who spoke openly and sometimes intemperately on controversial issues, and unlike his immediate predecessor, Dag Hammarskjöld, who projected an almost ethereal presence, Thant appeared considerably more restrained, down to earth, and colorless. This contrast was particularly striking in juxtaposition to Hammarskjöld, who, with his penchant for international globe-trotting, dramatic and personal diplomatic initiatives, and intellectually rich descriptions of his office, had cut a wide swath in the field of international diplomacy. Thant, by comparison, relied more heavily on subordinates to engage in sensitive negotiations and showed himself to be less intellectually reflective on his position. Thant was primarily a practitioner, not a conceptualizer, and to his detractors this was a major failing.

Apart from contrasts in demeanor and style, Thant suffered in comparison to his predecessor because, unlike Hammarskjöld, Thant was compelled to operate under the handicap of Hammarskjöld's political legacy, a legacy defined by Hammarskjöld's last, very turbulent year in office. At the time of Hammarskjöld's death, the broad powers the secretary-general had assumed were coming under serious review by the great powers and the position of secretary-general was itself being threatened. Thant helped to restore the credibility of his office, but he could not arrest the erosion in its powers. Upon his acceptance of a second term, the secretary-general expressed frustration with the Security Council's tendency to treat him like a "glorified clerk," but in practice, Thant appeared to understand the limits on his role in the post-Hammarskjöld era. To his critics, Thant's appreciation of the limits on his power was taken for undue reticence in the discharge of his office.

Another factor in the decline in Thant's reputation was the Arab-Israeli War of 1967. The secretary-general's image never recovered, particularly in the United States, from the beating it took over his decision to remove UNEF. To his detractors, Thant displayed an incredible lack of courage and wisdom in complying so quickly with Cairo's request that UNEF be redeployed. Even the Egyptians, looking for scapegoats in the wake of their disastrous military defeat, later claimed that Thant's decision to remove rather than just redeploy the peacekeeping force, as they had requested, was an important factor in allowing Israel to strike first. To many critics, the UNEF decision, with all it suggested about the secretary-general's timorousness, defined Thant's tenure as secretary-general.

Perhaps most important in explaining his relatively pallid historical reputation, Thant's tenure as secretary-general coincided with the end to that time of the American era in the UN's history. Much of the organization's great success in its first fifteen years, from Korea to Suez to the Congo, resulted, in large part, from Washington's desire to use the United Nations to further its own foreign policy objectives. This conjunction of interests between the United States and the

United Nations continued for several years into Thant's tenure as secretary-general and allowed Thant to organize peacekeeping operations in West Irian, Yemen, and Cyprus. The fiscal crisis, however, persuaded Washington that it could no longer exercise control over an organization dominated by a third world majority. That, along with Thant's public criticism of American policy in Vietnam, turned the United States increasingly away from the world organization. The change in American attitudes toward the United Nations could best be demonstrated by the American public's response to a Louis Harris Poll question about the UN's effectiveness. In July 1964, before the escalation of America's role in the Vietnam War and the gravest period in the political crisis over article 19, 81 percent of the American public registered their opinion that the UN was doing a good or fair job. In August 1967, two months after the Six Day War, only 44 percent answered that the world organization was performing effectively, and in October 1971, the month that Communist China was admitted into the United Nations, that number fell to 35 percent. With neither superpower particularly interested in employing the United Nations as a foreign policy instrument, the organization and its secretary-general could hardly engage in the kind of activism that characterized most of Hammarskjöld's tenure.

There is no question that Hammarskjöld was a more activist secretary-general than was Thant or that Hammarskjöld did more to develop the office of secretary-general than did his successor, but the image of passivity that has become associated with Thant's tenure at the United Nations is not supported by the facts. It neglects Thant's critical role in the Cuban missile crisis and his impassioned effort to broker an agreement to end the Vietnam War. It ignores also the energy and imagination he displayed in activating UN peacekeeping forces and observation teams in West Irian, Cyprus, Yemen, and Pakistan and in arranging a diplomatic solution to the Malaysian-Indonesian dispute over Sarawak and Borneo. The image of passivity does not correspond either to the strong statements made by the secretary-general against colonialism, the arms race, apartheid, and the unequal distribution of world resources. If Thant did not add to Hammarskjöld's expansive vision of the office they both held, he did not detract from it either. In fact, it appears that the Hammarskjöld conception of the secretary-generalship guided, with allowance for changing political circumstances, Thant's approach throughout his two terms at the United Nations.

On several occasions, for example, Thant, like Hammarskjöld, acted without consulting either the Security Council or General Assembly. The negotiations leading to the formation of UNYOM took place without specific UN authorization, and the diplomatic intercessions into the Indonesian-Malaysian and West Irian disputes occurred without Security Council guidance. In these and other instances Thant followed Hammarskjöld's interpretation of article 99 of the UN Charter, which permits the secretary-general to "bring to the attention of the Security Council any matter which in his opinion may threaten the maintenance of international peace and security."[2] In Hammarskjöld's view, article 99 extended beyond the formal submission of information to the Security Council. Instead, it permitted the secretary-general to engage in what Hammarskjöld and also Thant referred to as "preventive diplomacy." In the words of UN scholar Leon Gordenker, the task of the secretary-general became that of preventing "the worsening of international friction and to keep [controversies] off the agendas of other United Nations organs where it might become a Cold War issue."[3] Thant elaborated on this theme in September 1971, when he addressed a luncheon meeting of the Dag Hammarskjöld Memorial Scholarship Fund. "The right to bring matters to the Security Council implies a watching brief and a broad discretion to conduct inquiries and to engage in informal diplomatic activity in regard to matters relating to the maintenance of international peace and security."[4]

But Thant's activism did not go unopposed, especially by the Russians. Consistent with the Kremlin's post-Hammarskjöld view that the proper domain for peacekeeping lay within the Security Council, an inevitable clash erupted between Thant's interpretation of article 99 and the Soviets' zealous safeguarding of the council's authority. Moscow, for example, forced the Security Council to convene over the UNYOM deployment, even though Thant had already set in motion the details of the UN operation, including its financing. The Soviets were clearly uncomfortable with Thant's unilateral assertion of authority and did not allow instances of such activism to pass without registering their disapproval.

Nor were the Soviets entirely sanguine about peacekeeping operations mandated by the Security Council and consistent with their national interest but, in their view, too open-ended in their grant of authority to the secretary-general. The Soviets, for example, concurred in the formation of UNFICYP but abstained on that portion of the resolution granting Thant the authority to decide on the size, composition, and command of the force. In 1965, Moscow, along with Paris, bitterly assailed Thant for expanding the size of UNIPOM, even though the Kremlin fully supported the dispatch of observers to the India-Pakistan cease-fire line. Once again, the Soviets were asserting a principle at variance with the Hammarskjöld-Thant view of the secretary-general's prerogatives.

Thant survived the Soviet assault on his office, first, because the general outlines of his policy were not inconsistent with the Soviet national interest and, second, because the United States and other nations offered a spirited defense of his charter authority. Nonetheless, frustrated by the restraints he was experiencing, Thant in 1966 threatened not to stand for a second term. Whatever the secretary-general's frustrations, however, he seemed to understand the narrow political environment in which he was compelled to operate. Despite his personal agony over Vietnam, for example, he did not bring the matter before the Security Council. In the case of the Dominican invasion, where it was clear that the United States opposed UN action, Thant behaved in a fairly reactive way, following Security Council instructions but steering clear of personal initiatives. In his frustration with a Security Council dominated by the threat of a great power veto, Thant often called for investing the General Assembly with greater power, and so won the admiration of the third world bloc. Yet, in retrospect, it is clear that Thant appreciated the restraints on his role and the limitations of the UN. As he said in 1971, "There are two poles of the Secretary-General's world—at one extreme the idealism and the global objectives of the Charter; at the other the pragmatic, and on occasion downright selfish, nature of national sovereignty."[5]

Within the boundaries established by the charter and international realities, as Thant averred to in his final annual report, the secretary-general employed a variety of techniques in the discharge of his office. Thant saw the powers of inquiry and good offices as flowing logically from a "common-sense interpretation" of article 99, and he made frequent use of personal representatives, whether mandated by the Security Council or not, to inform himself of situations that threatened the peace. The Security Council's decision in 1965, for example, to request that Thant visit India and Pakistan was a direct result of reporting by Thant's personal representative, General Robert H. Nimmo. In keeping with his view that article 99 invested the secretary-general with an independent political role, Thant placed great emphasis on the mediative function of his office. In rare cases, Thant himself participated in direct negotiations with the parties to a conflict, as he did in 1965 when he visited Rawalpindi and New Delhi and in 1967 when he met with North Vietnamese officials in Rangoon. But Thant was less disposed than his predecessor to engage in high-stakes, highly personal diplomacy. Nowhere during Thant's tenure is there any personal involvement as dramatic and risky as Hammarskjöld's visit to the People's Republic of China in 1955 or his Congo flights. Thant, instead, relied more heavily on subordinates, such as Ralph Bunche and José Rolz-Bennett, or special emissaries, such as American diplomat Ellsworth Bunker, drafted for a specific mission. In a somewhat defensive manner Thant explained his aversion to public diplomacy in his final annual report. "The general public expects the Secretary-General to act in crisis situations, and when he makes no pronouncements there is a consequent reaction of disappointment and an assumption that the Secretary-General is doing nothing. The requirements of discretion and the essential need for 'quiet diplomacy,' if useful results are to be achieved, are not always adequately recognized."[6]

Another, although less dramatic instrumentality of mediation was the personal appeal, employed frequently by Thant to warn governments in conflict of the concern of the international community. On many occasions, Thant sent appeals, in writing or otherwise, to warring governments, admonishing them to find a peaceful way out of their impasse. Normally, the appeal would be general in nature, but sometimes would contain specific proposals, as occurred in May 1967 when Thant appealed to the Israelis and Egyptians to seek a cooling-off period. The most celebrated case of Thant's intervention through personal appeals was the Cuban missile crisis, during which the secretary-general sent several written messages to Khrushchev, Kennedy, and Castro, offering specific proposals for easing, if not resolving, the crisis. He also offered in 1962 specific proposals for resolving the Congo crisis and in 1965 a Three Point Plan for ending the war in Vietnam.

Many of Thant's responsibilities derived from mandates voted by the Security Council or General Assembly. Thant's administration of West Irian in 1962–1963 followed the passage of a General Assembly resolution, which essentially ratified arrangements brokered by Thant's representative Ellsworth Bunker prior to General Assembly involvement. Peacekeeping missions in the Congo and Cyprus derived from authorizations by the Security Council. Once authorized, the details of each mission fell, for the most part, within the jurisdiction of the secretary-general and his mission commander. The Security Council's authorization of UNFICYP was sufficiently vague to permit Thant a huge hand in specifying its mission, which, in Thant's view, did not entail subduing the Turkish minority on the island. In the Congo, on the other hand, where Thant regarded the Katangese secessionists as both irresponsible and near maniacal, he used Security Council resolutions to justify ONUC's successful effort to crush the rebellion.

It is difficult to measure the secretary-general's exact contribution in those cases where a peaceful outcome was, in fact, achieved, for it is likely that recourse to the good offices of the secretary-general often indicated a prior willingness to resolve a conflict. In the case of West Irian, for example, the Netherlands was searching for a face-saving measure that would allow it to withdraw honorably from West New Guinea, and in the Cuban crisis both Khrushchev and Kennedy were desperate to find some means of turning away from the brink of nuclear war. In both cases Thant's intervention served as a convenient mechanism for defusing a crisis. In the case of the Malaysian-Indonesian dispute, however, despite the ambitious role afforded Thant, it is not clear how seriously the parties to the conflict really regarded the secretary-general's mediation. Malaysia announced its intention to form a federation before Thant had the opportunity to announce the results of the plebiscite, and Indonesia virtually ignored Thant's conclusions after they were promulgated.

In cases where peacekeeping forces or observation teams were dispatched, the secretary-general's report card was mixed. In the Congo, with the strong support of the United States and the acquiescence of Russia, Thant was able to end the Katangese secession and effectively terminate the UN role. But, in other cases, the UN presence proved less decisive. In the case of Yemen, the observation team ended its mission unsuccessfully because the parties to the conflict were unwilling to live by the terms of their disengagement agreement. Thant had neither the resources nor political backing to force Egypt and Saudi Arabia to abide by their commitments. In Cyprus, the warring parties were, for the most part, kept apart, but a political solution remained elusive for decades, and still does. In the case of the India-Pakistan War, cease-fire violations continued after the deployment of UNIPOM, and it was not until both countries became physically exhausted from the war that they turned to the Soviet Union for help in ending their conflict. Several years later, the two countries fought again, with disastrous consequences for Pakistan.

Thant's tenure proved that the secretary-general can be only as useful as the international community, and especially the great powers, want him to be. In cases where governments are determined to find a political solution to their differences and require the good offices of a respected third party, the secretary-general can be most helpful. In cases where governments are searching for a respite from war but are unprepared to resolve the fundamental differences that divide them, the secretary-general can offer limited assistance, as Thant did in Cyprus and the India-Pakistan War. In cases where governments are determined to press their interest through the employment of superior force, there is little that the secretary-general can do, as Thant discovered in the case of the American war effort in Vietnam and when Nasser ordered UNEF removed. As UN scholar Leon Gordenker described the secretary-general's role in peacekeeping, "[t]he secretary-general is still at the mercy of governments which contribute troops and supplies. Cooperation by governments can turn into recalcitrance or sabotage in such matters as the refusal to withdraw invading forces or objectionable persons from the affected area."[7]

Throughout his ten years in office, Thant acted with a mixture of audacity and circumspection. He did not shrink from using the bully pulpit of the UN to promote his personal crusade against colonialism, war, the arms race, and the unequal distribution of world resources. Nor did he hesitate to criticize the great powers when he thought they were wrong. But he wisely recognized the limits of his office and engaged in substantive negotiations or mobilized UN peacekeeping organs only after having first secured through quiet diplomacy the support of the affected states. Thant, for example, orchestrated his military and diplomatic moves in the Congo and Yemen in tandem with the United States. He refused to conduct a plebiscite in Borneo without the formal assent of Great Britain. He chose not to send Ralph Bunche to mediate between India and Pakistan in 1965, because he saw little hope that the mission would succeed. He hesitated to bring the war in East Pakistan before the Security Council, because he feared that the council would deadlock and hence damage his ability to mediate the dispute.

It was this astute appreciation of political reality that permitted Thant to survive politically where his predecessors did not. In contrast to Lie and Hammarskjöld, whose last years in office were clouded by constitutional challenges to their authority and boycotts, Thant was accorded in his last years at the UN enormous respect by the member states and was even implored to serve a third term as secretary-general. True to the distinction he had once made between "impartiality" and "neutrality," Thant, for the most part, acted in a fair and open-minded manner without sacrificing his inclination to take sides on the moral questions of the day. He was critical of American policy in Vietnam and the Dominican Republic, but equally harsh in his treatment of the Soviet invasion of Czechoslovakia, which he likened to the American intervention in the Dominican Republic. Thant took sides on specific East-West issues but did not become identified with either superpower, as had been the case with both Lie and Hammarskjöld.

If there were biases in Thant's makeup, they were the products of his third world upbringing and worldview. On third world issues such as apartheid, income redistribution, and Vietnam, he was a tireless and relentless advocate, as evidenced by his promotion of the UN Development Decade, frequent statements condemning racism and colonialism, and relentless criticism of American war policy. But when Nigeria brutally prosecuted its war against rebellious Ibo tribesmen, Thant, unwilling or unable to offend the African states that supported the central government, refrained from public criticism of the Lagos regime. For Thant, the support of the third world was an important source of strength. It allowed him to speak out against the policies of the great powers without jeopardizing his position in the organization. Recognizing that Thant enjoyed the respect of a huge constituency that they themselves were eager to court, the superpowers were careful in their criticisms of him.

In retrospect, Thant's greatest contribution was to uphold the position of secretary-general in the face of assaults on its independence, authority, and integrity. Achieving this goal in an atmosphere of fiscal hardship and continuing superpower tensions was no easy task. It required restraint as much as it did initiative. Thant's quiet diplomacy conveyed to many the appearance of passivity, but his conception of the job of secretary-general was considerably more assertive. The Thant era may be most vividly remembered in the public mind for the UNEF disaster or the secretary-general's inability to involve himself in a meaningful way in ending the war in Vietnam, but it was also a turning point in the history of the organization. The United Nations ceased its almost exclusive preoccupation with the cold war and began to focus on the north-south conflict. U Thant, with his personal background under the shadow of colonialism, both symbolized and became a principal spokesman for the United Nations' new agenda.

NOTES

1. Andrew W. Cordier and Max Harrelson, eds., *Public Papers of the Secretaries-General of the United Nations, Vol. VIII, U Thant* (New York: Columbia University Press, 1977), 692.

2. Cited in Peter R. Baehr and Leon Gordenker, *The United Nations in the 1990s* (New York: St. Martin's, 1994), 180.

3. Leon Gordenker, *The UN Secretary-General and the Maintenance of Peace* (New York: Columbia University Press, 1967), 76.

4. Cordier and Harrelson, *Public Papers, Vol. VIII*, 594.

5. Cordier and Harrelson, *Public Papers, Vol. VIII*, 590.

6. Cordier and Harrelson, *Public Papers, Vol. VIII*, 644.

7. Gordenker, *The UN Secretary-General*, 332.

Chronology, 1961–1974

June 3–4   Soviet Premier Nikita S. Khrushchev and U.S. President John F. Kennedy meet for summit talks in Vienna, which only deepen cold war tensions.

June 21   Khrushchev threatens to sign a separate peace accord with East Germany, a challenge Kennedy rejects on June 28.

July 8   Khrushchev orders a 25 percent increase in Soviet defense expenditures for 1961.

July 25   Kennedy announces a U.S. military buildup, including increased defense spending and an increase in draft calls.

August 12–13   To stop the flow of refugees from East Germany into West Berlin, the Communists erect a wall dividing the city.

August 31   American Vice President Lyndon Johnson visits the Berlin Wall to express U.S. opposition to its existence.

August 31   The USSR ends its voluntary moratorium on nuclear testing and explodes devices on September 1, 4, 5, and 6.

September 3   Kennedy and British Prime Minister Harold Macmillan propose an immediate, total ban on atmospheric nuclear tests.

September 5–6   Leaders of twenty-five neutralist nations meet in Belgrade, Yugoslavia, to denounce colonialism and the arms race.

September 18   UN Secretary-General Dag Hammarskjöld dies in a crash of a chartered airliner near Ndola, northern Rhodesia, as he attempts to arrange a cease-fire between UN and Katangese troops.

September 19   Soviet Foreign Minister Andrei Gromyko announces that the USSR will not support any acting secretary-general to replace Hammarskjöld; he suggests a troika scheme for UN leadership. The General Assembly convenes its sixteenth session and adjourns following a moment of silence for Hammarskjöld.

September 20   Tunisian diplomat Mongi Slim is elected president of the General Assembly. A provisional agreement ends the fighting between Katangese and UN forces but is soon violated by Katangese forces and foreign mercenaries.

September 25   Addressing the General Assembly, President John F. Kennedy rejects the troika scheme. Gromyko in turn rejects Kennedy's plea for an immediate treaty banning nuclear tests and endorses "general and complete disarmament."

September 26   A meeting of Stevenson, Sir Patrick Dean of Great Britain, Armand Berard of France, and Valerian Zorin of the USSR breaks up after Zorin suggests the appointment of four UN undersecretaries, one of whom would be elected secretary-general by the other three on a rotating basis.

September 27   Sierra Leone is admitted as the one-hundredth member of the UN.

September 28   The United Arab Republic, a four-year union between Syria and Egypt, dissolves as Syrian army officers stage a coup against Egyptian rule. A United States-British draft resolution to the General Assembly endorses an end of all nuclear weapons tests.

September 29   Hammarskjöld is buried in Uppsala, Sweden.

September 30   Gromyko and U.S. Secretary of State Dean Rusk hold conversations on Berlin's future.

October 2   South Vietnamese President Ngo Dinh Diem announces to his National Assembly that the Viet Cong insurrection against his government has become a "real war."

October 6   Kennedy suggests that any "prudent family" should provide itself with a fallout shelter as a protection against nuclear attack.

October 10 The American Atomic Energy Commission announces detonation of its third postmoratorium underground nuclear test.

October 11 The General Assembly censures South African Foreign Minister Eric H. Louw after he defends his nation's apartheid policies.

October 15 U.S. General Maxwell Taylor, dispatched by Kennedy to Saigon, reports "any American would be reluctant to use troops [in Vietnam] unless absolutely necessary."[1]

October 17 As great power negotiations continue over West Berlin, Khrushchev agrees not to sign a separate peace treaty with East Germany and announces termination of Soviet nuclear tests; he discloses that the USSR will not detonate a 100-megaton weapon for fear of breaking "our own windows."

October 22 Armed U.S. military police enter East Berlin unmolested to protect the assistant chief of the U.S. Mission in Berlin from East German harassment.

October 23 The USSR detonates a thirty-megaton atmospheric nuclear test, igniting worldwide protests. The Nobel Peace Prize Committee grants its 1961 award posthumously to Hammarskjöld.

October 27 The Mongolian People's Republic (Outer Mongolia) and Mauritania are admitted into the UN. The General Assembly (87–11) appeals to the Soviet Union not to test its fifty-megaton bomb.

October 28 In Berlin, U.S. and Soviet tank formations withdraw after a week of nervous confrontation.

October 30 The White House announces that Russia has detonated a bomb exceeding fifty megatons, and Kennedy orders American scientists to prepare for the resumption of atmospheric tests.

October 31 Stalin's body is removed from its Red Square tomb and reinterred near the Kremlin Wall.

November 1 Eighty-three Algerian Muslims and three French soldiers die in riots marking the seventh anniversary of the Algerian nationalist rebellion.

November 3 U Thant is elected unanimously by the General Assembly to the post of acting secretary-general of the UN, for a term ending April 10, 1963. Maxwell Taylor returns from Saigon and asserts that President Diem can "prevail against the communist threat."[2]

DOCUMENT ONE

**U Thant's Statement in the General Assembly after Taking the Oath
of Office as Acting Secretary-General, New York, November 3, 1961**

Speaking for the first time in this hall, not in my familiar role as the representative of Burma but in the new role as Acting Secretary-General of
the United Nations, my first thought is to thank my fellow representatives for the honor they have done me and the confidence that they have
placed in me in electing me to this high office. May I at the same time
thank the President for his very gracious words of welcome, and also
the President and members of the Security Council for unanimously
recommending my name to the General Assembly for election as Acting Secretary-General.

Most of my colleagues present in this hall know me personally. They
know that I come from a relatively small country in Asia. They know
also that my country has steadfastly pursued over the years a policy of
nonalignment and friendship for all other nations, whatever their ideologies. In my new role I shall continue to maintain this attitude of objectivity and to pursue the ideal of universal friendship.

Having been the permanent representative of my country to the
United Nations for the last four years and more, I am not unaware of
the heavy responsibilities I am undertaking today. The debates in the
General Assembly have already shown that the international climate
can hardly be described as sunny. The Organization is also facing a serious financial problem. In the Congo operation, which is one of the major undertakings in the history of the Organization, we continue to en-
counter serious difficulties which clamor for an urgent solution.

If I am to discharge these responsibilities, surmount these difficulties
and resolve these problems I shall need, in the first instance, the whole-
hearted support, friendly understanding, and unstinting cooperation of
all my colleagues. I have enjoyed such friendly cooperation from all of
you for so long as a representative that I would fain hope that in my
new role I shall receive it in even greater measure. For my part I shall
endeavor to cooperate with you in every possible way. In addition to
your cooperation I shall also need the loyal support of my colleagues in
the Secretariat.

I know how hard the Secretariat has had to work during the last sixteen months, especially in connection with the Congo operation. The
Secretariat has shown itself capable of meeting all demands made on it
so far, and I count on the continued assistance and team spirit of my colleagues in the Secretariat, especially in the difficult days ahead that we
shall face together.

In particular it is my intention to invite a limited number of persons who are at present undersecretaries, or to be appointed as undersecretaries, to act as my principal advisors on important questions pertaining to the performance of functions entrusted to the Secretary-General by the United Nations Charter. In extending this invitation I am fully conscious of the paramount consideration of securing the highest standards of efficiency, competence and integrity, and with due regard to the importance of as wide a geographical basis as possible, as laid down in Article 101 of the Charter. I intend to include among these advisers Mr. Ralph J. Bunche and Mr. Georgy Petrovich Arkadev. It is also my intention to work together with these colleagues in close collaboration and consultation in a spirit of mutual understanding. I am sure that they will seek to work with me in the same manner. Of course, this whole arrangement is without prejudice to such future organizational changes as experience may reveal to be necessary.

Once again I thank the President, my fellow representatives in this hall, and the President and members of the Security Council for entrusting me with these heavy responsibilities. In discharging these responsibilities I shall count on the support of all men and women of good will all over the world, whose overriding interest in the peace, security, and progress of the world it will be my task to reflect and serve.

General Assembly Official Records, Sixteenth Session, 1046th plenary meeting

November 4   The Congolese government concedes that its October 30 invasion of Katanga has been repulsed.

November 6   The General Assembly approves a third world resolution, opposed by East and West blocs, calling for a resumed voluntary moratorium on nuclear weapons tests.

November 8   The General Assembly endorses a United States-British resolution calling for resumption of three-power Geneva negotiations on a nuclear test ban. China's congratulation of Albanian Communists on their twentieth anniversary flouts Soviet denunciations of the Albanian party and indicates growing tension between the Communist giants.

November 11   Eleven Italian nationals working for the UN are massacred by Congolese soldiers.

November 14   A UN investigating commission reports that Congolese Premier Patrice Lumumba was probably murdered on January 17, 1961, on orders of the Katanga Provincial Government. Forces of leftist Congolese Vice Premier Antoine Gizenga mutiny against the pro-Western central government of Premier Cyrille Adoula.

November 17   Thant presides for the first time as acting secretary-general over the Congo Advisory Committee, ambassadors from states contributing military contingents to the United Nations Operation in the Congo (ONUC).

November 24   The Security Council authorizes the acting secretary-general to take measures to rid the Congo of all forces, foreign and indigenous, not connected with the central government. The General Assembly passes a resolution (55–20–26) opposing any use of nuclear weapons. The United States votes against the proposal. The majority also instructs Thant to convene a conference to ban the use of nuclear weapons.

November 27   The General Assembly votes 97–0 (Great Britain, France, South Africa, and Spain abstaining) to create a committee to examine the members' adherence to its 1960 resolution calling for the termination of colonialism.

November 28   A UN subcommittee report condemns Portuguese rule in Angola. The General Assembly condemns apartheid. Geneva test ban talks resume. Two high UN officials, Brian Urquhart and George Ivan Smith, are beaten by Katangese soldiers in Elisabethville.

November 29   Thant proposes a UN bond issue to alleviate the organization's worsening fiscal crisis.

December 1   In his first press conference as acting secretary-general, Thant calls Katangese President Moise Tshombe a "very unstable man."

December 2   In a radio-television address to his people, Cuba's Fidel Castro declares himself a "Marxist-Leninist" and rejects neutralism.

December 5   UN and Katangese forces engage in heavy fighting despite a cease-fire, and Thant orders attacks on Katangese positions.

December 9   The British-administered trust territory of Tanganyika becomes independent with Julius K. Nyerere as prime minister; it joins the UN on December 14.

December 10   The Soviet Union orders the closing of Albania's embassy in Moscow. Thant publicly defends UN military operations in Katanga and blames Tshombe for the fighting.

December 15 Nazi war criminal Adolf Eichmann is sentenced by an Israeli court to death by hanging. The General Assembly rejects (37–48–19) a Soviet resolution to expel Nationalist China from the UN.

December 16 Tunisia, in Fifth Committee deliberations, offers a draft resolution for a UN bond issue.

December 18 UN forces in Katanga secure major military objectives in Elisabethville and a cease-fire permits President Moise Tshombe to meet with Adoula. Indian troops successfully invade the Portuguese enclaves of Goa, Damao, and Diu as Russia vetoes a Security Council cease-fire demand.

December 19 The General Assembly votes 90–1 in favor of independence and self-determination for the inhabitants of South-West Africa. The General Assembly approves the UN Development Decade first proposed by Kennedy on September 25.

December 20 The General Assembly (58–13–28) approves a $200-million bond issue to meet peacekeeping costs. It asks the International Court of Justice for an advisory opinion on members' obligations to pay for peacekeeping operations. It also approves a Soviet-American resolution to create an Eighteen Nation Disarmament Committee to explore the feasibility of general and complete disarmament.

December 20–21 Tshombe and Adoula reach an agreement in which Katanga recognizes the sovereignty of the central government. Upon his return to Elisabethville, Tshombe denies the pact is final.

1962

January 14 The Council of the European Economic Community (EEC) announces the "second stage" of Common Market integration, effective January 1.

January 15 After Dutch destroyers sink two Indonesian torpedo boats off the coast of New Guinea, Thant urges the two countries to peacefully resolve their dispute over the Netherlands New Guinea (West Irian).

January 17   France reaffirms its decision to relinquish control over Algeria.

January 18–19   Princes representing three rival Laotian factions announce agreement on the formation of a coalition government.

January 19   Kennedy and Thant meet privately, discuss a wide range of world problems, and find much ground for cooperation.

January 22–31   In a meeting at Punta del Este, Uruguay, the Organization of American States (OAS) effectively ostracizes Cuba from the community of Western Hemispheric states.

January 30   The General Assembly calls on Portugal, 99–2 (with Spain and South Africa opposed and Lisbon absent), to end its repression in Angola and prepare the African colony for independence.

January 31   The Organization of American States (OAS) votes to ban Cuba from participation in inter-American affairs.

February 9   London agrees to the establishment of an independent Jamaica, effective August 6.

February 10   American U-2 pilot Francis Gary Powers, shot down over the Soviet Union in May 1960, is exchanged for Soviet spy Rudolf Abel.

February 11–19   Negotiations between French government officials and Algerian rebels produce agreement on a cease-fire and creation of a provisional government.

February 20   American Astronaut John Glenn circles the earth three times in a *Mercury* space capsule.

February 22   The Security Council refuses to consider Cuba's complaint against the OAS Punta del Este meeting.

February 23   The General Assembly empowers its Committee on Decolonization to investigate whether Southern Rhodesia is, as claimed by Great Britain, a self-governing colony.

February 28   Andrew Cordier, UN undersecretary-general for General Assembly affairs, leaves the UN to become dean of the Columbia University School of International Affairs.

March 2   Kennedy announces that the United States will resume atmospheric nuclear testing.

March 15   Tshombe arrives in Léopoldville for talks on uniting the Congo and ending the Katangese secession.

March 17   The Eighteen Nation Disarmament Committee (ENDC) convenes, but France refuses to attend.

March 18   A truce signed at Evian-les-Bains ends Algeria's rebellion against France.

March 20–30   Talks on the West Irian dispute open outside Washington with American diplomat Ellsworth Bunker acting as Thant's representative. After ten days, Sukarno recalls his negotiators.

March 29   Kennedy admits that three-power test ban talks have reached a "real impasse."

April 8   French voters endorse President Charles de Gaulle's accord with Algeria.

April 9   The Security Council condemns Israel for its March 17 raid into Syria.

April 13   Khrushchev rejects a plea by Kennedy and British Prime Minister Harold Macmillan for a three power ban on nuclear tests.

April 16   Talks on reducing East-West tensions in Berlin resume in Washington, but in Geneva they reject a neutral nations' formula to end nuclear testing.

April 18   The UN's Economic and Social Council (ECOSOC) votes 17–0–1 to approve an experimental three-year World Food Program to supply $100 million worth of surplus commodities to poor nations.

April 25   The United States carries out its first atmospheric nuclear test since 1958.

May 12–15   American naval and ground forces are sent to Southeast Asia after pro-Communist Pathet Lao forces break a truce and drive all government forces from northern Laos.

May 15–20   Fighting breaks out between Indonesian paratroopers and Dutch forces on West Irian.

May 21   Thant's only son dies in a traffic accident.

May 23   In identical cables to Indonesian President Sukarno and Dutch Prime Minister Edward de Quay, Thant requests that both governments resume negotiations over West Irian with his representative, Ambassador Ellsworth Bunker.

May 31   Adolf Eichmann is executed in Israel.

June 9   In a speech at Massachusetts' Williams College, Thant attacks the weighted voting principle, which would give larger countries more votes in the General Assembly.

June 11   Three Laotian princes, representing competing factions, announce an agreement to end their civil war, and a coalition government is installed in Vientiane (June 22).

June 14   In a report on the UN Development Decade, Thant calls for a transfer of capital from developed to developing nations amounting to $8 billion per year by 1970.

June 15   The Eighteen Nation Geneva Disarmament Conference adjourns after an exchange of acrimonious speeches. The World Court rules in favor of Cambodia in its territorial dispute with Thailand.

June 26   Talks between Congolese and Katangese officials on ending Katanga's secession break down.

June 27   The General Assembly votes to grant independence to the Belgian Trust territory of Ruanda-Urundi, and two states (Rwanda and Burundi) officially become independent on July 1.

June 28   The General Assembly calls (73–1) on Great Britain to replace the Southern Rhodesian constitution that places power in the hands of the white minority. The United States abstains as Britain opposes the resolution.

July 3   An independent Algeria comes into existence following a self-determination vote on July 1.

July 2–8   West German Chancellor Konrad Adenauer visits France; the rapprochement between former enemy states changes the face of European politics.

July 9   The United States tests an H-bomb 200 miles above the Pacific; an angry Thant denounces the experiment on July 11. Thant opens the Economic and Social Council's debate on the Development Decade by presenting his own proposals in a speech at Geneva.

July 20   The World Court delivers an advisory opinion declaring that all UN members are responsible for peacekeeping costs, even if they oppose the operation.

July 23 An agreement guaranteeing the freedom and neutrality of Laos is signed in Geneva by a fourteen-nation conference. The accord represents a triumph for Ambassador Averell Harriman, Kennedy's special negotiator.

August 15 Dutch and Indonesian negotiators agree to transfer Netherlands New Guinea (West Irian) to Indonesia.

August 20 Thant unveils a "Plan for National Reconciliation" for a unified Congo.

August 23 Congolese Prime Minister Cyrille Adoula accepts Thant's "Plan for National Reconciliation."

August 27 The United States and Great Britain offer the USSR two test ban plans, one comprehensive, one partial, but the Soviets reject both.

August 30 In a speech broadcast by Moscow Radio Thant asserts, "the Russian people do not fully understand the true character of the Congo problem."[3]

September 2 Tshombe accepts Thant's "Plan for National Reconciliation."

September 4 Kennedy declares that the United States will use "whatever means necessary" to prevent Cuba from becoming an aggressor state.

September 4–9 De Gaulle visits West Germany as French-German rapprochement continues.

September 11 The Soviets warn the United States that an attack on Cuba or on Soviet ships carrying supplies to the Caribbean island might result in nuclear war.

September 13 Kennedy affirms that he will protect American security against any Soviet offensive military capability in Cuba.

September 18 Rwanda, Burundi, Jamaica, and Trinidad and Tobago are admitted into the UN, bringing the total membership in the world body to 108.

September 21 The General Assembly (89–0–14) approves the West Irian settlement between Indonesia and Holland.

September 26 A Yemeni military revolt touches off civil war in the Arab nation.

October 8 Algeria becomes the UN's 109th member.

October 9 The General Assembly calls on Great Britain to secure the release of black nationalist Joshua Nkomo, detained by Rhodesia's white minority government.

October 19 Thant sends a personal representative to mediate the ongoing border dispute between Thailand and Cambodia.

October 20 Full-scale fighting erupts between India and China over border dispute.

October 22 Kennedy, citing the construction of medium range Soviet nuclear missiles in Cuba, announces a United States naval quarantine of the island.

October 23 The Security Council meets to consider the Cuban missile crisis, as Stevenson makes America's case.

October 24 The naval quarantine of Cuba goes into effect as Thant sends Kennedy and Khrushchev separate but identically worded messages urging restraint.

October 25 The U.S. Navy halts a Soviet merchant ship headed toward Cuba; the ship passes through the quarantine without being boarded. Uganda becomes the UN's 110th member.

October 26 The U.S. Navy boards a Lebanese freighter on its way to Cuba, then allows it to pass. Thant accepts Castro's offer to visit Havana.

October 28 Khrushchev agrees to dismantle Soviet weapons in Cuba in return for a U.S. pledge not to invade the island.

October 30 The General Assembly again rejects (56–42–12) a Soviet resolution to expel Nationalist China.

October 31 Thant returns from Havana after a brief and unsuccessful visit.

November 6 The General Assembly votes, 67–16, to approve an Afro-Asian resolution calling on the UN to impose economic sanctions on South Africa; the United States and Britain vote against. Member states are encouraged to break diplomatic relations with Pretoria.

November 19 Negotiations on British entry into the Common Market are deadlocked.

November 20   The United States lifts its quarantine of Cuba.

November 21   A Peking-ordered cease-fire ends fighting between China and India, with China in control of the disputed territory.

November 30   Acting Secretary-General U Thant is elected unanimously to a full term to expire in November 1966.

December 3   Thant urges the Fifth Committee to endorse the World Court's decision affirming members' responsibility to pay for peace-keeping activities.

December 12   Khrushchev defends his Cuban policy against Chinese attack. The U.S. delegation to the Eighteen Nation Disarmament Committee proposes the installation of a "hot telephone" linking Washington and the Kremlin.

December 15   The General Assembly votes 82–7 to condemn Portugal's administration of its African territories.

December 19   *Pravda* accuses China of leading Communist opposition to the USSR's policy of peaceful coexistence. By a vote of 76–17–8, the General Assembly endorses the World Court's decision on peacekeeping expenses.

December 20   The Dominican Republic elects Juan Bosch as president in the country's first free election in thirty-eight years. The General Assembly accepts the credentials of the Yemen Arab Republic.

December 21   Kennedy and Macmillan issue a joint communiqué from Nassau, the Bahamas, scrapping the Skybolt air-to-ground missile and pledging to develop a NATO multilateral nuclear force.

December 23   Valerian Zorin is replaced by Nikolai T. Federenko as Soviet ambassador to the UN.

December 29   UN troops attack military objectives in Elisabethville in another effort to end Katangese secession.

1963

January 7   A joint letter from American Ambassador Adlai Stevenson and Soviet Ambassador Vassily V. Kuznetsov thanks Thant for his efforts to resolve the Cuban crisis.

January 9 UN forces win control of Katanga and detain Tshombe.

January 14 De Gaulle rejects a United States-British plan for a multilateral NATO nuclear force; he chooses instead to develop an independent *force de frappe*.

January 23 Indian Prime Minister Jawaharlal Nehru announces that his parliament accepts an Indian-Chinese border peace plan.

January 26 Iranian voters approve the shah's "White Revolution" reform plan.

January 29 France vetoes a continuation of talks to integrate Great Britain into the Common Market.

February 4 Thant tells the Security Council that the situation in the Congo has improved to the point where UN troops can be withdrawn.

February 5 Tshombe announces in Elisabethville that the UN plan to integrate Katanga into the Congo will be implemented.

February 8 The Iraqi government of Premier Abdul Karim Kassem is ousted, and Colonel Abdel-Salam Arif takes over.

February 18 The USSR informs the United States that thousands of Soviet troops will be removed from Cuba.

February 26 The UN announces that Ralph Bunche, undersecretary for political affairs, has been sent to the Middle East to discuss the Yemen crisis.

March 4 In a letter to Thant, Soviet UN Ambassador Nikolai T. Federenko calls for a complete removal of UN troops from the Congo.

April 2 Khrushchev rejects a Chinese proposal for a bilateral summit meeting in Peking.

April 10 Pope John XXIII issues his *Pacem in terris* encyclical, a plea for world peace. The U.S. Navy announces the disappearance of the nuclear powered submarine, USS *Thresher*, with 120 aboard.

April 11 Thant suggests talks to deal with a renewed outbreak of fighting in Laos.

April 12 The United Arab Republic, Iraq, and Syria sign an agreement to form a new United Arab Republic.

April 26   Following a Harriman visit to Moscow, Harriman and the Kremlin announce joint support for the 1962 accord on an independent Laos.

April 29   Thant reveals an agreement by Yemen, Saudi Arabia, and the United Arab Republic to deploy UN observers in Yemen and disengage Saudi and Egyptian forces from that country. Thant sends Major General Carl Carlson von Horn to reconnoiter the region.

May 1   The UN formally transfers the administration of West Irian to Indonesia.

May 3   Thant remarks at a press conference that the "primary function of the UN in the Congo has been fulfilled."[4]

May 14   Kuwait joins the United Nations.

May 15   Thant says the fiscal crisis is "perhaps the most vital issue before the United Nations,"[5] even as a special General Assembly session discusses the crisis.

May 25   Representatives of thirty-one African states form the Organization of African Unity (OAU).

May 31–June 1   Sukarno and Malayan Prime Minister Abdul Rahman confer in Tokyo over Malaya's plan to create a Malaysian federation. Rahman asserts that the plan will go through despite Indonesian and Philippine resistance.

June 3   Pope John XXIII, elected on October 28, 1958, dies in the Vatican Palace.

June 5   British Secretary of War John Profumo resigns his office after admitting that he lied to Parliament about a sex scandal.

June 8–11   In Manila, representatives of Malaya, Indonesia, and the Philippines agree to the formation of Malaysia but propose that Thant assay the wishes of the inhabitants of Borneo and Sarawak.

June 10   Kennedy announces the convening in Moscow of three-power talks on nuclear testing. At Washington's American University, the president, in a speech that leads to superpower détente, calls on the American people to rethink the cold war.

June 12   The Security Council instructs Thant to establish an observer mission to supervise Yemeni troop disengagements agreed to by Egypt and Saudi Arabia in April.

June 20   The United States and USSR agree to establish a direct communications link (hot line) between their two capitals.

June 21   The Archbishop of Milan, Giovanni Battista Cardinal Montini, is elected Pope Paul VI.

June 26   Kennedy addresses 150 thousand West Berliners and declares, *"Ich bin ein Berliner."*

June 27   Federenko rejects a series of General Assembly resolutions (passed May 19–June 27) affirming each member's obligation to pay for peacekeeping expenses.

July 4   The United Nations Observation Mission in Yemen begins operations.

July 9   An agreement is signed in London creating a federation of Malaysia (Malaya, Singapore, Sarawak, and North Borneo).

July 15   In a letter to English philosopher Lord Bertrand Russell, Khrushchev explains his refusal to pay for peacekeeping expenses.

July 20   Russian-Chinese ideological talks break up in failure after two weeks of acrimonious discussion.

July 22   Egyptian President Gamal Abdel Nasser renounces the April accord establishing a larger United Arab Republic.

July 30   Leaders of Indonesia, Malaya, and the Philippines meet in Manila to discuss differences over the proposed Malaysian federation.

July 31   The Security Council adopts by a vote of 8–0 (United States, United Kingdom, and France abstaining) a partial arms embargo against Portugal for its African colonial policies. The council then votes 9–0 (United Kingdom and France abstaining) for a complete embargo on the shipment of arms to South Africa.

August 5   Representatives of the United States, Great Britain, and the Soviet Union sign a pact banning nuclear testing in the atmosphere, seas, and outer space.

August 8   Thant agrees to a request from Indonesia, Malaysia, and the Philippines that he dispatch a mission to North Borneo and Sarawak to ascertain whether those populations wish to join the Malaysian federation.

August 12   Thant appoints Laurence V. Michelmore to head his eight-man mission to Sarawak and North Borneo.

August 20   Major General Carl Carlson von Horn, commander of United Nations Yemen Observation Mission (UNYOM), quits his post and denounces UN headquarters. Von Horn subsequently withdraws his resignation, but Thant refuses to reinstate the general.

August 26   The U.S. State Department blames South Vietnamese President Ngo Dinh Diem for his government's attacks on Buddhist pagodas and priests.

August 28   More than 200,000 people from around the United States convene in Washington in favor of civil rights. The assembly hears the Rev. Dr. Martin Luther King Jr. deliver his "I Have a Dream" address.

September 14   Thant announces that inhabitants of Sarawak and Borneo favor integration into the Malaysian federation, and the Federation of Malaysia formally comes into existence on September 16.

September 24   The U.S. Senate approves the Nuclear Test Ban Treaty.

September 25   The Dominican armed forces topple President Juan Bosch in a coup.

October 9   Kennedy authorizes the sale of U.S. wheat to the Soviet Union.

October 11   The General Assembly, by a vote of 106–1, urges South Africa not to execute eleven black nationalists convicted on charges of sabotage; the world body's appeal fails.

October 17   A resolution banning the deployment of nuclear weapons in space passes the General Assembly by acclamation.

October 18   At the request of the Congolese government, the General Assembly agrees to retain a UN troop presence in that country until June 30, 1964.

October 19   The General Assembly calls on Great Britain not to transfer power to Southern Rhodesia's white minority government. Harold Macmillan resigns as British prime minister to be followed by Sir Alec Douglas-Home.

October 21   A resolution to expel Nationalist China and seat the Peking government in its stead is defeated in the General Assembly by a vote of 57–41–12.

October 24   In Dallas, Texas, U.S. Ambassador Adlai Stevenson is jeered and hit on the head by right wing opponents of the UN.

October 30   A truce halts a month of border fighting between Algeria and Morocco.

November 1–2   The Army of the Republic of South Vietnam deposes and executes President Ngo Dinh Diem and Ngo Dinh Nhu, his security chief.

November 12–16   The USSR briefly detains Yale Professor Frederick C. Barghorn as a spy and precipitates a brief crisis in Soviet-American relations.

November 22   John F. Kennedy is assassinated in Dallas, Texas, and Lyndon Baines Johnson assumes the presidency.

November 27   The General Assembly endorses (64–18–25) an international conference to examine the feasibility of a comprehensive ban on the use of nuclear weapons.

December 4   Expanding on its August resolution, the Security Council bans the sale of equipment and materials for the "manufacture and maintenance of arms and ammunition" to South Africa.

December 16   Admission of Zanzibar and Kenya to the United Nations raises the Afro-Asian bloc to fifty-eight of the UN's 113 members. The new majority immediately calls on member states (99–2) to financially assist families of those persecuted by South Africa's white minority government for their opposition to apartheid.

December 17   The General Assembly votes to increase the size of the Security Council from eleven to fifteen.

December 18   Stevenson warns that unless the USSR pays peacekeeping assessments, the United States will attempt to deny Moscow voting rights in the General Assembly.

December 21   Violence erupts between Turkish and Greek communities on Cyprus.

December 26   The Security Council meets but fails to act on a Cypriot complaint that Turkey intervened in its internal affairs.

1964

January 9–12   After twenty-three people are killed in clashes between Panamanian mobs and American troops in the Canal Zone, Panama breaks diplomatic ties with the United States.

January 13   Thant informs the Security Council that Cyprus, Greece, Turkey, and Great Britain have requested that he send a personal representative to survey the situation in Cyprus. On January 17, Lieutenant General P. S. Gyani of India visits the troubled island on behalf of the secretary-general.

January 27   France recognizes the People's Republic of China.

January 30   A coup in South Vietnam brings Major General Nguyen Kahn to power.

January 31   London proposes the emplacement of ten thousand NATO troops on Cyprus to promote peace between the Turkish and Greek communities.

February 17–March 4   A Security Council debate of the Cyprus question results in unanimous approval of a peacekeeping force on Cyprus for three months. Thant is granted wide latitude to create the United Nations Forces in Cyprus (UNFICYP), which go into operation on March 27. Thant names Finnish ambassador to Sweden, Sakari Severi Tuomioja, as the UN mediator on Cyprus.

March 13   Thant warns Ankara against taking unilateral military action against Cyprus.

March 23   The UN Conference on Trade and Development (UNCTAD) convenes in Geneva with 116 nations participating.

March 27   The Soviets return three U.S. airmen shot down over East Germany on March 19.

March 28   Crown Prince Faisal Abdul Aziz of Saudi Arabia successfully seizes power from his brother, King Saud.

March 30   Thant publishes a letter urging that South Africa spare the lives of those charged with opposing apartheid.

April 1   The military stages a successful coup in Brazil, and the Congress elects General Humberto Castelo Branco as president on April 11.

April 9   Bunche confers with the warring parties on Cyprus.

April 19   Rightists stage a coup against the Laotian coalition government.

April 20   A five-member Panel of Experts from the UN's Special Committee on Apartheid, headed by Sweden's Alva Myrdal, advises Thant to organize a national convention of all of South Africa's racial groups.

April 26   Tanganyika and Zanzibar merge to form Tanzania.

April 29   Thant tells a news conference that military might will not defeat the Communists in Vietnam. Thant unveils a Cyprus peace plan.

May 9   Khrushchev arrives in Egypt for a two-week state visit.

May 11   Thant names former Ecuadorian President Galo Plaza Lasso as his special representative on Cyprus.

May 26   Thant derides those who suggest that the United States should use nuclear weapons in Vietnam.

May 27   Prime Minister Nehru dies. India's first prime minister was a close associate of Gandhi and a leader in the nonaligned movement. The UN's Special Committee on Apartheid recommends imposition of economic sanctions upon South Africa.

May 29   UNCTAD, by a vote of 72–0, calls on developed nations to transfer 1 percent of their annual GNP to developing states.

June 1–2   High-ranking U.S. officials meet in Honolulu to discuss the war in Vietnam.

June 2   Lal Bahadur Shastri is named to succeed Nehru.

June 4   The Security Council sends a mission to Cambodia and South Vietnam to report on continuing border conflict.

June 12   In Pretoria, Nelson Mandela and seven other South African black nationalists are sentenced to life imprisonment for plotting violent revolution.

June 20   UNFICYP is extended another three months, as sporadic ethnic fighting continues.

June 30   UN forces evacuate the Congo after a four-year intervention.

July 9   Cyrille Adoula quits as prime minister of the Congo and is replaced by Moise Tshombe.

July 16   Thant warns Cypriot, Greek, and Turkish leaders about the perils of intercommunal war.

July 22   Thant complains to Cypriot officials about limitations on the free movement of UNFICYP.

July 27   Cyprus President Archbishop Makarios urges the UN General Assembly to discuss the Cyprus problem.

July 28   The UN committee studying the Cambodian-South Vietnamese border dispute recommends emplacement of UN civilian observers on the border, but Cambodia rejects the solution.

July 29   In Moscow, Thant pleads with Khrushchev to resolve the fiscal crisis and pay Russia's peacekeeping assessment.

August 4–5   U.S. Navy planes bomb North Vietnam, following an alleged attack on the American destroyers *Maddox* and *C. Turner Joy* in the Gulf of Tonkin.

August 6   Thant urges President Johnson and Secretary of State Dean Rusk to begin direct negotiations with Hanoi.

August 7–9   Turkish planes bomb Cyprus to defend the besieged Turkish community on the island.

August 7   The Gulf of Tonkin Resolution, passed by the U.S. Congress, approves presidential actions taken in the Vietnam crisis.

August 10   A Security Council cease-fire resolution is accepted by Turkey and Cyprus.

August 19   Cyprus lifts its economic blockade of the Turkish community on the island.

August 20   Thant, despite recent visits to Washington, Moscow, and Paris, asserts that UN finances remain severely strained.

August 27   Moscow announces that it will pay nothing toward UN peacekeeping operations and ridicules America's threat to deprive it of an assembly vote.

September 4   UNYOM begins to evacuate Yemen after Saudi Arabia refuses to finance its deployment. The civil war and outside interventions continue for several more years.

September 10   The Arab League approves in principle the formation of a Palestinian refugee army to fight against Israel.

September 17   A Security Council resolution condemning Indonesia for airdropping guerrillas into Malaysia is defeated by the Kremlin's 102nd veto.

September 23   Thant tells Ambassador Stevenson he believes Hanoi would be willing to negotiate directly with the United States.

September 25   The Security Council extends the life of UNFICYP for another three months.

October 4   Congolese Prime Minister Tshombe, viewed as a tool of Belgian interests, is banned from a conference of nonaligned nations meeting in Cairo.

October 14   Dr. Martin Luther King Jr., the American civil rights activist, is awarded the Nobel Peace Prize for 1964.

October 14–15   Krushchev is deposed as Soviet leader as Leonid Brezhnev becomes first secretary of the Communist Party; Aleksei Kosygin becomes chairman of the Council of Ministers.

October 15   British elections return the Labor Party to power after thirteen years in opposition. Harold Wilson becomes the prime minister. Stevenson informs Thant that the U.S. response to his proposal for direct United States-North Vietnam talks will follow the presidential elections.

October 16   China tests its first atomic device.

November 1   Viet Cong forces raid an American air base at Bien Hoa.

November 3   Lyndon Johnson wins a landslide victory to become president in his own right.

November 16   At Geneva, representatives of seventeen industrial nations initiate the "Kennedy Round" of tariff cutting negotiations.

November 20   Thant announces that "valiant efforts" have been made to avoid a disaster over the article 19 crisis, occasioned by Washington's insistence that the charter provision be employed against members in arrears to the organization. Behind the scenes, Thant has arranged for the General Assembly to convene without conducting formal votes.

November 22   Riots erupt in Saigon against the government of Prime Minister Tran Van Huong.

November 24   Congolese rebels capture Stanleyville, in the eastern part of the Congo, and take one thousand hostages. Belgian paratroopers dropped from U.S. planes, assisted by Congolese ground troops, intervene on behalf of the Tshombe government.

November 30   Following South Africa's execution of three black nationalists, the UN's Special Committee on Apartheid recommends to the General Assembly and Security Council the imposition of immediate and complete sanctions on Pretoria.

December 1   The nineteenth General Assembly opens in a climate of uncertainty over the world organization's future; all votes are conducted by acclamation rather than roll call. Malawi, Malta, and Zambia become members of the UN.

December 4   Thant enters the hospital for treatment of a chronic stomach ulcer.

December 11   A bazooka shell fired at the UN from the Queens side of the East River falls two hundred yards short of its target. Anti-Castro Cuban exiles are arrested for the attack, which occurs during delivery of a speech by Cuban Industry Minister Ernesto (Che) Guevara.

December 15   The North Atlantic Council convenes in Paris to discuss the U.S. plan for a multilateral nuclear force.

December 29   Malaysia is elected by the General Assembly to a seat on the Security Council.

December 20   Following several weeks of bitter debate, the Security Council urges a halt to all foreign intervention in the Congo, a ceasefire, and the withdrawal of all foreign mercenaries.

December 31   Malaysia sends a note to the Security Council charging Indonesia with incursions into its territory.

1965

January 1   Indonesia informs Thant of Djakarta's intention to quit the world body over the Malaysian issue.

January 8   Reports circulate that the Congolese government has executed five hundred rebels in Stanleyville.

January 12   Indonesia orders all UN officials to leave its territory.

January 13   Stevenson asks Thant to arrange a secret meeting place for United States and North Vietnamese talks.

January 14   Indonesian President Sukarno proposes a new poll of the inhabitants of North Borneo and Sarawak to gauge their loyalty to the Malaysian federation.

January 18   Thant informs Stevenson that Burma is willing to host a meeting between representatives of Hanoi and Washington.

January 20   Johnson is sworn is as president of the United States.

January 21   Indonesia formally withdraws from the United Nations because Malaysia has been voted a seat on the Security Council.

January 24   Sir Winston Churchill dies in London. The former British prime minister led his nation through World War II. Chinese Premier Chou En-lai calls for the creation of a rival UN composed of "revolutionary" states.

January 30   Stevenson informs Thant that the United States will not meet with North Vietnam to discuss war issues.

February 4   De Gaulle proposes that a Five Power conference, including Communist China, discuss reform of the United Nations.

February 7   U.S. planes raid military bases in North Vietnam, following a Viet Cong attack on its military barracks at Pleiku. Stevenson writes to the president of the Security Council that Washington has no intention of widening the war, but raids continue on February 11.

February 10   The General Assembly approves by acclamation Thant's selection of Dr. Raul Prebisch as secretary-general of UNCTAD.

February 12   Calling for military restraint, Thant urges that the Geneva Conference on Indochina be reconvened.

February 18   The General Assembly considers an Albanian resolution calling for abandonment of the no-voting procedure and votes it down. Washington's decision to allow a procedural vote without invoking article 19 permits the assembly to survive its latest crisis.

February 21   At a White House meeting, Thant informs President Johnson that North Vietnam would begin peace talks in return for a halt in American bombing.

February 24 In a press conference, Thant laments his inability to bring Hanoi and Washington together: "I am sure that the great American people, if only they knew the true facts and the background in the developments in South Vietnam, will agree with me that further bloodshed is unnecessary."[6]

February 25 The UN confirms that Hanoi supports Thant's plan for direct negotiations between the United States and North Vietnam.

February 26 Thant's letter to Indonesian Minister for Foreign Affairs Dr. Roden Subandrio regretfully accepts Djakarta's decision to withdraw from the United Nations.

February 27 A Special Committee on Peace Keeping Operations is appointed to study the fiscal crisis.

March 4 When Asian students in Moscow protest at the American Embassy over Washington's Vietnam policy, Soviet police break up the demonstration, prompting strong protests from Peking.

March 8–9 U.S. Marines, the first 3500 American combat troops sent to Vietnam, arrive to protect the U.S. Air Force base at Danang.

March 9 The United States rejects Thant's plan for a peace conference on Vietnam until North Vietnam demonstrates a willingness to halt its "aggression."

March 30 The UN's Cyprus mediator, Galo Plaza Lasso, appointed in August 1964 to succeed the late Sakari Tuomioja, proposes a peace plan that rejects both the Greek call for enosis (unification with Greece) and the Turkish demand for partition.

March 31 Turkey denounces Galo Plaza Lasso for exceeding his mandate, and the UN mediator is ultimately compelled to relinquish his post.

April 5–12 Serious military clashes occur between India and Pakistan in the disputed Rann of Kutch, Kashmir.

April 7 In an address at Baltimore's Johns Hopkins University, President Johnson offers unconditional talks with North Vietnam and more than $1 billion in rehabilitation aid. He claims that North Vietnamese policy is directed by Peking.

April 12 After Moscow and Peking reject the Johnson peace plan, Hanoi does likewise.

April 17–20   Johnson rejects both foreign and domestic calls for a bombing halt, as U.S. officials plan in Honolulu to expand the Vietnam War.

April 24   Army rebels in the Dominican Republic loyal to ex-President Juan Bosch overthrow the government of Dr. J. Donald Reid Cabral. Civil war ensues as antirebel forces are led by Brigadier General Elias Wessin y Wessin.

April 28   In Santo Domingo, 405 U.S. marines land by helicopter to protect American citizens caught up in the civil war. After pro-Bosch forces surrender to Wessin y Wessin, a three-man military junta is formed.

April 30   Pro-Bosch and Wessin y Wessin forces sign a cease-fire agreement that fails to take hold across the island.

May 1   The Organization of American States (OAS) votes to send a five-man peace commission to Santo Domingo.

May 2   Johnson defends American intervention in the Dominican Republic as preventing the emplacement of another Communist state in the Caribbean.

May 3   The Security Council convenes to discuss a Soviet complaint against U.S. intervention in the Dominican Republic.

May 4   Rebels in Santo Domingo install Colonel Francisco Caamano Deno as provisional president, as two governments claim to control the nation.

May 5   Opposing Dominican forces sign a temporary truce, but sporadic fighting continues. There are approximately 19,000 American soldiers in Santo Domingo.

May 5–9   The buildup of U.S. forces in Vietnam reaches 42,000.

May 6   The OAS approves the formation of an inter-American peace force for the Dominican Republic.

May 7   Santo Domingo's three-man military junta dissolves in favor of a five-man military-civilian junta headed by Brigadier General Antonio Imbert Barreras.

May 13   Israel and West Germany formally establish diplomatic ties, prompting ten Arab nations to sever relations with Bonn.

May 14 After the Security Council unanimously calls on Thant to send a representative to the Dominican Republic, Thant appoints Jose Antonio Mayobre, a Venezuelan who has worked in the Secretariat since 1951, to the position.

May 16 A four-man U.S. peace mission, led by McGeorge Bundy, Johnson's national security adviser, arrives in Santo Domingo.

May 19–20 Mayobre arranges a truce, but the OAS criticizes the UN's role in Santo Domingo.

May 21 The Security Council, by a 6–5 vote, defeats a Soviet resolution calling for the withdrawal of U.S. and other troops from the Dominican Republic.

May 22 The Security Council, by a 10–0–1 vote, approves a French resolution calling for a permanent truce in the Dominican Republic. The United States abstains on the resolution, which invites the secretary-general to report on its implementation.

May 26 Three-man OAS observer teams fan out through Santo Domingo to supervise the latest truce.

May 27 Thant says that the replacement of the United Nations by the OAS in Santo Domingo could create a bad precedent for future UN peacekeeping operations.

June 3–June 22 The Security Council meets in response to Soviet charges that the Dominican junta is arresting and executing rebel sympathizers but is unable to act because of the split between Washington and Moscow.

June 11 The UN Disarmament Commission calls for a world disarmament conference, including the People's Republic of China.

June 14 Following the resignation of Vietnam's civilian government, a military triumvirate made up of Major General Nguyen Van Thieu, Air Vice Marshall Nguyen Cao Ky, and Brigadier General Nguyen Huu Co is formed.

June 15 The Security Council extends UNFICYP's mandate by six months.

June 16 American Secretary of Defense Robert McNamara announces the addition of 21,000 troops to American forces in South Vietnam.

June 17   The UN's Special Committee on Apartheid calls for total economic sanctions against South Africa and criticizes the United States, Great Britain, and France for blocking effective Security Council action.

June 19   Algerian President Ahmed Ben Bella is ousted in a military coup led by Colonel Houari Boumedienne.

June 24   A proposal to amend the UN Charter to increase the size of the Security Council from eleven to fifteen, and ECOSOC from sixteen to twenty-seven, is ratified. The amendments demonstrate the changing nature of the world organization.

June 25   Johnson and Thant meet in San Francisco to honor the UN's twentieth anniversary, a celebration marked by tension over Thant's public criticisms of America's Vietnam policy.

June 28   Ex-President Joaquín Balaguer returns to the Dominican Republic and declares his intention to run for the presidency.

June 29   India and Pakistan declare a cease-fire, which ends their fighting in the Rann of Kutch.

July 5   Thant calls for the creation of an International Youth Corps as part of the UN Development Decade.

July 10   The OAS proposes the appointment of Hector Garcia-Godoy as president of a provisional Dominican government.

July 14   Adlai Stevenson dies in London. The former governor of Illinois and two-time Democratic presidential candidate served as UN ambassador from January 1961 until his death.

July 16–20   The Security Council discusses the Dominican situation but once again the Soviet-American deadlock prevents action.

July 20   McNamara asserts, after a fact-finding visit to South Vietnam, that the military situation there has worsened. Supreme Court Associate Justice Arthur J. Goldberg replaces Stevenson as Washington's representative to the United Nations.

July 27   The Eighteen Nation UN Disarmament Committee reconvenes in Geneva.

July 28   American draft calls double as Johnson orders an increase in U.S. troop strength in South Vietnam from 75,000 to 125,000.

July 30   The United States asks the Security Council to help end the Vietnam War.

August 3   The Security Council meets to hear Turkish complaints about the Cypriot government's planned electoral reforms.

August 5–16   India and Pakistan resume fighting in the Kashmir region.

August 9   Ethnic tensions between Malays and Chinese force Singapore to withdraw from the Malaysian federation and become a sovereign state.

August 16   Goldberg announces that the United States will drop its insistence on invoking article 19 against financially delinquent member states. The decision permits normal functioning for the upcoming General Assembly.

August 17   The United States presents a draft treaty to limit proliferation of nuclear weapons to the Eighteen Nation UN Disarmament Committee.

August 18   All Dominican factions reject a new OAS peace plan.

August 24   India crosses the cease-fire line in Kashmir, and Thant decides not to send Ralph Bunche to Kashmir as a peacemaker. An agreement to end the Yemeni Civil War is reached in Jidda, Saudi Arabia.

September 1   Thant sends messages to Indian Prime Minister Shastri and Pakistani President Ayub Khan pleading for restraint in their widening war. In its last meeting of the nineteenth session, the General Assembly votes by consensus to encourage voluntary contributions to the UN.

September 3   A provisional government headed by Hector Garcia-Godoy takes power in the Dominican Republic after the August 31 approval of a Reconciliation Act, drawn up by the OAS.

September 4   A bleak report from Thant's representative leads the Security Council to call for an immediate cease-fire in Kashmir.

September 6   India invades West Pakistan and drives toward Lahore as subcontinent fighting spreads and intensifies.

September 7   Thant leaves for India and Pakistan, and from September 9 to 14 confers with officials in both nations.

September 9   De Gaulle announces that France will leave NATO by 1969. Brigadier General Elías Wessin y Wessin is exiled from the Dominican Republic.

September 9   Thant endorses the idea of inviting all nations, including the People's Republic of China, to a proposed world disarmament conference.

September 16   Thant returns to New York after failing to secure Pakistani and Indian acceptance of a cease-fire followed by direct talks.

September 20   The Security Council sets a cease-fire of September 22 in the Pakistani-Indian war.

September 21   UN membership reaches 117 as Singapore, the Maldive Islands, and The Gambia are admitted into the organization. Thant's *Annual Report* encourages the admission of Communist China into the UN.

September 22   The UN ordered cease-fire takes effect in the war between India and Pakistan, although sporadic fighting continues.

September 24   Thant announces formation of the United Nations India-Pakistan Observation Mission (UNIPOM) to patrol the cease-fire.

September 25   Juan Bosch returns to the Dominican Republic.

September 27   The Security Council appeals to India and Pakistan to observe their truce.

October 1   Indonesia announces that loyal military forces crushed an armed coup on September 30, but rebels claim they acted only to forestall a CIA-sponsored coup against President Sukarno.

October 2   Sukarno announces that he still commands Indonesia and appoints Major General Raden Suharto as the new chief of the army.

October 3   The Indonesian army, claiming that Communists were involved in the coup attempt, bans all Communist newspapers.

October 4   During his first visit to the United States, Pope Paul VI addresses the General Assembly.

October 10   As part of the army drive against Communists, more than one thousand Communists have been arrested in Indonesia.

October 12   A General Assembly vote encourages Great Britain to do anything possible to prevent a unilateral declaration of independence by Rhodesia, where white leaders intend to maintain minority control.

October 13   President Joseph Kasavubu dismisses the government of Prime Minister Moise Tshombe.

October 15–16   Nationwide student protests against the war in Vietnam are held in approximately forty U.S. cities.

October 25   In the Security Council, the Soviet delegate assails Thant for widening the size of UNIPOM and appointing members of NATO's General Staff to the mission's command.

October 30   British and Rhodesian negotiators agree to establish a three-man royal commission to study plans for granting independence to Rhodesia; it fails to bridge the gap between the two sides.

November 5   The Security Council unanimously calls on India and Pakistan to observe its September 20 truce call. Moscow abstains because of reservations over Thant's role.

November 6   Santo Domingo's nighttime curfew, in effect since April, is lifted.

November 11   Rhodesia unilaterally declares its independence from Great Britain.

November 12   The Security Council, including Great Britain, condemns Rhodesia and calls on all states not to recognize the white government.

November 15   Newsman Eric Sevareid, who interviewed Adlai Stevenson only a few days before the diplomat's death, reports that Washington rejected Thant's plan for direct negotiations between the United States and Vietnam.

November 17   A bid to expel Nationalist China and seat the Peking government is defeated 47–47–20 in the General Assembly. As in all previous tallies, the vote is deemed an "important question," requiring a two-thirds margin in favor of the resolution.

November 19   Britain announces that British Guiana will achieve independence on May 26, 1966, and thereafter be known as "Guyana."

November 20   The Security Council votes that all nations should sever economic relations with Rhodesia. The General Assembly votes

(112–0–2) to convene a world disarmament conference, including Communist China, but Peking announces that it will not take part.

November 22   The General Assembly votes 98–0 to merge the UN Special Fund and UN Expanded Program of Technical Assistance into the UN Development Program (UNDP).

November 25   General Joseph Mobuto seizes power from President Kasavubu in the Congo.

November 30   India reports on new clashes with China along the Sikkim frontier.

December 3   The General Assembly calls on all nations to stop nuclear testing.

December 8   The Soviet Union announces that Indian Prime Minister Shastri and Pakistani President Ayub Khan will meet in Tashkent in January.

December 9   Johnson pledges to search for peace in Vietnam despite Communist rejections of his peace feelers.

December 15   In the first American raid on an industrial target, U.S. warplanes destroy a North Vietnamese thermal power plant near Haiphong. The General Assembly condemns apartheid and calls on Thant to establish a UN Trust Fund to aid the victims of apartheid.

December 21   The General Assembly votes to request voluntary contributions to finance the United Nations Emergency Force (UNEF) in 1965 and 1966. The General Assembly, by a vote of 66–26–15, calls on all nations to sever diplomatic ties with Portugal, condemned for its colonial policies in Africa.

December 24–25   After a one-day Christmas truce expires, Johnson orders a bombing halt that endures until the end of January 1966.

December 29   As part of America's "peace offensive," Johnson sends high-ranking U.S. emissaries to meet with leaders around the globe.

1966

January 6   Provisional President Garcia-Godoy exiles left- and right-wing military officers from the Dominican Republic.

January 10   Ayub Khan and Shastri sign an accord ending the war between Pakistan and India. The White House confirms direct contacts between U.S. Ambassador Henry Byroade and a North Vietnamese representative in Rangoon. Thant convenes the first meeting of the UNDP's governing board in New York.

January 11   Shastri dies in Tashkent, and Nehru's daughter, Indira Gandhi, is elected prime minister of India on January 19.

January 20   Thant recommends that a solution to the Vietnam conflict should result in a coalition government, including the National Liberation Front (NLF).

January 21   Following a coup, a new military government is formed in Nigeria.

January 31   Johnson announces resumption of U.S. air raids against North Vietnam, as his "peace offensive" ends.

February 1   The Security Council meets to consider an American proposal that the UN convene an international conference on Vietnam.

February 6–8   President Johnson, South Vietnamese Premier Nguyen Cao Ky, and other Saigon officials meeting in Honolulu issue the "Declaration of Honolulu," calling for cooperation between the two governments in prosecuting the war effort.

February 8, 10   The U.S. Senate Foreign Relations Committee holds hearings on the war in Vietnam.

February 19   Breaking with President Johnson, U.S. Senator Robert F. Kennedy (New York) proposes the formation of a coalition government in South Vietnam that would include the NLF.

February 21   De Gaulle announces that France will henceforth exercise exclusive control over all military bases on its territory, including those of NATO.

February 22   Nasser threatens to keep his troops in Yemen for another five years.

February 24   A military coup overthrows Ghanian leader Kwame Nkrumah.

March 1   East Germany formally applies for membership in the UN, but the United States, France, and Great Britain issue a joint communiqué rejecting the East German request.

March 9   France formally announces its intention to withdraw all of its forces from NATO. A UN spokesman discloses Thant's three-point proposal for initiating Vietnam peace negotiations. The proposal involves: 1) an American bombing halt; 2) the de-escalation of military hostilities in South Vietnam; 3) the inclusion of all parties to the conflict in negotiations.

March 12   Sukarno relinquishes all governmental powers to Major General Suharto, who then bans the Communist Party.

March 16   The Security Council extends UNFICYP's mandate.

March 29–April 8   Hanoi but not Peking attends the Twenty-Third Congress of the Soviet Communist Party in Moscow.

April 7   The United States announces recovery of a missing twenty-megaton hydrogen bomb lost in January off the Spanish coast after a B-52 collided with a jet tanker.

April 9   South Vietnamese Buddhists announce a campaign to topple the government of Premier Nguyen Cao Ky.

April 10   The Security Council votes to strengthen its oil embargo against Rhodesia by permitting the British Royal Navy to take measures to enforce it.

April 14   Nguyen Cao Ky approves elections for a constituent assembly that will draw up a new constitution.

May 5   A thirty-two-member committee created to draft a South Vietnamese election law convenes in Saigon.

May 7   Romanian President Nicholas Ceausescu defends the Romanian policy of independence from the Soviet Union.

May 12   In a New York City speech, Thant explains that the UN is ill suited to deal with the situation in Vietnam because only one of the parties to the conflict, the United States, is a member of the world organization.

May 13   China charges that U.S. planes entered Chinese territory and shot down a Chinese plane on May 12.

May 15   Troops loyal to Nguyen Cao Ky seize the South Vietnamese city of Danang from soldiers loyal to Buddhist dissidents.

May 23   The Security Council defeats a resolution calling on Great Britain to forcibly end Rhodesian independence.

May 24 In a speech to an American audience, Thant calls for talks between the NLF and Washington.

May 28–June 2 Clashes between Ibo and Hausa tribesmen sweep the northern region of Nigeria.

May 29 Indonesia and Malaysia engage in peace talks.

May 30–31 U.S. warplanes stage a record number of air strikes against North Vietnam.

June 3 As part of the emerging cultural revolution, the Chinese press announces the purging of several leading Communist officials.

June 11 McNamara announces that a new U.S. troop buildup will bring American troop strength in South Vietnam to 285,000.

June 19 Communist Party newspapers in Peking publish letters by Defense Minister Lin Piao, calling for increased study of the works of Mao Tse-tung.

June 20 Thant's Three-Point Plan for ending the war in Vietnam includes a cessation of American bombing, de-escalation of the ground fighting, and participation of all parties in peace talks.

June 23 Nguyen Cao Ky's forces seize a Buddhist pagoda in Saigon that has served as a center for antigovernment activity.

June 24 The OAS calls for the withdrawal from Santo Domingo of the Inter-American peace force's remaining troops.

June 29 U.S. aircraft attack oil storage facilities in Hanoi and Haiphong.

July 1 France reasserts national control over all its forces assigned to NATO.

July 2 India accuses Pakistan of building up its forces in Kashmir.

July 5 The Indonesian Congress strips Sukarno of his "President for Life" title.

July 18 The World Court, contending that the plaintiffs have not established "any legal right or interest in the objective matter of their claim,"[7] rejects (8–7) a Liberian-Ethiopian complaint against South Africa's administration of South-West Africa.

July 25–30 Thant visits Moscow to discuss the war in Vietnam and the possible renewal of his term as secretary-general.

July 29   The Ironsi regime is overthrown in Nigeria and replaced by a regime headed by Lieutenant Colonel Yakubu Gawon.

August 10   Pakistan accuses India of an arms buildup along their common border.

August 11   A Malaysian-Indonesian Peace Pact is signed.

August 15   Israel and Syria fight a battle around the Sea of Galilee.

August 18   Red Guards loyal to Mao riot in the first of a series of violent demonstrations on Peking streets.

August 22   Rusk meets with Thant in New York and claims that U.S. peace efforts in Vietnam are stymied by the recalcitrance of North Vietnam.

August 25   Anglo-Rhodesian talks break down.

September 1   Thant says he will not seek a second term as secretary-general.

September 6   South African Prime Minister Hendrik F. Verwoerd is assassinated in Cape Town.

September 11   South Vietnamese Constituent Assembly elections draw a large turnout.

September 16   China again charges the United States with attacks on its territory.

September 19   Thant announces that he will be willing to extend his term as secretary-general beyond November 3.

September 20   Guyana, formerly British Guiana, joins the UN.

September 22   Ambassador Goldberg, at the UN, offers a bombing halt in return for a North Vietnamese de-escalation of the war.

September 28   Indonesia, with Sukarno stripped of his title and powers, formally rejoins the UN.

October 6   The Hanoi Communist Party newspaper reveals that North Vietnam rejects Thant's proposal calling for a de-escalation of ground combat in the south.

October 12   Goldberg recommends formation of a UN Commission for South-West Africa to facilitate the eventual advent of self-determination in that territory.

October 17 Botswana and Lesotho are admitted into the UN, bringing the world body's membership to 121.

October 24–25 Johnson and representatives of five other nations fighting in South Vietnam pledge to withdraw their troops from Vietnam within six months from the time North Vietnam ceases its infiltration of the south.

October 25 Guinean Ambassador Marof Achkar, chairman of the UN's Special Committee on Apartheid, charges the United States, France, Japan, and the United Kingdom with encouraging apartheid by trading with South Africa.

October 26 The General Assembly votes to condemn apartheid in South Africa, terminates South Africa's mandate, over South-West Africa (Namibia), and calls on Pretoria to transfer authority over Namibia to the UN.

October 27 China successfully tests a missile equipped with a nuclear warhead.

November 1 The General Assembly votes to extend Thant's term until the end of its session.

November 3 Egypt and Syria restore diplomatic relations broken after the breakup of the UAR in 1961 and establish a joint military command.

November 4 A Soviet veto defeats a Security Council measure calling on Syria and Israel to reduce tensions along their common frontier.

November 13 Israeli forces raid the Jordanian village of Es Samu, an action censured by the Security Council on November 25.

November 17 The General Assembly calls on London, by a vote of 89–2–7, to take all measures, including the use of force, to end the white Rhodesian rebellion.

November 23 Canada proposes to the General Assembly that Communist China replace Taipei on the Security Council but that both governments be represented in the assembly.

November 29 Reflecting concern over China's Cultural Revolution, the annual resolution to seat Peking in place of Taiwan is defeated in the General Assembly (57–46–17), and an Italian resolution to establish a committee to study whether Peking wants to enter the world organization is also defeated (63–34–25).

December 1   West German Chancellor Kurt Georg Kiesinger heads a grand coalition in Bonn uniting the Christian Democratic and Socialist Parties in one government.

December 2   A unanimous General Assembly appoints Thant to a second term to begin January 1, 1967.

December 9   Barbados is admitted into the UN.

December 12   By a vote of 70–13–22, the General Assembly proposes to the Security Council that all states be required to sever relations with Portugal over its policies in Africa.

December 16   The Security Council calls for mandatory sanctions against Rhodesia. The General Assembly calls apartheid a threat to peace and security in Africa.

December 17   The General Assembly chooses Vienna as the permanent headquarters for the newly formed United Nations Industrial Development Organization (UNIDO).

December 19   In a letter to Thant, Goldberg requests that the secretary-general intervene in the war in Vietnam. The General Assembly approves the Outer Space Treaty, banning weapons of mass destruction in outer space.

December 20   The General Assembly votes to end colonial rule on Gibraltar and calls on Spain and Great Britain to negotiate over its eventual status.

December 30   In a reply to Goldberg's letter of December 19, Thant calls for a bombing halt.

1967

January 3–10   Widespread rioting is reported in China as the Cultural Revolution spreads to the industrial and farming sectors.

January 5   A report circulates that Egyptian warplanes killed more than 250 people in a strike against a pro-royalist Yemeni village.

January 7   Jordanian Prime Minister Wafsi Tal charges Nasser with entering into a gentleman's agreement to avoid war with Israel.

January 10   Thant calls for an unconditional halt to U.S. bombing of North Vietnam.

January 11   Syria and Israel clash in the Galilee.

January 23   Red Guard posters announce that Mao has mobilized the army against dissenters.

January 27   Representatives of six countries, including the United States and USSR, sign an agreement banning the deployment of weapons of mass destruction in outer space.

January 31   West Germany and Romania agree to the establishment of full diplomatic relations.

February 13   U.S. bombing of North Vietnam resumes after being suspended for the Tet holiday.

February 14   Fourteen nations sign a treaty banning nuclear weapons in South America.

February 20   French Ambassador Roger Seydoux informs Thant that representatives of the North Vietnamese government will be willing to meet him secretly in Rangoon, and the session is held on March 2.

February 23   Mao orders Red Guards to stop attacking government and party officials.

February 25   A scheduled Syrian-Israeli meeting to deal with border problems in canceled as pointless by General Odd Bull, the head of the United Nations Truce Supervisory Organization (UNTSO).

March 9   The United States reports that American forces in South Vietnam suffered a record number of casualties (1,617) in the week ending March 4.

March 12   The Indonesian Congress formally strips Sukarno of all executive and ceremonial powers and names Suharto acting president.

March 13   A Congo court sentences Moise Tshombe to death in absentia for his role in killing civilians and his proclamation of Katangese independence.

March 14   A Thant aide-mémoire to the government of North Vietnam, South Vietnam, the United States, and the NLF offers new suggestions for ending the conflict.

March 28   Thant makes public his recent peace overtures.

April 2   Arab nationalists in Aden Colony begin general strikes against Great Britain in response to the arrival of a three-man UN team investigating proposed elections and independence for the British colony.

April 6   Six Syrian warplanes are shot down, and Damascus is buzzed in a clash between Israeli and Syrian air forces.

April 19   Former German Chancellor Konrad Adenauer, who presided over West Germany's growth into an industrial giant, dies.

April 21   A military coup in Greece overthrows the civilian government, initiating the seven-year rule of the colonels.

April 28   General William Westmoreland, commander of U.S. forces in South Vietnam, addresses the U.S. Congress and asserts that American forces will prevail.

DOCUMENT TWO

U Thant and Vietnam: Remarks to Speakers Research Committee, New York, May 10, 1967

Criticisms have been leveled at the United Nations for some time with regard to its obvious inability to become involved effectively in the greatest crisis facing mankind since the end of the Second World War. I am referring to the war in Vietnam. I have explained why the United Nations has not been able to be involved in that crisis and I have explained also why the United Nations, at least for the moment, as it is constituted at present, is not in a position to deal effectively with this tragic situation. Of course, I do not want to reiterate the reasons I have adduced on previous occasions, in view of the shortness of time. I just want to say that—taking account of the history of the last few years— the United Nations would not have been able to do anything with regard to the solution of the West Irian problem, for instance, if either the Netherlands or Indonesia had not been a Member of the United Nations at that time. The United Nations would not have been able to do anything in Kashmir in the past eighteen years if either Pakistan or India had not been a Member of the United Nations. The United Nations would not be able to do anything in the Middle East, through the United Nations Truce Supervision Organization in Palestine or the United Nations Emergency Force, if either Israel or the Arab states were not Members of the United Nations. The explanation is as simple as that.

Another criticism leveled at the United Nations for some time, which has come to my knowledge is that the 122 Member states are spending every year more than $100 million for the United Nations. The question has been posed: Is it worthwhile? My answer is this. If we take into consideration the various activities of the United Nations, not only in the political field, but also in the economic and social fields and in the colonial field, my conviction is that, even if the United Nations had not been able to do anything in the political field in the past twenty-two years, it is still worthwhile. Of course, that is not so. The United Nations has been able to do many things in the political field also. Even if the United Nations had not been able to do anything in the economic and social fields—which is, of course, far from true—again it is worthwhile. Even if the United Nations had not been able to do anything in the colonial field, that is, in facilitating the emergence of nonindependent states to independent status, it is worthwhile. But we have to consider this in the context of other developments.

To cite one very obvious example, we come back to the tragic situation in Vietnam again. I think it worth remembering that what the actual combatants are spending in the Vietnam war in two days is equivalent to what the United Nations has been spending in one whole year. I think it is a very obvious illustration of the need for a real perspective in regard to the expenditure of funds by the Member states vis-à-vis the United Nations and other activities. According to a rough calculation, the amount of money spent by the combatants in the Vietnam war— apart from the tremendous destruction, devastation, and loss of life, and only in terms of the money spent by the actual combatants—for two days is equivalent to the amount of money spent by 122 Members of the United Nations for 365 days. In other words, the money that is being spent in Vietnam for one whole year is sufficient to operate the United Nations for another 185 years. I think we should look at this problem from such relative perspectives.

I believe I would be doing an injustice to this distinguished gathering, particularly to my colleagues, the permanent representatives and the members of this Committee, if I did not make even a brief reference to the war in Vietnam. I have been stating my views for the past three and a half years, as you are all aware, and I still maintain the same views. First of all, I am convinced that cessation of the bombing of North Vietnam is a prerequisite to meaningful talks. I have maintained this since February 7, 1965, when North Vietnam was bombed for the first time—we are told, in retaliation for an attack on Pleiku.

While on this subject, I want to draw a demarcation line in the Vietnam war. I want to divide the Vietnam war into two phases. The first phase is prior to February 7, 1965. The second phase is post-February 7, 1965. In the first phase, as you are no doubt aware and as many governments are no doubt aware now, Hanoi showed a willingness to talk. That was in the first phase, prior to February 7, 1965. In the second phase, post-February 7, 1965, Hanoi has not shown any willingness to talk. So the explanation is obvious. It is not only obvious, it has been reiterated by leaders of Hanoi from time to time, particularly in the Foreign Minister's statement of January 28, 1967, that so long as the bombing of North Vietnam is going on there will be no talks. Of course, the argument against this is that the cessation of bombing of North Vietnam will increase the infiltration rate to the South. That is the argument, but if we consider this problem objectively, in true perspective, we have to come to the conclusion that that is not the case.

You will perhaps recall that, in January 1965, one official estimate of the strength of North Vietnamese regulars in South Vietnam was about 10,000. Two years later, two years after the bombing of North Vietnam— that is, in February 1967—one official estimate of the strength of North Vietnamese regulars in South Vietnam was 50,000. Of course, the government in North Vietnam has never accepted these figures, but that is beside the point. The point I want to bring home is the fact that after two years of bombing of North Vietnam the strength of the North Vietnamese regulars in the South is estimated to have increased by five times.

You will also remember that even the Secretary of Defense, Mr. McNamara, said last January—and his statement is in the official records— that the bombing of North Vietnam did not and does not have the desired result of stopping or reducing the rate of infiltration from the North to the South. So my point is that, although the cessation of the bombing of North Vietnam might have certain limited risks, the alternative is far more dangerous and far more disastrous. That is why I have been advocating—and many people and many governments have also been advocating—the taking of that limited risk and the cessation of the bombing of North Vietnam. Of course, "unconditionally" or "indefinitely" do not have any meaning for me. It does not mean that the bombing has to be stopped for one year or ten years or one hundred years. I have been saying that for the past three or four months that I am convinced that, once there is a cessation of bombing in North Vietnam, there will be talks in a few weeks' time. So I want to take this opportunity of reiterating my appeal from this platform that the first step to achieve peace in Vietnam is the cessation of bombing of North Vietnam.

I also want to reiterate another point: that the objective of all the combatants in Vietnam should be a return to the essentials of the Geneva Agreements of 1954. On this, of course, there is no dispute. As you will remember, last month I visited five Asian countries, and in the course of my visits I had very useful discussions with the leaders of their governments. Of course, Vietnam dominated our talks, naturally, and all the five governments—of Ceylon, India, Nepal, Afghanistan, and Pakistan—agree with me on certain basic concepts regarding the Vietnam war. First of all, all five of those governments agree that the cessation of bombing of North Vietnam should be the initial step which could lead to meaningful talks. Second, all five of those governments agree that military methods will not bring about a peaceful solution of the problem. Only diplomatic and political methods of discussion and negotiation can and will bring about peaceful solutions. All five governments also agree that in the final analysis the people of Vietnam should solve their problems without foreign interference. All five governments also agree that the objective should be the implementation of the Geneva Agreements of 1954.

I hope that these few remarks of mine will be relevant to the occasion, because I know your sentiments, your approach to the problem, your obsession with this very tragic problem, and I can assure you, Ladies and Gentlemen, that I will never cease to endeavor to contribute toward a peaceful solution of this very tragic conflict.
UN Press Release SG/SM/707

May 11   Thant warns that in Vietnam the world is "witnessing the initial phase of World War III."[8] Thant condemns Arab raids into Israel and claims that they reflect a more specialized training than heretofore displayed by the Arabs, while Israeli Prime Minister Levi Eshkol warns that Israel will use air power in its continuing border dispute with Syria. Great Britain renews its bid for full membership in the EEC.

May 13   The Soviets warn that Israel is massing for an attack on Syria, but UNTSO confirms the Israeli position that no attack appears imminent.

May 14   Egyptian General Mahmoud Fawzi travels to Syria to consult with Syrian officials and to check reports that Syria is about to be attacked by Israel.

May 15   Egyptian forces pass through Cairo, and the next day Nasser declares a state of emergency.

May 16   The UNEF commander, General Indar Jit Rikhye, informs Thant that the Egyptian government has requested the removal of UNEF from its Sinai border posts.

May 17   After meeting with representatives of UNEF states, Thant asks the Egyptian ambassador to request that Cairo reconsider its demand for the removal of UNEF.

May 18 Egyptian forces move on UNEF contingents, and Israel refuses to accept UNEF on its territory. Thant receives Egypt's formal request that UNEF be removed and informs the UNEF Advisory Committee that he intends to comply. He alerts the General Assembly the next day.

May 19 The General Assembly establishes a UN Committee for South-West Africa to administer the territory of Namibia.

May 20 Twelve Arab League states sign a resolution supporting the UAR's military action.

May 21 As the UAR mobilizes 100 thousand army reserves, Prime Minister Eshkol announces that his government has completed a partial mobilization of reserves.

May 22 As Thant leaves for talks in Cairo, Eshkol denounces the secretary-general's hasty withdrawal of UNEF. The prime minister claims that only the Advisory Committee should have had the right to make such a decision. Nasser closes the Straits of Tiran, thus blocking the Gulf of Aqaba and Israel's port city of Eilat.

May 23 President Johnson asserts that the Strait of Tiran is an international waterway and criticizes Thant's decision to comply with Cairo's ultimatum on UNEF.

May 23–25 Thant meets with Egyptian officials in Cairo in efforts to defuse the crisis.

May 24 Egypt mines the Strait of Tiran. Israeli Foreign Minister Abba Eban meets with French President de Gaulle, who warns the Israeli that his country should not strike at the Arabs first.

May 24–30 The Security Council meets to discuss the Middle East crisis, but a United States-Soviet deadlock prevents the council from acting.

May 25–26 Eban meets with Johnson and Rusk in Washington.

May 26 Syria and Iraq sign an agreement calling for bilateral action against Israel. Nasser warns that an Israeli attack will lead to a war aimed at destroying the State of Israel.

May 27 Thant, claiming that Nasser has assured him that Egypt will not initiate hostilities, calls for a "breathing spell" in the Middle East crisis, urges Israel to join the Egyptian-Israel Mixed Armistice

Commission, which it has boycotted since 1956, and calls on Israel and Syria to resume meetings of the Israel-Syria Mixed Armistice Commission.

May 28 Nasser rules out any political settlement that fails to repatriate Palestinian refugees. Eshkol, in a radio address to his nation, asserts that he is pursuing a diplomatic solution to the crisis.

May 29 The Security Council supports Thant's call for a breathing spell. Goldberg calls for freedom of navigation through the Straits of Tiran, but the Egyptians claim that the Gulf of Aqaba is not an international waterway.

May 30 Jordan and Egypt sign a defense pact. Biafra declares its independence from Nigeria.

June 1 General Moshe Dayan is named the new Israeli defense minister as the Gahal coalition, a collection of right wing parties headed by Menachem Begin, becomes part of a national unity government.

June 3 In his "Notes on Withdrawal of United Nations Emergency Force," Thant justifies his decision to comply with the Egyptian ultimatum on UNEF.

June 5 Israel destroys Arab air forces in a surprise raid. As fighting breaks out in the Sinai and along the Israeli-Jordanian frontier, Egypt, Jordan, Algeria, Iraq, Syria, Sudan, and Kuwait declare themselves at war with Israel. France suspends arms shipments to the Middle East.

June 6 The Security Council votes for an immediate cease-fire in the Arab-Israeli war, as Russia calls for Israel's withdrawal from occupied territories. The UAR closes the Suez Canal and breaks diplomatic relations with the United States. Kuwait and Iraq suspend oil shipments to the United States and Great Britain.

June 7 Fighting breaks out on the Syrian front. The Israelis seize the Gaza Strip from Egypt and East Jerusalem and all Jordanian territory on the west bank of the Jordan River. Jordan accepts the UN cease-fire call, while Israel promises to observe the cease-fire in return for Arab compliance. Israel claims victory in the entire Sinai Peninsula.

June 8 Claiming that the assault is an accident, Israel attacks the U.S. electronics ship, the USS *Liberty*. A defeated Egypt accepts the UN call for a cease-fire.

June 9   Heavy fighting breaks out between Syria and Israel. Nasser resigns the Egyptian presidency, a resignation retracted the next day in response to large pro-Nasser demonstrations in Cairo. Israeli forces penetrate twelve miles into Syria, capture the entire Golan Heights, and force Syria to accept the UN cease-fire. The Soviet Union and other East bloc countries break diplomatic relations with Israel.

June 14   The Security Council votes down a Soviet resolution calling for condemnation of Israel and for its withdrawal to the 1949 armistice lines. The council adopts a resolution calling on Israel to facilitate the return of Palestinian refugees.

June 17–July 5   The General Assembly meets in emergency session to consider the Middle East crisis. It adopts two resolutions, one dealing with the treatment of Palestinian refugees, the other opposing Israel's unification of the Israeli and Jordanian sectors of Jerusalem.

June 19   Johnson issues a Middle East peace plan. The Security Council extends the life of UNFICYP by six months.

DOCUMENT THREE

U Thant Addresses the General Assembly on the Middle Eastern War in New York on June 20, 1967

During the last five and a half years I have never had reason to comment upon a statement made to this Assembly by a representative of any government. But I feel it necessary to reply very briefly to certain statements made by the Foreign Minister of Israel [Abba Eban] in his address to the General Assembly on the morning of June 19 with regard to my decision to comply with the request of the United Arab Republic for the withdrawal of UNEF.

Mr. Eban's remarks on this subject were highly critical, but it is not for that reason that I speak now. I personally welcome criticism when it is just, based on fact, and does not obscure or ignore essential facts. The concern behind this intervention is that the picture which Mr. Eban gave yesterday can be very damaging to the United Nations with regard to its peace-keeping function, past and present. I seek only to restore in that picture the balance which the facts warrant.

I have to say at the outset that I was rather surprised at the breadth and vigor of the Foreign Minister's dissatisfaction with the withdrawal decision, since in a quite recent meeting we had discussed that issue and at that time I had given a rather full explanation of just why the decision I took had to be taken in the way that it was and I heard no such reaction as Mr. Eban projected to the General Assembly yesterday; nothing like it. I wish now to say that I do not accept as having validity Mr. Eban's strictures on this matter.

My position on the decision to withdraw UNEF and the reasons for it have been set forth clearly in reports which I have submitted to the General Assembly and the Security Council.

Beyond this, I need make only the following specific comments.

The Foreign Minister of Israel, I note, made no mention in his critical analysis of my decision of certain decisive facts and factors with which he is certainly very well acquainted. Mr. Eban must know, for example, that the indispensable basis for the effective buffer function exercised by the United Nations Emergency Force for more than a decade was the voluntary decision of the government of the United Arab Republic to keep its troops away from the line, with only United Nations troops in the buffer zone which was exclusively on the United Arab Republic side of the line.

On the other hand, the Foreign Minister also knows, I am sure, that Israel extended no such cooperation on the United Nations Emergency Force to the United Nations; that, despite the intent of the General Assembly resolution that United Nations troops should be stationed on both sides of the line, Israel always and firmly refused to accept them on Israel territory on the valid grounds of national sovereignty. There was, of course, national sovereignty on the other side of the line as well.

There can be no doubt that it would have been a helpful factor of considerable importance if Israel had at any time accepted the deployment of the United Nations Emergency Force also on its side of the line. I may report in this connection that prior to receiving the United Arab Republic request for withdrawal and prior to giving my reply to it, I had raised with the permanent representative of Israel to the United Nations the possibility of stationing elements of the United Nations Emergency Force on the Israel side of the line. I was told that the idea was completely unacceptable to Israel. Moreover, for all of those ten years Israel's troops regularly patrolled alongside the line and now and again created provocations by violating it.

Finally, may I say that Mr. Eban cannot help but know that the government of the United Arab Republic had never accepted any limitation or restriction with regard to the exercise of its sovereign powers concerning the presence of the United Nations Emergency Force on its territory. It can also be emphasized that there was no limitation of any kind on the right of the United Arab Republic to move its troops up to the line at any time with the inevitable result of immediately making academic the question of withdrawal of the United Nations Emergency Force or its continued presence.

In this regard, Mr. Eban referred to the alert order issued to the Egyptian troops on the morning of May 17. He failed to mention, however, that it was on that same morning that Egyptian troops began to move up to the line, thus eliminating the buffer zone, as I have previously reported to this body.

I have noticed Mr. Eban's picturesque simile of the "fire brigade which vanishes from the scene as soon as the first smoke and flames appear!" Mr. Eban would agree, I am sure, that for more than ten years the United Nations Emergency Force had been remarkably effective in preventing clashes along the line and in extinguishing the flames of the raids across the line, the terror of the fedayeen. But I am sure that Mr. Eban did not mean what he seemed to imply, namely that the United Nations Emergency Force was on Egyptian territory to stay as long as the United Nations saw fit and to fight against United Arab Republic troops, if necessary, to prevent them from moving up to line in their own territory.

On the matter of consultation, Mr. Eban should know that I did engage in consultations before taking my decision, to the full extent required of me and even somewhat more.

I conclude these observations by quoting a statement on the same subject made in the Security Council on June 3, 1967, by the permanent representative of Israel:

The crisis in the Middle East erupted without warning on May 16 when an Egyptian general sent an ultimatum to the Commander of UNEF. At the same time as he asked for the removal of the United Nations Force, he moved his own forces into the positions held by the United Nations. The course of events that followed is by now common knowledge and well documented in the reports of the Secretary-General.

The Secretary-General tried to prevent the crisis from getting out of hand. He failed. It was not his fault . . .

In view of the fact that important questions have been raised before the General Assembly on the withdrawal of the United Nations Emergency Force, I wish now to inform the Assembly that it is my intention to issue within a day or two a report giving a full account of my actions on this matter.

General Assembly Official Records, Fifth Emergency Special Session, 1527th meeting

June 21 De Gaulle accuses Israel of starting the war with the Arab states.

June 23, 25 Johnson and Soviet Premier Kosygin meet in Glassboro, New Jersey. No major, substantive breakthroughs take place, although the president reports some progress on arms control.

June 28 Israel formally unites the Israeli and Jordanian sectors of Jerusalem.

June 30 An airplane carrying Moise Tshombe is hijacked and diverted to Algeria, where Tshombe is incarcerated while Algeria considers the Congolese government's request for his extradition.

July 1–9 As Israeli and Egyptian forces exchange fire across the Suez Canal, the Security Council meets to discuss the fighting.

July 6 Fighting breaks out in Nigeria between the central government and Ibo tribesmen determined to establish their independence from the central government.

July 11 Israel agrees to Thant's proposal calling for the stationing of UNTSO observers along the Suez Canal.

July 12 The General Assembly votes a second resolution calling on Israel to rescind its unification of the two sectors of Jerusalem.

July 21 The special General Assembly session on the Middle East convenes again.

July 24 On a visit to Canada, de Gaulle calls for a "free" Quebec, thus roiling Canadian-French relations.

July 27 The International Committee of the Red Cross charges Egypt with the use of poison gas in the Yemen war.

August 1 The celebration of the fortieth anniversary of the People's Liberation Army in Peking is notable for the absence of key officials, among them head of state Liu Shao-chi, caught up in the Cultural Revolution.

August 15 Thant appoints Swiss diplomat Dr. Ernesto Thalmann to investigate the effects of the Israeli annexation of East Jerusalem on the Arab inhabitants of the city.

August 16 After several days of anti-Soviet violence in Peking, *Pravda* prints a long article attacking the Chinese leadership.

August 24 The United States and USSR submit to the Eighteen Nation Disarmament Committee in Geneva a draft treaty to curb the proliferation of nuclear weapons.

August 25 Hanoi, after weeks of stepped-up American bombing, evacuates nonessential citizens from the capital city.

August 29–September 1   Arab heads of state meet in Khartoum and issue three "nos": 1. No peace with Israel; 2. No negotiations with Israel; 3. No recognition of Israel.

September 1   In an effort to curb Red Guard lawlessness, the Peking Municipal Revolutionary Committee orders severe punishments for looters and asks people to return to work. A UN committee condemns a British plan to conduct a plebiscite on Gibraltar and affirms the 1966 General Assembly resolution calling for negotiations between Spain and Great Britain on Gibraltar's status.

September 4   Michigan Governor George Romney, a front-runner for the 1968 Republican presidential nomination, announces that on a 1965 visit to South Vietnam he received "the greatest brainwashing that anyone can get."[9] The remark hurts his campaign, and Romney is forced to pull out of the race on February 28, 1968.

September 6   Raoul Prebisch assails the Kennedy Round June 30 accord lowering tariffs on 60,000 items valued at $40 billion annually. He claims that the agreement favors developed countries because most of the items are "industrial" rather than "primary" products.

September 7   Nguyen Van Thieu is elected president and Nguyen Cao Ky vice president in South Vietnamese elections observed by a group of Americans.

September 10   In a British-sponsored plebiscite, Gibraltarians overwhelmingly favor remaining under British sovereignty.

September 11–14   Indian and Chinese troops exchange gunfire on the border between Tibet and Sikkim.

September 14   McNamara announces that the United States will deploy a "light" antiballistic missile (ABM) to protect against an accidental or Chinese attack.

September 19   In his annual report, Thant admits, "The international political situation has not only not improved; it has in fact deteriorated considerably."[10]

September 26   Hanoi rejects Johnson's latest peace offer, made in a speech in San Antonio.

October 8   Ernesto (Che) Guevara, the Cuban revolutionary leader, is killed in a clash with Bolivian army troops.

October 12   Secretary of State Dean Rusk sets off a furor by referring to the Chinese Communists as a "yellow peril."

October 21   The Israeli destroyer *Elath* is sunk by missiles fired from Egypt.

October 24   Israel retaliates for the *Elath* sinking by launching a three-hour shelling of Egyptian oil installations in the port city of Suez.

October 25   The Security Council calls on Israel and Egypt to observe the UN-sponsored cease-fire.

November 2   Goldberg says that the United States favors the inclusion of the NLF in peace talks. The General Assembly, by a vote of 92–2–18, condemns Great Britain for not doing enough to topple the white minority government in Rhodesia.

November 7   The General Assembly approves the "Declaration on the Elimination of Discrimination against Women."

November 14   A Canadian newspaper reports that 20,000 Nigerians and Biafrans have died in the civil war in Nigeria.

November 15–16   Communal clashes on Cyprus threaten war between Greece and Turkey.

November 17   The General Assembly, by a vote of 82–7–21, condemns Portuguese policies in Africa and calls on Portugal's NATO allies to prevent the sale and supply of arms to Lisbon.

November 18   Britain devalues the pound by 14.3 percent because of a widening balance of payments deficit.

November 22   The Security Council approves British-sponsored Resolution 242 as a basis for a Middle East peace and urges the secretary-general to appoint a special representative to the region.

November 23   Thant names Swedish diplomat Gunnar Jarring as his Middle East negotiator.

November 25   The Security Council calls on all sides in the Cyprus conflict to exercise restraint.

November 28   The South Arabian Federation, renamed the People's Republic of South Yemen, achieves its independence. A resolution to expel the Nationalists and seat the Communist Chinese is defeated in the General Assembly by a vote of 58–45–17.

November 29   Robert McNamara announces his intention to step down as U.S. secretary of defense and assume the presidency of the World Bank.

December 1   In resolution of yet another crisis over Cyprus, Greece and Turkey sign an agreement ending the threat of war between the two nations.

December 7   The General Assembly condemns (91–21–17) colonial exploitation of peoples and natural resources in the third world.

December 8   The General Assembly (77–0–29) calls for a ban on the use of nuclear weapons. The United States, Great Britain, and France, which see nuclear weapons as an important deterrent to Soviet aggression, are among those nations who abstain.

December 13   An impatient assembly, now dominated by third world nations, asks the Security Council to take more effective measures against apartheid.

December 14   The People's Republic of South Yemen is admitted into the United Nations. The General Assembly calls on its specialized agencies (81–2–18) to extend aid to people fighting against colonialism.

December 16   The General Assembly condemns South Africa for not abiding by previous resolutions on South-West Africa.

December 19   The General Assembly votes (105–0) to extend emergency aid to all persons displaced during the 1967 Arab-Israeli war. The General Assembly (73–19) condemns the Gibraltar plebiscite as a contravention of previous assembly resolutions. The General Assembly urges the Eighteen Nation Disarmament Committee to complete a treaty to prevent the proliferation of nuclear weapons.

December 28   Turkish Cypriots form a "transitional administration" to have jurisdiction over the island's Turkish community.

1968

January 1   North Vietnam's foreign minister says Hanoi will begin talks with the United States after Washington agrees to an unconditional bombing halt.

January 5   The American troop presence in South Vietnam reaches

486,000 men. Alexander is Dubček elected first secretary of the Czech Communist Party and launches a reform movement.

January 8   Israel and Jordan fight in their heaviest clash since the 1967 war.

January 12   The United States and Cambodia sign an agreement designed to prevent Cambodia from becoming involved in the war in Vietnam.

January 15   South Vietnamese President Thieu expresses regret at American peace feelers.

January 18   The United States and USSR submit a nonproliferation pact, with new inspection provisions, to the Eighteen Nation Disarmament Committee in Geneva.

January 23   The U.S. intelligence ship *Pueblo* is seized by North Korean vessels in the Sea of Japan, with Pyongyang claiming that the ship was seized within its twelve-mile territorial sea boundary.

January 24   Secretary of State Rusk calls the *Pueblo* seizure an act of war, but North Korea broadcasts an alleged confession by the ship's commander, Lloyd Bucher, acknowledging that the vessel had deliberately violated North Korean waters.

January 26–27   The Security Council meets to hear a U.S. complaint against North Korea about the *Pueblo* seizure, but the council adjourns for private negotiations.

January 30   Communists launch the "Tet" offensive against key targets throughout South Vietnam, including the U.S. embassies in Saigon, Hué, Da Lat, and Quang Tri. The United States reports on February 6, that 21,330 communist troops and 546 Americans have died in a week of fighting that reversed initial Communist gains. The Tet offensive becomes a turning point in the U.S. public's support for the war. Israeli and Egyptian guns fire across the Suez Canal and prevent the implementation of a UN-sponsored plan to free vessels stranded in the waterway.

February 1–March 29   Delegates from 132 nations meet in New Delhi for an UNCTAD Conference characterized by deep divisions between developed and developing states. UNCTAD's secretary-general, Dr. Raul Prebisch, in his report to Thant on May 12, assails the industrial nations for their lack of commitment to the developing states and says that the conference achieved "very limited positive results."

February 8   Thant meets with North Vietnamese officials in Hanoi and obtains their pledge to participate in peace talks in return for an unconditional American bombing halt.

February 15–16   Israeli and Jordanian troops clash in an intense tank and artillery duel.

February 21   Thant discusses his Asian trip with President Johnson in Washington.

February 24   In Hué, Allied forces recapture the Imperial Palace seized by the Communists during the Tet offensive.

February 25   Archbishop Makarios is elected to a second five-year term as president in Cyprus.

February 27   The Trucial States, Bahrein, and Qatar agree to form a union upon Great Britain's departure from the area, scheduled for 1971.

February 28   Saudi Arabia threatens to resume aid to Yemeni royalists because of Soviet Union, Syrian, and South Yemeni assistance to the republicans.

March 7   UAR Foreign Minister Mahmud Riad tells UN Middle East peace envoy Gunnar Jarring that Egypt will not meet with Israeli representatives.

March 18   In New York Thant opens a UN conference on the legal status of the seabed.

March 21   Fifteen thousand Israeli troops enter Jordan in a retaliatory raid against Arab guerrilla bases in Karameh, Jordan.

March 22   General Westmoreland is named chief of staff of the United States Army.

March 23   Eastern European Communist Party leaders meet in Dresden where reformist leader Alexander Dubček is called upon to explain his party's liberal policies in Czechoslovakia.

March 24   The UN Security Council condemns the Israeli raid into Jordan and all acts of violence in violation of the cease-fire.

March 31   Johnson orders a partial bombing halt of North Vietnam and shocks the world by pulling out of the race for the 1968 Democratic Party presidential nomination.

April 1   A joint United States-South Vietnamese force lifts the siege of the American marine base at Khesanh.

April 3   The United States and North Vietnam agree to face-to-face talks on ending their war.

April 4   American civil rights leader, the Reverend Dr. Martin Luther King Jr., is assassinated in Memphis, Tennessee.

April 6   Justice Minister Pierre Elliott Trudeau is named head of the Canadian Liberal Party and is sworn in as new prime minister on April 20.

April 13   U.S. officials announce news of a new Communist drive in Laos.

April 17   The UN Council for South-West Africa abandons its efforts to establish authority over the disputed territory of Namibia when South Africa prevents the twenty-six-member committee from entering the territory.

April 19   North Vietnam rejects sites proposed by the United States for holding talks and proposes Warsaw instead.

April 24   Mauritius is admitted into the UN.

April 25   George Ball replaces Goldberg at the UN.

May 2   The Security Council unanimously passes a resolution condemning an Israeli military parade in Jerusalem.

May 3   The United States and North Vietnam agree on Paris as a site for negotiations.

May 3–5   Dubček visits Moscow for talks on Czechoslovakia's reform movement.

May 6   Representatives of Nigeria and Biafra meet in London to discuss a civil war that has produced widespread deaths, starvation, and displacement.

May 9   Israel and Egypt agree to meet with Jarring in New York.

May 10   The Paris Peace Conference opens.

May 13   Thant calls for an American bombing halt.

May 14   Waves of antigovernment strikes fanned by students and workers break out in France, threatening the de Gaulle government.

May 21   The Security Council, with the United States and Canada abstaining, opposes Israel's administrative unification of the Israeli and Jordanian sectors of Jerusalem.

May 22   The Gaullist government in France survives a censure vote in the General Assembly.

May 24   De Gaulle calls for a vote of confidence referendum in June and on May 30 disbands the National Assembly.

May 29   The Security Council unanimously votes a total embargo on trade with and travel to Rhodesia.

May 31   At the Paris Peace Talks, North Vietnam rejects an American call for a reciprocal gesture in return for a unilateral bombing halt.

June 12   The General Assembly approves a ban on the proliferation of nuclear weapons submitted to the Eighteen Nation Disarmament Committee in March.

June 18   The British House of Lords, in a move assailed by Prime Minister Wilson, vetoes the government's decision to implement the Security Council's May 29 resolution imposing an embargo on Rhodesia.

June 23, 30   Gaullists sweep elections for the National Assembly, winning an absolute majority for the first time in the history of the Fifth Republic.

July 1   Johnson announces that Moscow and Washington will discuss limitations on nuclear weapons.

July 6   Thant meets separately in Paris with American and North Vietnamese negotiators.

July 8   Thant blames both the developed and developing states for "what went wrong" at the UNCTAD conference.

July 10   Thant appeals to Biafra to cooperate with Lagos in ending the famine in Nigeria's eastern province.

July 16   The Soviet Union and four of its East bloc allies warn Czechoslovakia that its liberalization drive is unacceptable.

July 17 The Iraqi government falls in a coup led by Major General Ahmad Hassan al-Bakr.

July 22 After the Dubček government rejects a summons to travel to Moscow, the entire Soviet Politburo agrees to travel to Cierna, Czechoslovakia, to confront the Czech Presidium.

July 23 The Soviets announce their largest peacetime military maneuvers, scheduled to be conducted on the border with Czechoslovakia. The Popular Front for the Liberation of Palestine hijacks an Israeli commercial airliner to Algiers. On July 28, Israeli Foreign Minister Eban discloses his visit to the UN to solicit Thant's help in gaining the release of the hijacked airliner and its Israeli captives.

July 29–31 Meetings between the Soviet Politburo and Czech Communist Party Presidium are held and appear to ease the growing East bloc crisis.

July 31 France announces its support of Biafra in the Ibos' war against the Nigerian central government.

August 2 Thant charges Israel with preventing a UN mission from investigating Israeli treatment of Arabs under Israel's rule.

August 3 At a meeting of Soviet, Czech, and selected East bloc officials, a Soviet recommendation that Czechoslovakia be permitted to continue its policies is approved.

August 7 The Republican Party platform declares, "Under existing conditions, we cannot favor the recognition of Communist China or its admission to the United Nations."[11]

August 9–11 Yugoslavian leader Marshal Tito visits Prague in a show of support for the reform movement.

August 16 The Security Council condemns Israel for its August 4 retaliatory strike against Jordan.

August 20–21 Two hundred thousand Soviet, East German, Polish, Hungarian, and Bulgarian troops invade Czechoslovakia. Communist Party officials, including Dubček, are seized and taken to Moscow.

August 22 The USSR vetoes a UN resolution condemning its invasion of Czechoslovakia, with Hungary joining the Soviet Union in opposition and India, Algeria, and Pakistan abstaining.

August 23   Czechoslovakia asks that the Security Council call on Thant to send a representative to ensure the safety of Czechoslovak leaders seized by the Russians.

August 24   Nigeria mounts what it calls the final assault on Biafran rebels.

August 26   Soviet and Czech officials meet in Prague.

August 27   Dubček returns to Prague.

August 29   Czechoslovakia, in response to Soviet pressure, announces de-liberalization, including the reimposition of press censorship.

August 31   Algeria releases the last of the Israeli hostages seized in the July airline hijacking.

September 1   A new presidium is named in Czechoslovakia.

September 6   Swaziland, the last British dependency in Africa, is granted independence.

DOCUMENT FOUR

U Thant Statement to Heads of State and Government of the Organization of African Unity, Algiers, September 13, 1968

If I am unable to conceal my concern about developments stemming from the persistence of colonial and racial policies in Africa, even less can I refrain from expressing my distress and dismay at the mounting toll of destruction, starvation, and loss of life resulting from the tragic fratricidal strife in Nigeria over the past year. As has been verified from impartial sources, a very large number of people, combatants and non-combatants alike, are either dying or undergoing acute suffering; many, particularly children, are dying from, or are on the verge of, starvation. In the name of humanity, it is essential that everything be done to help relieve the impact of this tragic conflict.

It will be recalled that I had the privilege of attending the fourth session of the Assembly of Heads of State and Government of OAU in Kinshasa last year when this issue was discussed. The Assembly adopted a resolution which recognized the "sovereign and territorial integrity of Nigeria" and pledged "faith in the Federal Government." It further recognized the Nigerian crisis as an internal affair and expressed "concern at the tragic and serious situation in Nigeria." This resolution is a basis for my attitude and approach to this problem, and I believe that the OAU should be the most appropriate instrument for the promotion of peace in Nigeria. In order to coordinate efforts and thus undertake the most effective action, it has been agreed by a number of organizations, both governmental and private, that all humanitarian aid to the victims of the Nigerian conflict should be channeled through the International Committee of the Red Cross and this arrangement still stands.

In addition, deeply disturbed by the extent of human suffering involved in the present conflict, and wishing to determine in what way I might contribute toward a solution of the relief problems, I appointed a representative who proceeded to Nigeria over a month ago in order to assist in the relief and humanitarian activities for the civilian victims of the hostilities. Similarly, in coordination with the International Committee of the Red Cross, other organs within the United Nations family have been active in sending supplies and in trying to speed up their distribution to distressed areas. However, it would appear that, apart from the need for larger shipments of relief supplies, there is an urgent need for greater efforts and fuller cooperation on the part of those bearing responsibility in the areas of conflict as regards facilities for the movement and distribution of supplies.

Even so, it goes without saying that there can be no quick end to the present plight of the people in the areas affected by the conflict unless concrete measures are taken with a view to bringing about the cessation of hostilities and the negotiation of arrangements for a permanent settlement. In this connection, I wish to pay tribute to the efforts of the OAU and in particular to its six-member Consultative Committee under whose auspices useful preliminary talks recently took place in Niamey [Niger] and Addis Ababa [Ethiopia]. It is my earnest hope that, pursuant to the practical steps and procedures thus far agreed upon, fruitful negotiations will take place leading to a just solution which would guarantee the security of all the people of Nigeria.

In expressing this hope I am also taking into account the possibility that situations of this type can be easily—as indeed the present situation has been in some circles—misrepresented or exaggerated to the disadvantage of Africa as a whole. Already the Nigerian conflict has created difficulties in relations between African states, and its continuance is bound to affect badly needed cooperation and unity among African countries. As I have said elsewhere, the many problems that the African peoples are facing are by no means all of their own making. Nevertheless, few, if not all of them, can be solved except by the African countries themselves showing the qualities of maturity and restraint which they have often displayed, and using these qualities to engender the greatest spirit of cooperation and willingness to work together,

which is essential to the fulfillment of Africa's destiny. This task is so important that governments and peoples must agree to put aside their differences in the higher interests of Africa and of the world as a whole . . .
UN Press Release SG/SM976

September 14   After heavy artillery fire across the Suez Canal on September 8, the Security Council calls on Israel and the Arab states to observe their truce.

September 19   Malaysia breaks diplomatic relations with the Philippines, after the Philippines claims Sabah.

September 23   Thant irritates the United States by speculating that the General Assembly would support a call for a United States bombing halt in Vietnam.

September 24   Swaziland is admitted as the United Nations' 125th member.

September 26   Thant equates the Soviet invasion of Czechoslovakia with the U.S. invasion of the Dominican Republic.

September 27   The Security Council votes that Israel be asked to allow Thant's representatives to observe its treatment of Arabs firsthand. France excludes Great Britain from the Common Market.

October 3–4   After talks in Moscow, Czech Communist leaders agree to end their liberalization policies and to permit Warsaw Pact troops to remain in their country indefinitely.

October 8   West German and Soviet foreign ministers Willy Brandt and Andrei Gromyko confer at the UN in the first high-level meeting between representatives of the two countries since 1962.

October 9–13   British Prime Minister Wilson and white Rhodesian leader Ian Smith meet aboard a British warship in unsuccessful talks aimed at ending the Rhodesian rebellion.

October 16   Soviet Premier Aleksei Kosygin flies to Prague to sign a treaty allowing Soviet troops to remain on Czech territory.

October 25   The General Assembly calls on Great Britain to deny Rhodesia its independence unless a government based on the principle of majority rule is first formed.

October 31   In the wake of new fighting, Israeli commandos strike at a transformer station and two bridges three hundred miles from Cairo. China's chief of state, Liu Shao-chi, is expelled from the Communist Party.

November 1   Five days before U.S. presidential elections, Johnson suspends all bombing of North Vietnam, a concession designed to allow South Vietnam and the NLF to participate in the Paris Peace Talks.

November 5   Richard M. Nixon is elected thirty-seventh president of the United States.

November 7   The General Assembly, with Washington and London abstaining, overwhelmingly calls on Great Britain to forcibly eliminate the Rhodesian government.

November 11   Thant appears before a committee of the General Assembly to call for renewal of the mandate for the United Nations Relief and Works Agency for Palestine Refugees in the Middle East (UNRWA) and a "just settlement" for the refugees.

November 12   During a Saigon visit, Secretary of Defense Clark Clifford announces that the United States will participate in Vietnam peace talks even without South Vietnam. Equatorial Guinea becomes the 126th state to join the United Nations.

November 19   By a vote of 58–44–23, the General Assembly defeats a resolution calling for the expulsion of Nationalist China and its replacement by Peking.

November 26   Saigon agrees to attend the Paris Peace Talks.

November 29   By a vote of 85–3–15, the General Assembly condemns Portugal's colonial policy in Africa.

December 2   Harvard Professor Henry A. Kissinger is named President Nixon's special assistant for national security affairs. By a vote of 85–2–14, the General Assembly condemns apartheid and criticizes South Africa's "trading partners" for encouraging Pretoria's resistance to the UN.

December 9   Nixon representative, William Scranton, on a tour of the Middle East, calls for a more "even-handed" U.S. policy in the region, provoking Israeli protests.

December 12   Malaysia and the Philippines agree to resume diplomatic relations and suspend for at least one year their dispute over Sabah.

December 13   As an "important question" requiring a two-thirds vote in its favor, an Afro-Asian resolution calling for the expulsion of South Africa from UNCTAD fails in the General Assembly by a tally of 55–33–28. Most Western governments oppose the resolution, while Communist bloc states abstain.

December 16   The General Assembly calls on Great Britain to terminate its rule over Gibraltar by October 1, 1969, and to negotiate with Spain over the disputed territory's final status. By a vote of 96–2–16, the General Assembly recommends to the Security Council that it take action to force South Africa out of South-West Africa.

December 20   Nixon names Charles Yost to be Washington's new ambassador to the UN.

December 22   North Korea releases the *Pueblo* crew.

December 24–25   Three American astronauts circle the moon in the *Apollo 8* spacecraft.

December 28   In retaliation for an Arab terrorist attack on an Israeli aircraft in Athens on December 26, Israeli commandos raid the Beirut Airport and destroy thirteen civilian airplanes.

December 30   The UN's first secretary-general, Trygve Lie, dies in Norway at age seventy-two.

December 31   The Security Council unanimously condemns Israel for its Beirut raid.

1969

January 3   Thant appeals to the leaders of the USSR, United States, France, and Great Britain to meet on ways of easing Middle East tensions.

January 7   France bans the sale or shipment of all arms and spare parts to Israel.

January 8   *The New York Times* publishes a draft of a new Chinese Communist Party constitution designating Lin Piao as Mao's successor.

January 10 A Soviet peace plan, calling for the complete withdrawal of Israel from territories seized during the 1967 war, is published in a Beirut newspaper.

January 17 France proposes a "Big Four" meeting on the Middle East.

January 18 South Vietnam and the NLF participate in expanded Paris peace negotiations.

January 20 Nixon is inaugurated as U.S. president. The Soviets announce that they are prepared to begin talks on containing the number of nuclear weapons in the superpowers' arsenals.

January 27 Thant expresses shock as Baghdad publicly hangs fourteen Iraqis, including nine Jews, as Israeli spies. Nixon announces his opposition to the admission of Red China to the United Nations.

January 28 Thant blames Biafran leaders for the widespread famine in Nigeria and defers to the OAU demand that the United Nations and member states not become involved in Nigeria's civil war.

January 30 North Vietnam rejects a U.S. proposal calling for the restoration of the neutrality of the demilitarized zone (DMZ) between North and South Vietnam. Secretary of Defense Melvin Laird endorses the Sentinel ABM system, first proposed by President Johnson.

February 5–6 The "Big Four" hold preliminary meetings to consider holding a Middle East peace conference.

February 10 In an interview published in *Newsweek*, Nasser unveils a five-point peace plan, including a call for Israeli withdrawal from occupied territories, a declaration of nonbelligerency, freedom of navigation in international waterways, and a just solution to the Palestinian problem.

February 19 Israel's UN Ambasssdor Yosef Tekoah submits an informal aide-mémoire to Thant, requesting that the secretary-general ask the governments of Iraq, Jordan, Lebanon, Syria, and the United Arab Republic whether they dissociate themselves from terrorist actions against the State of Israel. Thant, contending that he would only play such a role with the prior consent of the governments involved, refuses the Israeli request.

February 20   The World Court rules in favor of the Federal Republic of Germany in its dispute with Denmark and the Netherlands over their continental-shelf boundaries.

February 21   Terrorist bombs kill two Israelis in a Jewish supermarket in Jerusalem, thus highlighting the changed nature of the Arab threat to Israel in the aftermath of the 1967 war. The anti-Israel initiative shifts from established Arab states to the Palestine Liberation Organization (PLO) and its constituent units. After weeks of antigovernment violence, Pakistani President Mohammad Ayub Khan, in power since October 27, 1958, announces that he will not run in scheduled March 1970 elections.

February 23   Communist forces launch a major offensive throughout Soviet Vietnam.

February 23–March 2   Nixon visits Western Europe on a five-nation tour.

February 26   Israeli Prime Minister Levi Eshkol dies of a heart attack in Jerusalem, and Deputy Premier Yigal Allon becomes acting prime minister.

March 2, 15   Soviet and Chinese forces fight two big battles on the Manchurian border, involving a dispute over custody of islands in the Ussuri River.

March 3   The UN Commission on Human Rights condemns Israeli rule in occupied Arab territories, with Israel dissenting and the United States abstaining.

March 4   Thousands of demonstrators march against the Soviet embassy in Peking.

March 8   Thant dispatches a representative to Equatorial Guinea to resolve a dispute between that nation and Spain.

March 8–9   Israel and Egypt engage in artillery duels across the Suez Canal.

March 10   Thant dispatches UN official Marcial Tamayo to resolve a dispute between Spain and Equatorial Guinea (a former Spanish colony) over the former's deployment of troops to the newly independent country. The situation is resolved and all Spanish troops withdrawn by the beginning of April 1969.

March 11 In a meeting with Ayub Khan, Sheik Mujibur Rahman, leader of East Pakistan's Awami League, warns that unless the East gains more autonomy from the central government, a separatist movement will evolve.

March 11–14 Hundreds of thousands stage demonstrations against the Soviet embassy in Peking.

March 13 The U.S. Senate ratifies the Nuclear Non-Proliferation Treaty.

March 14 Nixon announces plans to proceed with a revised missile defense system.

March 17 Golda Meir is named Israel's new prime minister.

March 18 In a message to the Eighteen Nation Disarmament Committee, Thant calls on the United States and Soviet Union to negotiate bilateral cuts in nuclear weapons.

March 20 The Security Council, with the United States and Great Britain abstaining, condemns South Africa for its continuing hold on South-West Africa.

March 24 The U.S. proposes that bilateral talks among "Big Four" nations be expanded into a "Big Four" conference on the Middle East. Former Congolese President Joseph Kasavubu dies.

March 25 After months of large-scale protests against his regime, Pakistani President Ayub Khan transfers power to General Agha Mohammed Yahya Khan.

March 27–31 British Prime Minister Harold Wilson visits Lagos to discuss the Biafran war with Nigerian officials.

March 28 Former U.S. President Dwight David Eisenhower dies.

March 28–29 Anti-Soviet demonstrations break out in Prague after a Czech hockey team defeats a Russian squad.

April 1 The Security Council condemns Israel for a raid on a Jordanian town.

April 3 A "Big Four" conference on the Middle East convenes and expresses support for the Jarring mission.

April 10   Israel's ambassador to the UN charges that the "Big Four" conference reduces chances for Jarring's success.

April 11   Jordan's King Hussein visits the United States and offers a six-point plan for peace in the Middle East. Moscow proposes new border talks with Peking.

April 14   The Ninth Congress of the Chinese Communist Party names Lin Piao as Mao's future successor.

April 14–25   Portuguese Premier Marcello Caetano is the first Portuguese leader to visit Lisbon's colonial territories in Africa.

April 17   Dubček resigns as leader of the Czech Communist Party, and hard-liner Gustav Husak is elected to replace him. The Husak regime lasts twenty years. Thant reaffirms his unwillingness to involve the UN in resolving the Nigerian Civil War and tells a press conference audience, "If the United Nations were to give endorsement to the principle of secession there would be no end to the problems besetting many Member states."[12]

April 21   In the wake of widespread religious/political disorders in Northern Ireland, British troops guard public utilities. Thant warns both Israel and Egypt that truce observers will be removed if fighting continues along the Suez Canal.

April 22   In a report to the Security Council, Thant asserts that a "virtual state of active war" exists along the Suez Canal. The council, however, does not meet to deal with the issue.

April 23   Cairo voids its 1967 truce with Israel.

April 28   De Gaulle quits the French presidency after a referendum dealing with local government and Senate reforms is rejected by the voters.

April 29   Israeli commandos strike deep inside Egypt.

May 1   The Biafran Assembly mandates continued war against Nigeria.

May 7   Indonesia reports it has subdued a revolt of 30,000 Papuan tribesmen in West Irian.

May 8   In Paris, the NLF presents a peace plan for ending the Vietnam War; Nixon offers a counterplan on May 14.

May 22 The United States presents a draft treaty banning the deployment of weapons of mass destruction on the sea bed to the Eighteen Nation Disarmament Committee.

May 25 Left-wing officers led by Colonel Jaafar Muhammed el-Nimeiry topple the Sudanese government.

May 26 The United States submits a Middle East peace plan to the Soviet Union. Moscow is "disappointed," and Egypt rejects the plan on June 27.

May 30 President Thieu swears that he will never participate in a coalition government with the NLF. Britain issues Gibraltar a new constitution declaring it a non-self-governing territory but granting its inhabitants control over local affairs.

June 5 Despite the lack of support from Latin-American countries, Cuba wins an ECOSOC election to the governing board of the UNDP.

June 6 Moscow warns Arab "extremists" against military adventures aimed at recapturing land occupied by Israel.

June 8 Nixon announces on Midway Island that 25,000 American troops will be withdrawn from South Vietnam.

June 10 The NLF announces the formation of a Provisional Revolutionary Government over South Vietnam.

June 11 Cambodia and the United States agree in principle to restore diplomatic ties.

June 13 Laotian Premier Souvanna Phouma acknowledges that the United States had been bombing targets in his country in efforts to halt North Vietnamese infiltration into South Vietnam.

June 15 Gaullist candidate Georges Pompidou is elected president of France.

June 18 Indonesia claims to have aborted a plot by West Irian rebel tribesmen to assassinate UN observers.

June 20 White Rhodesian voters approve a new constitution inspired by the South African apartheid system, which Thant labels "the product of the kind of racism which is abhorrent to the vast majority of mankind."[13]

June 29 Moise Tshombe dies in Algerian captivity at age forty-nine.

July 2 Thant calls on all governments to end the development, production, and stockpiling of chemical and biological weapons.

July 3 The Security Council unanimously condemns Israel for changing the legal and political status of East Jerusalem and creating a united city.

July 5 Fighting breaks out between Honduras and El Salvador, following a soccer match between teams representing the two Central American countries; the subsequent "Soccer War" produces, in Thant's words, "a grievous toll in loss of life and property."[14]

July 7 Thant tells the Security Council that "open warfare has been resumed" on the Suez Canal.

July 8 Thant undergoes ulcer surgery. The secretary-general's illness, coupled with the transfer of his chief of staff, Indian diplomat C. V. Narasimhan, to the post of deputy administrator of UNDP, prompt speculation that Thant is about to resign his office. A Secretariat spokesman denies the rumors on July 29.

July 11 A Thieu proposal for free elections in South Vietnam with the participation of the NLF is rejected by the Communists.

July 14 El Salvador's forces invade Honduras.

July 14–August 2 Indonesia permits 1,025 delegates chosen by tribal chiefs to represent the 800,000 inhabitants of West Irian in a plebiscite observed by UN officials. Thant's representative, Bolivian diplomat Frenando Ortiz-Sanz, expresses concern about the "tight political control" exercised by Indonesia over West Irian.

July 15 Thant appeals for a cease-fire and negotiations in separate but identical messages to the foreign ministers of Honduras and El Salvador.

July 18 After heavy fighting, El Salvador and Honduras accept an OAS peace plan.

July 20 For the first time since the 1967 war, Israeli jets bomb Egyptian positions along the Suez Canal. *Apollo 11* astronauts land on the moon.

July 26 Nixon, in Guam, asserts that the United States will avoid Vietnam type wars in the future but will continue to help its friends with material and diplomatic support. Democratic Senate Leader

Mike Mansfield (D-Montana) expresses support for Nixon's "Guam Doctrine."

July 29 El Salvador agrees to withdraw its troops from Honduras. General Odd Bull announces that UNTSO has abandoned two observation posts along the Suez Canal.

August 2–3 Nixon receives a tumultuous welcome in Romania, which, despite its austere Marxist political system, steers an independent course in foreign policy and receives "most favored nation" trade privileges from the United States.

August 2–4 The worst religious rioting in years breaks out in Belfast, Northern Ireland.

August 8 Paris devalues the franc.

August 12–16 British troops put down Belfast disturbances, as London rejects an Irish idea for a UN force in Northern Ireland.

August 13 New battles break out along the Suez Canal.

August 19 The British army assumes responsibility for all security in Northern Ireland. Ambassador Yost suggests to the Security Council that the UN consider "associate membership" for microstates.

August 21 A fire, set by a Christian pilgrim, damages the Al-Aksa Mosque in East Jerusalem, and triggers Muslim criticism of Israel for this violation of a Muslim shrine.

August 25 Israel rejects Thant's proposal to station UN observers along its border with Lebanon.

August 28 The Soviet Union hints at the use of nuclear weapons in its conflict with China.

August 29 Two Arabs hijack a TWA flight from Rome and divert it to Damascus. Burma's U Nu, in exile in London, announces the formation of a coalition to drive Ne Win from office.

September 3 North Vietnamese leader Ho Chi Minh dies at age seventy-nine.

September 6 In a meeting with the president of the International Federation of Air Line Pilots' Associations, Thant disagrees with the federation's proposal to suspend all airline service for twenty-four hours in protest against airline hijackings.

September 7 In an address before the Organization of African Unity (OAU), Thant calls on Nigerian and Biafran authorities to facilitate the flow of relief supplies to people suffering from the war.

September 10 The OAU calls for an end to the tribal fighting in Nigeria and the convening of peace talks. An Israeli armored force crosses the Suez Canal and carries out a devastating ten-hour attack against Egypt.

September 14 Kosygin, returning from Ho Chi Minh's funeral in Hanoi, meets Chinese Foreign Minister Chou En-lai in Peking. Israel claims to have downed eleven Egyptian planes over the Suez Canal.

September 15 Meeting to discuss the fire at the Al-Aksa Mosque, the Security Council calls on Israel to reverse the unification of Jerusalem.

September 16 Nixon announces the pullout of another 35,000 American troops from South Vietnam.

September 19 Nixon orders a 50,000-man cut in United States draft calls for the remainder of 1969.

September 20 The "Big Four" agree to resume talks on the Middle East, suspended since July 1.

September 25 A report prepared for the UN's Special Committee on Apartheid faults trading by the United States, Japan, Great Britain, and West Germany for the failure of UN economic sanctions against South Africa.

September 25–27 The Central Committee of the Czech Communist Party purges reformers Dubček and Josef Smrkovsky.

October 1 In a letter to Thant, the Spanish Foreign Ministry asks the UN to take action against Great Britain for its failure to observe the General Assembly resolution on Gibraltar.

October 7 The United States and USSR submit a seabed pact to the UN ENDC in Geneva. China and the Soviet Union agree to hold border talks.

October 10 Israeli Defense Minister Moshe Dayan charges Soviet advisers with participating in combat along the Suez Canal. By a vote of 26–0, with the United States, Britain, Canada, and Nigeria abstaining, the UN Economic and Social Council (UNESCO) condemns Israel for its archeological excavations in the Old City of Jerusalem.

October 13 Israeli Deputy Premier Yigal Allon proposes a peace plan granting West Bank Arabs responsibility for internal affairs and retaining security control for Israel.

October 18–November 1 The Lebanese government clashes with Palestinian commandos loyal to PLO leader Yasser Arafat, who is emerging into a major figure in the Arab-Israeli conflict. Sympathetic to the commandos, Muslim Prime Minister Rashid Karami resigns, as Syria puts pressure on the Lebanese government and Egypt tries to mediate the dispute.

October 21 The West German Bundestag selects Socialist Willy Brandt to head a coalition government joining the Socialists with the Free Democratic Party.

October 28 The United States Army charges a lieutenant and staff sergeant with wartime atrocities against South Vietnamese civilians in the hamlet of My Lai.

November 3 Nixon announces the United States and South Vietnam have agreed to a timetable for the complete withdrawal of U.S. troops from South Vietnam. The Lebanese government and PLO agree to end their fighting.

November 11 In a UN forum, the United States charges North Vietnam with mistreating American prisoners of war.

November 17 Strategic Arms Limitation Talks (SALT) negotiations begin in Geneva.

November 19 The General Assembly endorses the decision of West Irian to become part of Indonesia.

November 20 Henry Cabot Lodge, former American ambassador to the UN, resigns as head of the U.S. delegation to the Paris Peace Talks.

November 26 Clashes erupt between Saudi Arabia and South Yemen.

December 8 Soviet and West German officials discuss a pact affirming each country's willingness to renounce the use of force against the other.

December 9   American Secretary of State William Rogers calls for Israeli withdrawal from occupied territories in return for peace, and elicits Israelis' criticism of his proposal.

December 12   Greece, in response to criticisms of its military government, withdraws from the Council of Europe. The General Assembly's Political Committee votes not to endorse the United States-USSR seabed proposal. The General Assembly, by a vote of 67–1–17, with Cuba voting against, calls upon member states to prosecute those accused of aircraft hijacking.

December 15   Nixon orders a further reduction, by 50,000 men, of the American troop presence in South Vietnam. Dubček is appointed the Czech ambassador to Turkey.

December 18   An eleven-point plan for peace between Israel and Jordan is submitted by the United States to the "Big Four" nations. Israel condemns the proposal.

December 25   Israeli commandos capture an Egyptian radar, dismantle it, and return the parts to Israel. Israel spirits five French-made gunboats, originally sold to Israel but subsequently embargoed, out of a French harbor, and provokes an angry French reaction.

1970

January 2   The Nigerian government asserts that its latest military offensive has divided Biafra into three as a consequence of a major military offensive.

January 4   Thant backs the OAU stand against the Biafran secession and calls on Biafran leaders to negotiate on the basis that there is one Nigeria.

January 12   The Biafran government surrenders to Nigeria, ending the secession and civil war, and on January 15 Biafra ceases to exist as a state.

January 13, 16, 18   Israeli jets bomb military targets near Cairo.

January 14   Brandt calls for talks between the two Germanies.

January 21   France agrees to sell Libya one hundred jets.

January 22 Israel raids and disables an Egyptian military base on the Red Sea.

January 30 The Security Council condemns South Africa's presence in Namibia following South Africa's failure to heed a 1969 resolution calling for Pretoria's withdrawal from the disputed territory by October.

February 10 Arab terrorists attack passengers from an Israeli aircraft in Munich.

February 12 In what it calls an accident, Israel bombs a scrap metal processing plant seventeen miles from Cairo and kills seventy Egyptians.

February 14 Nixon bans the production and use of toxins for chemical weapons.

February 21 A Swissair passenger plane bound for Israel explodes in midair, as Palestinian groups first claim, then disclaim responsibility.

March 2 Rhodesia declares itself a republic.

March 6 Denying charges that there are U.S. combat troops in Laos and charging the North Vietnamese with violating the 1962 Geneva agreement neutralizing Laos, Nixon asks London and Moscow to help sustain the Laotian accord.

March 8 Gunmen unsuccessfully attempt to assassinate President Makarios in Cyprus.

March 9 Thant addresses the opening session of the Preparatory Committee on the Human Environment.

March 16 In talks with North Vietnamese and Viet Cong representatives, Cambodia demands the removal of Communist troops from its territory.

March 17 Indonesia and Malaysia sign a treaty of friendship.

March 18 A military coup led by Lieutenant General Lon Nol ousts Prince Norodom Sihanouk, who is out of the country, from the Cambodian leadership.

March 20 The United States steps up its attack on communist troops operating in Cambodia.

March 21 Dubček is suspended from Communist Party membership in Czechoslovakia.

March 26 Representatives of the United States, USSR, Great Britain, and France meet for the first time since 1959 to discuss Berlin.

March 30 The Cambodian government asks Thant to call on North Vietnam and the Viet Cong to withdraw from Cambodia.

April 1 France calls for an international conference to discuss the entire Indochinese problem. Communists launch a major assault in South Vietnam.

April 16 SALT (Strategic Arms Limitation Talks), suspended since December 1969, resumes in Vienna.

April 20 Nixon says 150,000 more American troops will be removed from South Vietnam by the spring of 1971. Vietnamese Communist forces reach fifteen miles from Phnom Penh in an attack on the Cambodian government, as Lon Nol asks Nixon for arms.

April 23 Saigon ships the Phnom Penh government thousands of rifles in response to the Lon Nol government's appeal for help against the Communists.

April 29 Israel charges Soviet pilots with flying combat missions against Israeli forces in the Suez Canal area.

April 29–30 To fight Communist forces, 20,000 U.S. and South Vietnamese troops move into Cambodia in areas close to the Vietnam border.

April 30 Nixon announces he is sending U.S. troops into Cambodia, triggering massive demonstrations in the United States.

May 11 The U.S. Senate Foreign Relations Committee passes an amendment cutting off funds for future Cambodian operations.

May 12 After Israeli raids into Lebanon, the Security Council calls on Israel to withdraw its forces. President Nixon declares the Cambodian operation an "enormous success."

May 12–16 Some U.S. troops are withdrawn from Cambodia.

May 16 Joaquín Balaguer wins reelection to the Dominican presidency.

May 22 Arab terrorists fire on an Israeli school bus near the Lebanese border, killing twelve, and Israel retaliates with the shelling of a Lebanese village.

May 26 The United States announces that American operations in Cambodia will end by June 30. Thant says in a speech that unanimous Security Council resolutions should be binding on all states.

May 27 Cambodia and South Vietnam agree that Saigon's army should have the right to pursue military objectives against the Communists in Cambodia.

June 1 Martial law is imposed in Cambodia.

June 3 Announcing American troop withdrawals, Nixon addresses the nation and calls the operation in Cambodia "the most successful operation of this long and very difficult war."[15]

June 5 France, which had boycotted the Western European Union (WEU) since February 1969, attends a WEU meeting.

June 6–10 Fighting breaks out between Jordanian troops and Palestinian guerrillas.

June 9 Yasser Arafat is selected as head of the Central Committee of the PLO in a reorganization of the guerrilla group.

June 18 Parliamentary elections in Britain restore the Conservative Party to power.

June 19 The U.S. Air Force announces that it has deployed multiple warheads on ICBMs at Minot Air Force Base, North Dakota.

June 21 The United States acknowledges that it has been conducting bombing raids deep inside Cambodia.

June 24 The U.S. Senate repeals the Gulf of Tonkin Resolution.

June 25 The United States makes a new proposal to end the Middle East impasse, but both Egypt and Israel are critical of the plan.

June 25 All U.S. troops are withdrawn from Cambodia.

June 30 The Senate passes the Cooper-Church amendment, limiting American intervention in Cambodia.

July 1 Nixon names veteran American diplomat David Bruce head of the U.S. delegation in Paris after a long vacancy in the post.

July 6 Israel claims that Soviet missile experts shot down three Israeli aircraft over the Suez Canal.

July 7 In deference to a new Washington diplomatic initiative, Thant announces a temporary suspension of the Jarring mission.

July 9 The House of Representatives rejects the Cooper-Church amendment designed to cut off funds for the American war effort in Indochina.

July 10 Moscow reacts somewhat favorably to Washington's latest Middle East peace proposal.

July 20 Nixon says at a news conference that the United States is proposing a ninety-day truce along the Suez Canal to defuse tensions in the Middle East.

July 23 Egypt accepts the U.S. truce proposal and calls for renewed negotiations with Jarring as the mediator.

July 26 Jordan accepts the U.S. truce proposal.

July 27 West Germany and the Soviet Union begin negotiations on a mutual nonaggression pact.

July 31 Israel accepts the American truce proposal, but the right wing Gahal coalition withdraws from the government in protest. Lieutenant General Odd Bull resigns as head of UNTSO and is replaced by Major General Ensio Siilasvuo.

August 3 Thant, Rogers, and Jarring meet at the UN to discuss Washington's peace initiative.

August 7 A truce along the Suez Canal goes into effect, as Jarring begins meeting with the envoys of Israel, Egypt, and Jordan. Palestinian groups oppose the truce.

August 12 West Germany and the Soviet Union sign a mutual nonaggression pact and agree to accept as legitimate existing European boundaries.

August 13–18 Israel charges Egypt with truce violations.

August 25 Jarring opens peace talks in New York in separate discussions with delegates from Egypt, Israel, and Jordan.

August 27–28 A meeting of the Palestine National Council, the chief legislative body of the PLO, rejects the U.S. peace initiative and calls for a war against Israel.

August 28   The United States conducts its first major test of an ABM.

August 30–31   Israel charges Egypt with constructing missile sites in violation of the truce, as peace talks are suspended.

September 1   King Hussein escapes an assassination attempt in Jordan. The Senate defeats the Hatfield-McGovern amendment that would have ended the war by late 1971. The United States and USSR propose a new seabed treaty in the United Nations.

September 3   The United States confirms Israeli charges of Egyptian truce violations.

September 6   Israel withdraws from the peace talks. The Popular Front for the Liberation of Palestine (PFLP) hijacks three commercial jets bound for New York from Europe, as a fourth hijacking attempt of an El Al airliner is foiled. Two of the jets are flown to the Jordanian desert, and the other is flown to Cairo, where, after the passengers and crew are evacuated, it is blown up on the airport tarmac. Another jet is hijacked by the same group on September 9 and flown to Jordan. The hijackers demand the release of fellow guerrillas imprisoned in Israel.

September 9   The Security Council passes a resolution calling for the release of all passengers and crews taken hostage in hijackings.

September 12   After evacuating the passengers and crews, Arab guerrillas blow up the three planes in the Jordanian desert. The Central Committee expels the PFLP from the PLO.

September 16   King Hussein installs a military government after two weeks of fighting between the Jordanian army and Palestinian commandos in Jordan and declares martial law. Commandos refuse to recognize the new government. The PFLP is readmitted into the PLO Central Committee.

September 17   Jordanian army tanks and infantry move on guerrilla bases in Amman, as Nixon expresses support for Hussein in the latter's battle with the Palestinians. The Viet Cong offer a new peace proposal in Paris.

September 20   Jordan radio asserts that Syrian tanks have entered Jordanian territory in behalf of the PLO, provoking an American warning to Syria.

September 21   Syrian tanks back Palestinian commandos in fighting in the northern part of Jordan.

September 25   A cease-fire takes effect in Jordan after other Arab governments help to mediate the Jordanian-Palestinian clash.

September 26   Hussein appoints a civilian government.

September 27   Arafat and Hussein sign a peace accord in Cairo.

September 28   Nasser dies in Cairo at age fifty-two. An acknowledged leader of the nonaligned movement, the Egyptian president inspired the adulation of millions of Arabs.

October 3   The Arab Socialist Union, Egypt's only political party, names Anwar Sadat president.

October 6   Palestinian commandos begin withdrawing from northern Jordan.

October 7   Nixon proposes a cease-fire in Indochina and an expanded peace conference, but Hanoi counters that a cease-fire must accompany a political settlement.

October 8   Dissident Russian writer Aleksander Solzhenitsyn is awarded the Nobel Prize for Literature.

October 13   Hussein's sovereignty is recognized in a new pact between Jordan and Palestinian commandos. Canada recognizes the People's Republic of China. After gaining independence from Great Britain on October 8, Fiji is admitted as the 127th member of the UN.

October 15   Sadat is elected president of Egypt in a nationwide plebiscite.

October 23   The U.S. Defense Department discloses a deal to supply Israel with $500 million in arms.

October 24   A joint session of the Chilean Congress elects leftist Salvador Allende Gossens president after he polls a plurality of the popular vote in September 4 elections.

October 31   Thieu opposes serving in a coalition government with Communists.

November 4   The General Assembly calls for an extension of the Middle East truce and the withdrawal of Israeli troops from occupied territories.

November 5   Italy and the People's Republic of China establish diplomatic relations.

November 9 Charles de Gaulle dies at age eighty. The wartime resistance hero saved France from political chaos when, in 1958, he became president of the Fifth Republic.

November 12 Chile reestablishes ties with Cuba. The United States reverses twenty years of UN policy and expresses support for a "two China" policy.

November 13 A cyclone and tidal wave in East Pakistan kill 168 thousand people, as East Pakistanis criticize the relief efforts of the government of President Yahya Khan. A coup, led by Defense Minister Hafez al-Assad, topples Syria's left wing government. By a vote of 60–42–12, the General Assembly refuses to accredit the South African delegation to the UN.

November 17 The General Assembly's Political Committee endorses a draft treaty banning the deployment of weapons of mass destruction on the seabed.

November 18 West Germany and Poland sign a mutual nonaggression pact recognizing the Oder-Neisse line as the western border of Poland.

November 20 As an important question requiring the support of two-thirds of the assembly, an Algerian resolution to expel the Chinese Nationalists fails.

November 21 U.S. forces unsuccessfully attempt to free American prisoners of war from a detention camp in North Vietnam.

November 21–22 The United States launches heavy air raids against North Vietnam as Secretary of Defense Melvin Laird warns of heavier bombing unless negotiations in Paris improve.

November 25 By a vote of 105–0–8, the General Assembly condemns "all acts of hijacking and other interference with civil air travel."[16]

November 26 The United States proposes to the General Assembly's Political Committee that a conference on the law of the sea be convened in January 1972.

November 27 Syria agrees to join a proposed federation with Egypt, Libya, and Sudan.

December 2 Delegates from France, Uruguay, and Saudi Arabia get into a fistfight during a session of the General Assembly's Social Committee.

December 7 In Pakistan's first general elections, the separatist Awami League wins a majority of the seats in the National Assembly, leading Sheik Mujibur Rahman to claim that East Pakistanis should enjoy the right to full autonomy.

December 8 By a vote of 11–0–4, the Security Council condemns Portugal for sponsoring an unsuccessful invasion of Guinea. (The United States, Britain, France, and Spain abstain.)

December 14 A new accord between Hussein and Palestinian commandos operating in his country goes into effect after the breakdown of the old agreement.

December 15 As workers' revolts spread across Poland, Wladyslaw Gomulka is replaced by Edward Gierek as leader of the Polish Communist Party.

December 28 The Organization of Oil Exporting Countries (OPEC) demands a greater share of oil revenues from oil companies.

1971

January 4 Pompidou says that it is in Europe's interest for Great Britain to join the EEC.

January 5 Arab-Israeli negotiations, with Jarring acting as go-between, resume in New York.

January 8 The Jordanian government launches a major military drive against Palestinian guerrillas in Jordan.

January 8–9 In a visit to Jerusalem, Jarring receives an Israeli peace proposal.

January 11 After voting against a 1970 revolution calling all forms of colonialism "crimes against humanity," the United States and Great Britain withdraw from the UN's Special Committee of Twenty-Four (established by the General Assembly in 1961 to implement its December 1960 Declaration on the Granting of Independence to Colonial Countries and Peoples).

January 18 Thant expresses "cautious optimism" over Middle East peace talks. Thant refuses to seek a third term as secretary-general.

January 20   Egypt rejects the latest Israeli peace proposal as does Jordan on January 25.

January 21   Senators John Sherman Cooper (D-Kentucky) and Frank Church (D-Idaho) accuse the Nixon Administration's escalation of the air war of violating the spirit of their amendment to end a U.S. ground combat presence in Cambodia. A coup led by Major General Idi Amin topples the government of Milton Obote in Uganda.

February 2   Talks between OPEC and major oil companies break down in Tehran, as the oil-producing countries threaten to raise oil prices unilaterally. Talks resume in Libya on March 2.

February 4   Sadat proposes an Israeli pullback from the Suez Canal followed by an Egyptian reopening of the waterway.

February 5   The Middle East cease-fire is extended by one month.

February 8   Supported by U.S. air and logistical support, five thousand South Vietnamese troops invade Laos and attack North Vietnamese supply lines to South Vietnam. Jarring submits his own peace plan to Israeli and Egyptian UN representatives.

February 11   Sixty-three nations sign the Seabed Treaty.

February 12   Israel accuses Jarring of overstepping his mandate, but Thant supports his negotiator.

February 15   Cairo tells Jarring it is willing to sign a peace agreement with Israel in return for a complete withdrawal from Arab territories. Zulfikar Ali Bhutto, head of the Pakistan People's Party, threatens to boycott the National Assembly, unless East Pakistan's Awami League compromises on the issue of regional autonomy.

February 22   London announces it will sell helicopters to South Africa.

February 26   Nixon's national security adviser, Henry Kissinger, says the United States has no plans to invade North Vietnam. Israel responds to the Jarring proposal: the government is willing to discuss all issues but will not precommit to the complete withdrawal from Arab territory.

March 1   President Yahya Khan indefinitely postpones the opening of Pakistan's first popularly elected National Assembly. Sheik Mujibur Rahaman, head of the Awami League, calls a strike in protest.

March 2 Riots break out in Dacca, the capital of East Pakistan.

March 5 Thant, to Israel's annoyance, applauds Egypt's response to the Jarring mission and urges Israel to withdraw from occupied territory.

March 7 Sheik Mujibur refuses to attend a National Assembly meeting rescheduled for March 25.

March 12 Prime Minister Meir indicates that Israel's border demands include retention of Sharm el Sheik, the Golan Heights, and East Jerusalem and the demilitarization of the Sinai. Turkish Prime Minister Suleyman Demirel resigns after the military threatens to intervene to stem rising political violence in the country.

March 15 Sheik Mujibur assumes administrative control of East Pakistan.

March 16 Yahya Khan and Sheik Mujibur meet in Dacca to discuss Pakistani tensions.

March 22 The opening of Pakistan's National Assembly is postponed again.

March 24 The South Vietnamese military campaign in Laos comes to an end.

March 25 When peace talks break down, central government troops launch a drive to gain control over East Pakistan. Sheik Mujibur is arrested. Jarring resumes his duties as Swedish ambassador to the Kremlin, his peace negotiations having failed.

March 26 Yahya Khan outlaws the Awami League, but rebels declare the existence of a new state in East Pakistan called Bangladesh.

March 29 India appeals to Thant to stop the massacre in East Pakistan. A United States military court finds American Lieutenant William L. Calley Jr. guilty of murdering South Vietnamese civilians at My Lai, and he is sentenced to life imprisonment.

March 31 The Indian Parliament accuses Pakistan of "genocide" in its eastern territory.

April 2 Libya and twenty-five Western oil companies sign an accord raising the price of oil from $2.55 to $3.45 a barrel.

April 4 Israel rejects Sadat's proposal to open the Suez Canal.

April 7   Nixon announces his intention to bring home 100,000 more troops between May 1 and December 1.

April 12   China sends a note to Yahya Khan expressing Peking's support for his policies in East Pakistan.

April 14   Nixon relaxes trade restrictions with China. Chou En-lai receives a visiting U.S. table tennis team and expresses hope for better relations between China and the United States.

April 15   Karachi Radio reports that all "principal towns" in East Pakistan are under control of the army.

April 17   The agreement of Egypt, Syria, and Libya to form the Union of Arab Republics is announced.

April 21   Haiti's President François (Papa Doc) Duvalier dies and is succeeded by his son, Jean-Claude (Baby Doc).

April 22   New Delhi asks the UN to help deal with the influx of several million refugees from East Pakistan into India, as Thant offers Pakistan UN assistance.

April 26   India and Pakistan withdraw their respective missions in Calcutta and Dacca. A presidential commission headed by former UN Ambassador Henry Cabot Lodge supports a "two China" policy for the United States. The State Department calls for negotiations between the two Chinas, but Peking rejects the Lodge report and State Department recommendation.

May 3   Walter Ulbricht resigns as head of East Germany's Socialist Unity Party and is replaced by Erich Honecker. Yahya Khan rejects Thant's offer of aid but pledges to consider future international assistance.

May 4   European speculation against the U.S. dollar, caused by America's growing balance of payments deficit and inflation concerns, drives down the value of the dollar.

May 6   India asks ECOSOC to finance relief costs for Pakistani refugees in India. Estimating the total number of refugees from East Pakistan at 2.6 million, India warns Pakistan that the situation is a threat to the peace. The Special Committee on Apartheid reports that France is South Africa's principal arms supplier.

May 17   Secretary of State Rogers discusses his just-completed Middle East trip with Thant and Jarring in New York. Thant appoints the UN High Commissioner for Refugees as coordinator of relief efforts in India and Pakistan.

May 20   The United States and USSR announce that they will seek an ABM accord.

May 20–21   A meeting between Pompidou and British Prime Minister Edward Heath paves the way for Great Britain's entry into the Common Market.

May 22   Despite initial hesitation, Pakistan requests relief assistance from the United Nations. Thant dispatches the assistant secretary-general for interagency affairs to Pakistan.

May 24–25   Clashes are reported between Pakistani and Indian troops along India's East Pakistan border.

May 27   Egypt and the Soviet Union sign a treaty of friendship in Cairo.

June 2   Hussein orders a final push against Palestinian commandos in Jordan.

June 4   NATO welcomes Soviet proposals on initiating talks to reduce troop levels in Europe. Mutual Balanced Force Reduction Talks begin in Vienna in 1972.

June 5   Thant tells newsmen that he will not serve past December 31.

June 7   Three Soviet cosmonauts dock with the Salyut orbiting laboratory to create humankind's first space station. Upon their return to earth on June 30, the cosmonauts are found dead in their space capsule, after a leak in the spacecraft's seal deprives them of oxygen.

June 13–15   *The New York Times* publishes the "Pentagon Papers," a history of America's escalating involvement in the Vietnam War, but halts publication after the Justice Department wins an injunction against the newspaper.

June 17   Washington cedes sovereignty over Okinawa to Tokyo, but the United States retains military base rights.

June 19   Suffering from extreme fatigue, Thant cancels a visit to the Soviet Union.

June 21   A World Bank report urges the suspension of aid to Pakistan because of the situation in East Pakistan. The World Court rules that South Africa's control over Namibia is illegal.

June 23 Great Britain reaches an agreement to join the EEC. The OAU votes 28–6 not to open a dialogue with South Africa.

June 30 The U.S. Supreme Court upholds the right of newspapers to publish the "Pentagon Papers"; "prior restraint" is held unconstitutional. Nixon announces that Turkey, which supplies two-thirds of the heroin that reaches the United States, will prohibit poppy cultivation beginning in 1972.

July 1 In Paris, the Viet Cong offers a prisoner swap in return for a U.S. troop withdrawal by the end of 1971, but the United States rejects the proposal on July 8. London and Buenos Aires agree to permit air travel between Argentina and the disputed Falkland Islands. (Eleven years later the two countries will fight a short but bitter war over the Falklands.)

July 11 The Chilean Congress authorizes nationalization of the copper industry, which is owned primarily by American companies.

July 15 Nixon announces he will visit Communist China in 1972.

July 18 Six Persian Gulf states agree to combine in a federation before the end of 1971, when Britain is scheduled to withdraw from the region.

July 19 Jordan's premier announces that Palestinian commandos have lost all their bases in Jordan after the newest government offensive.

July 19–24 A leftist coup against Sudan's President Mohammed Gaafar el-Nimeiry is defeated with the help of Egypt and Libya.

July 20 In a secret memo, Thant urges the Security Council to intervene in the India-Pakistan dispute.

July 28 Following a deterioration in relations between the island's Greek and Turkish populations, UNFICYP is placed on a low-level alert.

July 31 The United States announces a UN-Pakistani agreement on UN relief efforts in East Pakistan.

August 2 The United States announces it will vote in the General Assembly for Communist Chinese admission to the UN but will seek to retain membership in the world organization for the Nationalists. Peking accuses Washington of playing a "clumsy . . . two-China trick."[17] American officials acknowledge that the CIA maintains a 30,000-man force of "irregulars" in Laos. New Delhi rejects Thant's proposal to place a representative of the UN High Commissioner for Refugees on both sides of the Indo-Pakistani border.

August 3   Abandoning its traditional insistence on three miles, the United States proposes a twelve-mile territorial sea limit.

August 5   The United States and USSR unveil a joint draft treaty banning the development, production, stockpiling, and acquisition of biological weapons.

August 9   Heavy sectarian fighting breaks out in Northern Ireland after the British army cracks down on Irish Republican Army (IRA) terrorists. India and the Soviet Union sign a friendship treaty.

August 11   Sheik Mujibur is placed on trial for treason.

August 12   Syria breaks ties with Jordan after fighting between the two countries.

August 15   Nixon ends the convertibility of the dollar to gold, imposes an import surcharge, and orders a ninety-day wage price freeze; the dollar becomes a floating currency.

August 17   U.S. Ambassador George Bush asks Thant to place a "two China" resolution on the General Assembly agenda for the fall.

August 18   Thant appeals for more funds to deal with the Pakistani refugee crisis.

August 23   A "four power" agreement is reached on the status of Berlin, and the Soviets promise the West "unimpeded" access.

August 27   Japan floats the yen.

September 1   The Federation of Arab Republics comes into existence after voters in Egypt, Syria, and Libya approve its creation in a plebiscite.

September 11   Khrushchev dies at seventy-seven. The disgraced Soviet leader had moved from a policy of confrontation to peaceful coexistence with the United States before he was deposed in 1964.

September 21   Bhutan, Bahrain, and Qatar are admitted to the United Nations. UN membership is at 130.

September 22   The United States proposes two resolutions in the General Assembly: 1) Peking should be admitted to the Security Council in place of Taiwan; 2) Any move to oust Taiwan from the UN should be an "important" question requiring a two-thirds vote. The UN General Committee, however, places an Albanian resolution to expel the Nationalists ahead of the U.S. resolution on the General Assembly calendar. The United States had requested simultaneous consideration of the two resolutions.

September 26   By a vote of 14–0–1 (Syria abstains), the Security Council calls on Israel to halt further changes in the character of Jerusalem and instructs the secretary-general to send observers there.

September 28   Joseph Cardinal Mindszenty ends his fifteen-year exile in the U.S. Embassy in Budapest and flies to the Vatican.

October 1   Thant's trusted deputy, Ralph Bunche, resigns due to illness.

October 3   Thieu, the only candidate, wins 90 percent of the presidential vote in South Vietnam.

October 4   The Labor Party opposes British membership in the EEC.

October 6   Thant tells the UN Administrative and Budget Committee that the UN is nearing insolvency.

October 7   Oman is admitted into the United Nations.

October 12   Moscow and Washington announce that Nixon will visit the Soviet Union in May 1972.

October 19   Japan's Premier Eisaku Sato calls for closer ties with China, but Peking is cool to Tokyo's overtures.

October 23   Heavy casualties result from fighting between India and Pakistan in East Pakistan and Kashmir.

October 25   The General Assembly, by a vote of 76–35–17, admits Communist China and expels the Nationalists after defeating, 59–55–15, a U.S. motion to make the issue an "important question." Thant regrets the "departure of the Republic of China from the halls of the UN" but nonetheless welcomes the assembly decision. President Nixon expresses annoyance at the glee with which delegates greet the outcome of the assembly vote.

October 28   The British Parliament approves in principle the entry of Great Britain into the EEC.

October 29   In the wake of the U.S. defeat in the General Assembly over Taiwan's expulsion, an angry U.S. Senate, by a vote of 41–17, defeats a foreign aid authorization bill.

November 8   The "Group of 77," composed of ninety-five third world nations, meets to plan strategy for the next UNCTAD, to be held in Santiago, Chile, in 1972, and calls on the United States to revoke its 10-percent surcharge on imports from less-developed countries.

November 9   The General Assembly, by a vote of 109–2, condemns apartheid.

November 12   Nixon announces a further troop cut of 45,000 in Vietnam before February 1.

November 15   Chiao Huan-hua, chief delegate of the People's Republic of China, delivers his government's first address to the General Assembly.

November 21   Fighting in East Bengal escalates, with Pakistan claiming an invasion by more than 100,000 Indian troops. UN relief efforts are halted.

November 22   Israel does not allow a UN commission sent by Thant to visit East Jerusalem.

November 24   Britain and Rhodesia sign an accord designed to end their dispute. The principle of majority rule is affirmed, but the struggle over Rhodesia continues until 1979, when Zimbabwe comes into existence.

November 28   Jordan's Prime Minister Wafsi Tal is assassinated by Palestinians in Cairo.

November 29   Khan asks Thant to consider stationing observers on the Pakistan side of his country's border with India, but Thant, saying he is not competent to decide on the request, refers the matter to the Security Council.

November 30   Responding to the vacuum created by Britain's departure from the region, Iran seizes three Persian Gulf islands.

Prime Minister Indira Gandhi calls on Pakistan to pull out of East Pakistan.

December 2 Six Trucial States form the Union of Arab Emirates.

December 3 War erupts between India and Pakistan.

December 5 The Soviet Union vetoes a resolution calling for a cease-fire in the India-Pakistan war.

December 6 When New Delhi recognizes Bangladesh, the United States suspends aid to India, which Washington refers to as the "clear aggressor."

December 7 The General Assembly, by a vote of 104–11–0, calls on India and Pakistan to observe a cease-fire and withdraw from each other's territory. China calls the Kremlin the "boss behind the Indian aggression."

December 8 The Union of Arab Emirates is admitted into the UN.

December 13 Following a debate in which a representative from Bangladesh is prohibited from speaking, the Soviets veto another Pakistan-India truce resolution in the Security Council. The General Assembly calls on Israel to withdraw from the occupied territories and urges the reactivation of the Jarring mission.

December 15 Accusing the UN of "legalizing Indian aggression," Pakistani Foreign Minister Ali Bhutto walks out of the Security Council

December 15–16 Jarring resumes Middle East talks.

December 16 Pakistani forces surrender in East Pakistan.

December 17 Pakistan accepts a cease-fire in the west.

December 20 Yahya Khan resigns and is succeeded by Ali Bhutto.

December 21 The Security Council, by a vote of 12–0–2 (the USSR and Poland abstaining), calls for a cease-fire and troop withdrawals in Pakistan. Austrian diplomat Kurt Waldheim is selected by the Security Council as its choice for secretary-general.

December 22 Thant delivers a farewell address to the General Assembly and calls for the creation of a deputy secretary-general to act as chief administrative officer of the organization.

December 26–30   The United States launches a major air strike against North Vietnam.

1972

February 3   Thant is named a senior fellow at Chicago's Adlai Stevenson Institute for International Affairs.

1974

September 17   Bangladesh is admitted to the United Nations.

November 25   Thant dies in New York at age sixty-five.

December 5   Students protesting against the Ne Win regime seize Thant's coffin and bury him on the grounds of Rangoon University.

December 8   Police storm Rangoon University and retrieve Thant's body. He is reburied near a major Buddhist shrine.

NOTES

1. *Facts on File Yearbook 1961* (New York: Facts on File, 1962), 379.
2. *Facts on File Yearbook 1961*, 415.
3. *Facts on File Yearbook 1962* (New York: Facts on File, 1963), 331.
4. Andrew W. Cordier and Max Harrelson, eds., *Public Papers of the Secretaries-General of the United Nations, Vol. VI, U Thant* (New York: Columbia University Press, 1976), 325.
5. Cordier and Harrelson, *Public Papers, Vol. VI*, 345.
6. *Facts on File Yearbook 1965* (New York: Facts on File, 1966), 66.
7. *Facts on File Yearbook 1966* (New York: Facts on File, 1967), 395.
8. *Facts on File Yearbook 1967* (New York: Facts on File, 1968), 161.
9. *Facts on File Yearbook 1967*, 395.
10. Andrew W. Cordier and Max Harrelson, eds., *Public Papers of the Secretaries-General of the United Nations, Vol. VII, U Thant* (New York: Columbia University Press, 1976), 536.
11. *Facts on File Yearbook 1968* (New York: Facts on File, 1969), 332.
12. Andrew W. Cordier and Max Harrelson, eds., *Public Papers of the Secretaries-General of the United Nations, Vol. VIII, U Thant* (New York: Columbia University Press, 1977), 202.

13. *Facts on File Yearbook 1969* (New York: Facts on File, 1970), 396.
14. Cordier and Harrelson, *Public Papers, Vol. VIII*, 309.
15. *Facts on File Yearbook 1970* (New York: Facts on File, 1971), 393.
16. *Facts on File Yearbook 1970*, 886.
17. *Facts on File Yearbook 1971* (New York/: Facts on File, 1972), 581.

Appendix A

United Nations Members

1945 Argentina, Australia, Belarus (Byelorussia), Belgium, Bolivia, Brazil, Canada, Chile, China, Colombia, Costa Rica, Cuba, Czechoslovakia,* Denmark, Dominican Republic, Ecuador, Egypt, El Salvador, Ethiopia, France, Greece, Guatemala, Haiti, Honduras, India, Iran, Iraq, Lebanon, Liberia, Luxembourg, Mexico, Netherlands, New Zealand, Nicaragua, Norway, Panama, Paraguay, Peru, Philippines, Poland, Russian Federation,‡ Saudi Arabia, South Africa, Syrian Arab Republic,† Turkey, Ukraine, United Kingdom of Great Britain and Northern Ireland, United States of America, Uruguay, Venezuela, Socialist Federal Republic of Yugoslavia§
1946 Afghanistan, Iceland, Sweden, Thailand
1947 Pakistan, Yemen″
1948 Myanmar
1949 Israel
1950 Indonesia
1955 Albania, Austria, Bulgaria, Cambodia, Finland, Hungary, Ireland, Italy, Jordan, Lao People's Democratic Republic, Libyan Arab Jamahiriya, Nepal, Portugal, Romania, Spain, Sri Lanka
1956 Japan, Morocco, Sudan, Tunisia
1957 Ghana, Federation of Malaya (Malaysia)#
1958 Guinea
1960 Benin, Burkina Faso, Cameroon, Central African Republic, Chad, Congo, Côte d'Ivoire, Cyprus, Democratic Republic of the Congo, Gabon, Madagascar, Mali, Niger, Nigeria, Senegal, Somalia, Togo
1961 Mauritania, Mongolia, Sierra Leone, Tanganyika (United Republic of Tanzania)**
1962 Algeria, Burundi, Jamaica, Rwanda, Trinidad and Tobago, Uganda
1963 Kenya, Kuwait, Zanzibar (United Republic of Tanzania)**
1964 Malawi, Malta, Zambia
1965 Gambia, Maldives, Singapore#
1966 Barbados, Guyana, Lesotho

1967 Democratic Yemen"
1968 Equatorial Guinea, Mauritius, Swaziland
1970 Fiji
1971 Bahrain, Bhutan, Oman, Qatar, United Arab Emirates
1973 Bahamas, German Democratic Republic and Federal Republic of Germany (Germany)
1974 Bangladesh, Grenada, Guinea-Bissau
1975 Cape Verde, Comoros, Mozambique, Papua New Guinea, Sao Tome and Principe, Suriname
1976 Angola, Samoa, Seychelles
1977 Djibouti, Vietnam
1978 Dominica, Solomon Islands
1979 Saint Lucia
1980 Saint Vincent and the Grenadines, Zimbabwe
1981 Antigua and Barbuda, Belize, Vanuatu
1983 Saint Kitts and Nevis
1984 Brunei Darussalam
1990 Liechtenstein, Namibia
1991 Democratic People's Republic of Korea, Estonia, Federated States of Micronesia, Latvia, Lithuania, Marshall Islands, Republic of Korea
1992 Armenia, Azerbaijan, Bosnia and Herzegovina,§ Croatia,§ Georgia, Kazakhstan, Kyrgyzstan, Republic of Moldova, San Marino, Slovenia,§ Tajikistan, Turkmenistan, Uzbekistan
1993 Andorra, Czech Republic,* Eritrea, Monaco, Slovak Republic,* The former Yugoslav Republic of Macedonia§
1994 Palau
1999 Kiribati, Nauru, Tonga
2000 Tuvalu, Federal Republic of Yugoslavia§

---

* Czechoslovakia dissolved (1992) to create two independent member states: Czech Republic and Slovak Republic.
† Egypt and Syria were original members under the union, United Arab Republic. Syria assumed its independent status in 1961. In 1971 the United Arab Republic changed its name to the Arab Republic of Egypt.
‡ Union of Soviet Socialist Republics dissolved to into eleven member countries, most of which became UN member states.
§ The Socialist Federal Republic of Yugoslavia dissolved to create independent member states, Bosnia and Herzegovina, Croatia, Slovenia, former Yugoslav Republic of Macedonia, and Federal Republic of Yugoslavia.
" Yemen and Democratic Yemen merged in 1990 and represent a unified state in the UN under the name "Yemen."
Formerly part of the Federation of Malaya, Singapore became an independent state as well as a member of the UN.
** Tanganyika and Zanzibar united to create the United Republic of Tanganyika and Zanzibar and became UN member under the new name (1964); now United Republic of Tanzania.

Appendix B

Excerpt from the Charter of the United Nations[1]

CHAPTER XV

Article 97

The Secretariat shall comprise a Secretary-General and such staff as the Organization may require. The Secretary-General shall be appointed by the General Assembly upon the recommendation of the Security Council. He shall be the chief administrative officer of the Organization.

Article 98

The Secretary-General shall act in that capacity in all meetings of the General Assembly, of the Security Council, of the Economic and Social Council, and of the Trusteeship Council, and shall perform such other functions as are entrusted to him by these organs. The Secretary-General shall make an annual report to the General Assembly on the work of the Organization.

Article 99

The Secretary-General may bring to the attention of the Security Council any matter which in his opinion may threaten the maintenance of international peace and security.

Article 100

1. In the performance of their duties the Secretary-General and the staff shall not seek or receive instructions from any government or from any other authority external to the Organization. They shall refrain from any action which might reflect on their position as international officials responsible only to the Organization.
2. Each member of the United Nations undertakes to respect the exclusively international character of the responsibilities of the Secretary-General and the staff and not to seek to influence them in the discharge of their responsibilities.

Article 101

1. The staff shall be appointed by the Secretary-General under regulations established by the General Assembly.
2. Appropriate staffs shall be permanently assigned to the Economic and Social council, the Trusteeship Council, and, as required, to other organs of the United Nations. These staffs shall form a part of the Secretariat.
3. The paramount consideration in the employment of the staff and in the determination of the conditions of service shall be the necessity of securing the highest standards of efficiency, competence, and integrity. Due regard shall be paid to the importance of recruiting the staff on as wide a geographical basis as possible.

NOTE

1. From the *Charter of the United Nations and Statute of the International Court of Justice*, Department of Public Information, United Nations, 2000.

Bibliography

BIOGRAPHY AND AUTOBIOGRAPHY

Bingham, June. *U Thant: The Search for Peace,* New York: Alfred A. Knopf, 1966. A favorable, almost hagiographic account of Thant's life and career. Written by the wife of Representative Jonathan Bingham, former U.S. representative to the Economic and Social Council, the book is especially useful in integrating the details of Thant's life into a review of Burma's fight for independence and for its description of Buddhist beliefs and values.

Nassif, Rames. *U Thant in New York.* New York: St. Martin's, 1988. This memoir by Thant's press officer offers insights into the relationship between the secretary-general and the press and a chronicle of Thant's years at the UN.

Thant, U. *View from the UN.* Garden City, N.Y.: Doubleday, 1978. Thant recounts the major events of his tenure as secretary-general, including the Cuban missile and article 19 crises, the Indo-Pakistani War, the Arab-Israeli conflict, and the search for peace in Vietnam. There is little here about Thant's life before 1961, and some important issues, such as apartheid and the Cyprus Civil War, receive scant attention, but the book sheds considerable light on the secretary-general's philosophy as a man of the third world.

Urquhart, Brian. *A Life in Peace and War.* New York: Harper and Row, 1987. Urquhart reviews his years at the UN. While the section on Thant is relatively brief, it is generally favorable. The career diplomat offers some insight into Thant's actions during the Six Day War.

———. *Hammarskjold.* New York: Alfred A. Knopf, 1972. This brilliant biography sets the stage for Thant, who inherited Hammarskjöld's conception of the office and many of his problems—including the Congo, the fiscal crisis, and the Soviet assault on the Secretariat.

HISTORY AND SOURCE MATERIALS

Cordier, Andrew, and Max Harrelson, eds. *Public Papers of the Secretaries-General of the United Nations.* Vol. VI, *U Thant, 1961–1964.* New York: Columbia University Press, 1976. A collection of Thant's speeches, press conferences, official correspondence, interviews, and annual reports. The editors provide useful introductions to each section.

————. *Public Papers of the Secretaries-General of the United Nations.* Vol. VII, *U Thant, 1965–1967, 1976.* New York: Columbia University Press, 1976. A collection of Thant's speeches, press conferences, official correspondence, interviews, and annual reports. The editors provide useful introductions to each section.

————. *Public Papers of the Secretaries-General of the United Nations.* Vol. VIII, *U Thant, 1968–1971, 1977.* New York: Columbia University Press, 1976. A collection of Thant's speeches, press conferences, official correspondence, interviews, and annual reports. The editors provide useful introductions to each section.

Rovine, Arthur, ed. *The First Fifty Years: The Secretary-General in World Politics, 1920–1970.* Leyden, Netherlands: A. W. Sijthoff, 1970. A chronicle and assessment of the careers of the secretaries-general of the League of Nations and United Nations, beginning with Sir Eric Drummond and concluding with Thant.

Stoessinger, John G. *The United Nations and the Superpowers: China, Russia, and America.* New York: Random House, 1977. Professor Stoessinger, a former Secretariat official, examines some of the key crises and issues of the Thant years, including the article 19 imbroglio and the 1967 Arab-Israeli War. Thant's role is not examined deeply, but the cases are described clearly and interestingly.

THANT AND THE UNITED STATES

Finger, Seymour Maxwell. *Your Man at the UN: People, Politics, and Bureaucracy in the Making of Foreign Policy.* New York: New York University Press, 1980. Ambassador Finger, who served between 1956 and 1971 in various capacities at the U.S. mission to the UN, provides a readable and perceptive insider's account of U.S. policy under fifteen U.S. ambassadors. The Thant years are covered in much detail, although the emphasis is on the U.S. mission and the permanent representatives who headed it.

Johnson, Lyndon Baines. *The Vantage Point: Perspectives of the Presidency, 1963–1969.* New York: Holt, Reinhart and Winston, 1971. Thant's relationship with the United States deteriorated as the secretary-general stepped up his opposition to the war in Vietnam. Johnson offers his own perspective on his administration's differences with Thant. The secretary-general's efforts to end the war are played down here.

Martin, John Bartlow. *Adlai Stevenson and the World: The Life of Adlai E. Stevenson*. Garden City, N.Y.: Anchor/Doubleday, 1978. The last 330 pages of Martin's meticulously researched and brilliantly written biography of the former U.S. ambassador and two-time presidential candidate cover Stevenson's years at the UN. The emphasis is on Stevenson, not Thant, but their good relationship is well chronicled. The section on Thant's aborted Vietnam peace effort of 1964–65, in which Stevenson figured prominently, is especially useful.

Walton, Richard. *The Remnants of Power*. New York: Coward-McCann, 1968. In this sympathetic account of Adlai Stevenson's years as American ambassador to the UN, the author portrays Stevenson as a tragic figure, torn between his loyalty to Johnson and opposition to the administration's policies in Vietnam and the Dominican Republic.

Weintal, Edward, and Charles Bartlett. *Facing the Brink: A Study of Crisis Diplomacy*. London: Hutchinson, 1967. Two journalists discuss the major crises of the Kennedy-Johnson years. Treatment of the Cyprus and Yemen situations shed light on the relationship between Thant and Washington and the extent to which the secretary-general relied on U.S. diplomatic and logistical support in some of his early initiatives.

Yesselson, Abraham, and Anthony Gaglione. *A Dangerous Place: The United Nations as a Weapon in World Politics*. New York: Grossman, 1974. In this critical study, the authors see the UN as an arena for conflict rather than an instrument of cooperation. Events occurring during Thant's tenure are covered here.

PEACEKEEPING AND
THE SECRETARY-GENERAL

Gordenker, Leon. *The UN Secretary-General and the Maintenance of Peace*. New York: Columbia University Press, 1967. An analytical study of the various functions of the secretary-general, this book provides insights into Thant's view of his office.

Higgins, Roslyn. *United Nations Peacekeeping: Documents and Commentary*. Oxford: Oxford University Press, 1969–81. A two-volume set edited by a leading scholar of international law, this important collection of documents details the major UN peacekeeping operations between 1946 and 1987.

Rikhye, Indar Jit. *The Theory and Practice of Peacekeeping*, New York: St. Martin's Press, 1974. Rikhye examines the basic principle of peacekeeping and includes in his study examples from multinational UN operations in the third world.

———. *The Thin Blue Line: International Peacekeeping and Its Future.* London: Yale University Press, 1974. Drawing on his own experiences, Thant's chief military adviser, Lt. General Rikhye, reviews past peacekeeping operations and offers thoughts about the future of peacekeeping.

INTERNATIONAL ORGANIZATIONS

Bennett, A. Leroy. *International Organizations: Principles and Issues.* 4th ed. Englewood Cliffs, N.J.: Prentice Hall, 1988. A basic introduction to the UN, this book provides valuable background material on the organization's activities in combating colonialism, particularly in Africa, and in promoting economic development.

Claude, Inis L., Jr. *The Changing UN.* New York: Random House, 1967. Written in the mid-1960s by a respected scholar of international relations, this book chronicles and analyzes the "qualitative" and "quantitative" effects of decolonization on the UN. The third world agenda is effectively described and explored.

Murphy, Craig. "What the Third World Wants: An Interpretation of the Development and Meaning of the New Economic Order Ideology." In *Politics of International Organization,* edited by Paul I. Diehl, 226–41. Chicago: Dorsey, 1989. An analysis of the development of the third world as a political force, the article focuses on the thinking that underlay the creation of UNCTAD, Group of 77, and NIEO. The author summarizes the writings of Raul Prebisch, UNCTAD's first secretary-general and a leading ideological force in the evolution of the third world's stance on trade.

Ransey, Michael. "UNCTAD's Failures: The Rich Get Richer." In *The Politics of International Organization,* edited by Paul F. Diehl, 308–19. Chicago: Dorsey, 1989. A critical analysis of UNCTAD's performance since its formation in 1964. The author explores the conventional explanations for UNCTAD's failure—i.e., the "group" system of voting and the Secretariat's weaknesses—but lays most of the blame on the unwillingness of member governments to effect a real redistribution of global resources and wealth.

Sauvant, Karl P. *The Group of 77: Evolution, Structure, Organization.* New York: Oceana, 1981. A history and analysis of the emergence of the third world as a political bloc from the proclamation in 1961 of a UN Development Decade to the creation of UNCTAD to the formation of the Group of 77 and NIEO.

Sharma, D. N. *Afro-Asian Group in the UN.* Allahabad: Chaitanya Publishing House, 1969. The author looks at the evolution of the Afro-Asian bloc, beginning with the Bandung Conference of 1955. Sharma analyzes the voting patterns and diplomatic activities of third world governments on North-South issues such as decolonization, apartheid, and the Congo.

THE CHINA QUESTION

UNA-UN National Policy Panel. *China, the United Nations, and United States Policy: A Second Report of a National Policy Panel.* New York: United Nations Association of the United States of America, 1967. Against the backdrop of two new developments—the testing of China's first thermonuclear weapon and the advent of the Cultural Revolution—the policy panel issues a second report, once again calling for formula by which Communist China can be integrated into the UN.

————. *China, the United Nations, and United States Policy: A Report of a National Policy.* New York: United Nations Association of the United States of America, 1966. Primarily an advocacy statement in favor of a "Two China" policy, this report contains a valuable analysis, supported by statistical detail, of the "China question" in the General Assembly. The authors fully explore both sides of the seating question.

THE CONGO

Burns, Arthur Lee, and Nina Heathcote. *Peacekeeping by UN Forces: From Suez to the Congo.* New York: Praeger, 1963. A critical analysis of the UN role in the Suez and Congo. The authors question the authority of UN forces to engage in offensive operations, particularly in the Congo.

Colvin, Ian. *The Rise and Fall of Moise Tshombe.* London: Leslie Frewin, 1968. A sympathetic account of a politician, regarded by Thant as a "clown," by a journalist who was close to him. The UN comes under sharp attack in this interesting but one-sided polemic.

Jacobson, Harold Karan. "ONUC's Civilian Operation: State-Preserving and State-Building." In *From Collective Security to Preventive Diplomacy,* edited by Joel Larus, 423–44. New York: John Wiley and Sons, 1965. While most studies of the Congo focus on the UN's military effort against the Katanga secessionists, Jacobson concentrates on the organization's nonmilitary role in the Congo, designed to build and preserve a political and economic infrastructure.

O'Brien, Conor Cruise. *To Katanga and Back: A UN Case History.* New York: Simon & Schuster, 1962. An interesting and well-written account of O'Brien's ill-fated experience as a UN official in Katanga.

CUBAN MISSILE CRISIS

Blight, James G., Joseph S. Nye, Jr., and David A. Welch. "The Cuban Missile Crisis Revisited." *Foreign Affairs* 66 (Fall 1987): 170–88. This article contains

Dean Rusk's revelation that Kennedy instructed him to contact Andrew Cordier, who, on a signal from Washington, was to advise Thant to propose a trade of missiles in Cuba for American Jupiters in Turkey. The missile crisis was revealed before Thant was involved, and the secretary-general never learned of the role he might have played.

Bundy, McGeorge. *Danger and Survival: Choices about the Bomb in the First Fifty Years.* New York: Random House, 1988. While hundreds of books have been written about the Cuban missile crisis, Bundy's seventy pages in a book devoted to the history of the nuclear age make it among the best accounts and assessments of the Caribbean showdown. While the UN figured somewhat marginally in the final resolution, Bundy repeats Dean Rusk's assertion that Kennedy planned to employ Thant to float a proposal that would end the crisis.

CYPRUS

Salih, Halil Ibrahim. *Cyprus: The Impact of Diverse Nationalism on a State.* University: University of Alabama Press, 1978. A study of the roots of the Cyprus Civil War, this book provides an extensive and relatively clear treatment of UN involvement in the troubled country.

THE FISCAL CRISIS

Stoessinger, John G. "Who Pay." In *From Collective Security to Preventive Diplomacy,* edited by Joel Larus, 490–501. New York: John Wiley and Sons, 1968. Written during the height of the fiscal crisis in 1964, Stoessinger's article traces the evolution of the UN's financial problems and suggests solutions. The author effectively places the fiscal crisis into its political context.

THE INDO-PAKISTANI CONFLICT

Falit, D. K. *The Lightning Campaign: The Indo-Pakistani War.* New Delhi: Thompson, 1972. An Indian perspective on the 1971 war, this book provides a useful overview of the conflict and a commentary on India's victorious military campaign.

Jackson, Robert Victor. *South Asian Crisis: India, Pakistan, and Bangladesh.* London: Praeger, 1974. A political and historical analysis of the war, with an emphasis on the roots of the conflict.

THE MALAYSIAN CONFLICT

Macke, J. A. C. Konfrontasi. *The Indonesian-Malaysian Dispute: 1963–1966.* Oxford: Oxford University Press, 1974. Macke provides background material on the formation of the Malaysian Federation and Sukarno's decision to pull Indonesia out of the UN.

THE MIDDLE EAST

Bar-Zohar, Michael. *Embassies in Crisis: Diplomats & Demagogues behind the Six Day War.* Englewood Cliffs, N.J.: Prentice Hall, 1970. A day-by-day account of the diplomatic efforts expended by Thant and others to avert war in the three weeks preceding the outbreak of the Six Day War.

Lall, Arthur S. *The UN and the Middle East Crisis, 1967.* New York: Columbia University Press, 1968. The veteran diplomat describes diplomatic activity in the UN preceding and during the Six Day War.

THE DISARMAMENT

Bechhoefer, Bernhard G. *Postwar Negotiations for Arms Control.* Washington, D.C.: Brookings Institution, 1961. A useful review of UN disarmament activities leading up to Thant's tenure as secretary-general.

Jacobson, Harold Karan, and Eric Stein. *Diplomats, Scientists and Politicians: The United States and the Nuclear Test Ban Negotiations.* Ann Arbor: University of Michigan Press, 1966. While the emphasis is on the American policy-making process, this book explores in some detail disarmament efforts in the UN and Eighteen Nation Disarmament Committee leading up to 1963 Partial Nuclear Test Ban Treaty.

OTHER SOURCES

Baehr, Peter R., and Leon Gordenker. *The United Nations in the 1990s.* New York: St. Martin's, 1994.

Bennett, A. Leroy. *International Organizations: Principles and Issues,* 5th ed. Englewood Cliffs, N.J.: Prentice Hall, 1991.

Claude, Inis L., Jr. *Swords into Plowshares.* New York: Random House, 1959.

Facts on File Yearbook 1965. New York: Facts on File, 1966.

Facts on File Yearbook 1966. New York: Facts on File, 1967.

Facts on File Yearbook 1970. New York: Facts on File, 1971.

Facts on File Yearbook 1971. New York: Facts on File, 1972.

Stebbins, Richard P. *The United States and World Affairs 1961.* New York: Harper and Brothers, 1962.

Index

About the Author

Dr. Bernard J. Firestone is Dean of the College of Liberal Arts and Sciences and Professor of Political Science at Hofstra University in Hempstead, New York. A specialist in International Relations and the American presidency and recipient of the university's Distinguished Teaching Award, Dr. Firestone is the author of *The Quest for Nuclear Stability: John F. Kennedy and the Soviet Union* and editor of *Lyndon Baines Johnson and The Uses of Power* and *Gerald R. Ford and the Politics of Post-Watergate America*. His recent article on Kennedy's national security policy was published in *Kennedy and Europe,* by Louisiana State University Press.